OSSIE

LEON OSMAN
MY AUTOBIOGRAPHY

Sport Media

For Mum, Dad, Jenny, Cole, Deacon,
Kendall and anyone who has beaten
the odds by never giving in...

Sport Media

Ossie: My Autobiography

© Leon Osman

Written with Alan Jewell.
Special thanks to Darren Griffiths and Everton Football Club.

Production Editor: Adam Oldfield.
Cover Design: Rick Cooke.
Production: Harri Aston, James Cleary, Gary Gilliland.

First Edition
Published in Great Britain in 2014.
Published and produced by: Trinity Mirror Sport Media, PO Box 48,
Old Hall Street, Liverpool L69 3EB.

Publishing Director: Steve Hanrahan
Commercial Director: Will Beedles
Executive Editor: Paul Dove
Executive Art Editor: Rick Cooke
Senior Marketing Executive: Claire Brown
Sales and Marketing Manager: Elizabeth Morgan

ISBN: 978-1-908695-49-9

Photographic acknowledgements:
Front cover image: Tony Woolliscroft
Other images: Trinity Mirror, PA Photos,
The Cumberland News, Leon Osman collection.

Statistics: Gavin Buckland.

Printed and bound by CPI Group (UK) Ltd, Croydon, CR0 4YY.

Contents

CONTENTS

Acknowledgements

It's been a great experience putting this book together and it's really reminded me of the many special times I've enjoyed at Everton Football Club.

I was first approached to do a book some four years ago but at the time I wanted to wait until I had finished playing.

It wasn't until I was granted a testimonial that I thought it could actually work. It seemed like a nice way to wrap things up – even though I've got no intentions of retiring.

I feel incredibly privileged to have had such a great career with Everton Football Club – and it's not over yet. I'm sure there will be more good times ahead under Roberto Martinez.

I am one of the many, many people who have never heard a truer phrase than the one Alan Ball said: 'Once Everton has touched you, nothing will be the same'.

And that's coming from someone who started life as a Liverpool fan. I now know exactly what Bally meant. Once you wear the royal blue, there is no going back.

I have also been very lucky to have such love and support from my own family throughout my life. Mum and Dad are still together 30-plus years on and they're very happy.

I hope I can provide the same stability for my own family.

After all these years, I am still living five minutes away from Mum, Dad, my brother and my sister. My nan Osman (nana Sylvie to the kids) is also in the area. Playing for Everton suits me.

My wife Jenny has been to virtually all my matches over the

years. The only major one she missed was Wolves when I made my full debut! She was at all my Carlisle and Derby games – she'd travel with Mum and Dad.

Now we have three children and we're very happy. Jenny has always supported me and I'm thankful that I found someone like her.

I'd like to take this opportunity to publicly thank her for everything…because I forgot to do so when I made my wedding day speech!

Much of my family time is spent taking Cole and Deacon to football training and their Sunday league matches. As well as the boys, we now have our daughter, Kendall, who will be three in a few months and is starting to go to nursery. She already attends baby ballet classes and whatever she's interested in as she gets older, I will show the same commitment to her as I have to the boys. That's what you do for your family. That's what my parents did for me.

I'd also like to thank Alan Jewell, who has co-operated with me on the writing of this book, spending hours and hours listening to my stories.

Thanks also to the Media & Publications Manager at Everton, Darren Griffiths, for all his help and guidance.

It was my agents, Peter McIntosh and Dave Lockwood, who first mentioned the book idea to me. They've always been supportive not just with this project, but the many other aspects of my career, so thanks, as always, to them for all their hard work. They've been with me since I was 19 and as well as having a professional relationship, I consider them to be very good personal friends.

I should also thank my publishers Trinity Mirror Sport Media.

ACKNOWLEDGEMENTS

Publishing Director Steve Hanrahan and Commercial Director Will Beedles were really enthusiastic about the book idea when we first met at the Stanley Gate pub in Bickerstaffe as I ate ice cream! Thanks for giving me the opportunity to tell my story. Thanks also to Paul Dove, Adam Oldfield, James Cleary and Harri Aston on the production and editing side of things; to Rick Cooke who designed the jacket and Tony Woolliscroft who took the photos.

My journey from Elmers Green JFC through to the full England team would not have been possible without the contribution of so many fantastic players, coaches and friends. I hope I don't forget any of them in this book.

Hope you enjoy my story!

Leon Osman, October 2014

Foreword

When Ossie asked me to do the foreword for his book I didn't hesitate. 'No thanks lad,' I said. 'Why are you writing a book anyway?' But he persisted and so, to get him off my case because I know how he goes on and on when he wants something, I agreed.

Anyone who knows me is aware that this type of thing isn't really my style. In fact there's only one person I would even think about doing this for…and that's Ossie.

We've come such a long way together that we're more like brothers than mates.

We used to train together as kids at Bellefield and then Netherton, when our dads would watch the first bits and then nip off for a few pints, and if someone had said that we'd both play more than 300 first team games for Everton we would never have believed them. And if we'd have been taken to one side and told that we'd both end up getting testimonials at Goodison we'd have laughed our heads off.

Everything that has come Ossie's way in his career he has earned. He had injury setbacks before he even made the first team but his determination to be a professional footballer was unbelievable. Even at a young age he had that focus and desire that you don't often see in a kid and I knew that he would make it one day. I just didn't think it would take him so long!

When he scored that first goal at Wolves I was one of the first people to jump on his back because I was just so pleased for him. I knew what he'd been through and I knew it would be the first of many.

I know how proud he was to play the same number of games as Colin Harvey and, for me, Ossie deserves to be mentioned in the same bracket as players like that. He's been one of the best Everton midfield players of the Premier League era.

He maybe doesn't get the praise that he should because he's a local lad who didn't cost the club a transfer fee but I can tell you that he's always been appreciated greatly by every single player he's played alongside.

Nobody needs me to tell them just how good a footballer Ossie is. Anyone who has watched him over the years will know that he's a great player with a great attitude and I have enjoyed watching him become a leader in the dressing room.

We've had our ups and downs along the way, as all players do, but one thing that has never wavered has been our friendship and loyalty to each other. We'd battle for one another as much as we'd battle for ourselves. And that's the sign of a true friendship.

Our families have become close over the years as well and the Hibberts have had some good nights with the Osmans!

I can't begin to tell you how pleased I was when he got his England call-up. No player deserved it more – it's just a shame he looked ridiculous with that charity moustache he was trying to grow! He's always wanted a good 'tache but I don't think it's ever going to happen.

If this book is anything like Ossie himself then I'm sure everyone will enjoy it.

And if there are any lies in it about me, we may well have our first ever falling out!

Tony Hibbert, October 2014

I

Pre-match

Sunday, August 3, 2014.
Goodison Park.
Everton v Porto.

Even now I can't put into words what I was feeling when I heard the familiar sound of Z-Cars start to reverberate around Goodison Park.

Usually, there'd be me and ten team-mates bristling with excitement, determination and focus as we trotted down the players' tunnel and turned left to take the steps out onto the pitch.

On Sunday, August 3, 2014, there was just me and my three children.

The rest of the Everton team were already out there and they and 20,000 supporters were waiting for me to make my entrance.

What was going through my head?

Watching my dad playing Sunday League and being fascinated by the game from a very young age…playing well enough for Elmers Green to be spotted by Skem Boys…representing England Schoolboys at Wembley…tears, tantrums and frustration after picking up injury after injury as an Everton youth… making my debut at White Hart Lane…scoring my first goal at Wolves…qualifying for the Champions League…playing a full international.

All of these and more flitted briefly into my mind and straight back out again.

I held the hands of my son Deacon and daughter Kendall, instructed my eldest boy Cole to accompany us and I started up the steps and into the Goodison Park sunshine. My favourite stadium in the world for a game that was so much more than Everton versus Porto in a pre-season friendly.

My old mate Tony Hibbert picked me up from home on the day of the game. We go back a long way and he'd been through it two years earlier when he caused a sensation (and a riot) by scoring a goal at the Gwladys Street end.

"Are you feeling nervous?" he asked.

Hibbo and I have no secrets so I was being completely honest when I said 'no'.

The journey to Goodison Park is one I have made hundreds of times. I still love my first sight of the place as I drive up Walton Lane, past the police station and point the car in the direction of the stadium.

As I get closer and closer it still sends a shiver down my spine.

To think that a boy from a Skelmersdale housing estate had played for the Everton first team almost 400 times is scarcely believable. But I never gave up hope…and I never gave in.

On Sunday, August 3, 2014, the feeling of nervous excitement and anticipation were magnified many times. Forty-feet posters adoring the side of the perimeter walls advertising 'Leon Osman's Testimonial' and featuring a gigantic image of me did little to ease my edginess.

Imagine your wedding day but with 20,000 guests. That's what it was like and, like my wedding, it's a day that I will never forget.

By the time Hibbo parked his car in the Bullens car park we were surrounded by well-wishers. I had 10 times the normal requests for autographs and getting through the crowds and into the stadium took me about 20 minutes.

It would have been longer had a steward not helped to usher me through. I remember thinking that it must be like this for Cahill, Ferguson, Arteta or Rooney everywhere they go. Or for Robbie Williams or One Direction. But not for Leon Osman.

I'd never experienced it on that scale. Everyone wanted a bit of me that day and I'm not used to that level of attention. I've never been the main star of the team.

One of the thousands of nice things about playing for Everton is the warm friendliness of everyone associated with the club. It's my extended family and on my testimonial day, they were all genuinely pleased to see me. The handshakes, the greetings, the smiles and the back-slapping from all the staff inside Goodison were more enthusiastic than ever before.

I was handed a match programme when I got inside and, as you'd expect, it was all about me. I read what my youth-team coach Colin Harvey had said and a few other comments from team-mates past and present. Duncan Ferguson was quoted: "He's done well for a lad who is 4ft 2ins and can't run..." Thanks Dunc! Don't worry, we had words and I put him right in his place!

I continued to read through it and was horrified to find a double page spread of some of my childhood and toddler photographs. Thanks Mum! Don't worry, we had words and SHE put ME right in my place!

I laughed and thought about how much she would have enjoyed supplying those images for the programme editor. This day was for her and my dad as much as anyone. I could never repay them for what they've done for me over the years and I hoped that the whole day would go well for their sake. I knew Dad would be fine but I knew Mum would be ten times more nervous than me. She always has been…

There was a Leon Osman quiz in the programme and I tested a few of the lads in the treatment room. Hibbo, Phil Jagielka, Leighton Baines, Darron Gibson, Steven Naismith and John Stones took part, plus all the medical staff. It was surprising how well the lads knew me.

In the team meeting, the manager, Roberto Martinez, addressed the team and talked about the "standards I had set" and told the lads "Don't let him down." It was very humbling and I appreciated the words and the sentiment but not the fact that, yet again, it was all about me.

The team left the dressing room and I was suddenly alone with my thoughts. I was trying to stay focussed on everything I had to do because I knew if I dwelled on things there was every chance I'd get emotional.

As I walked into the players' tunnel, my children were waiting for me with the mascots. They were very excited. I had to wait with them in the tunnel until everything was ready out on the pitch. The wait seemed to take an age. I had our daughter Kendall in one hand, son Deacon in the other and our eldest Cole was stood in front of me.

Kendall is only two but I thought she would be okay as long as Deacon, who is six, was out there. I also knew that there'd be no holding Cole back once he heard Z-Cars. Keeping him close to the rest of us was my biggest problem. He loves being in the spotlight. Deacon on the other hand doesn't like it one bit. He has a hearing problem and doesn't like being around people. He also struggles to deal with noise so walking out with me that day was a massive thing for him to do. I know he was dreading it and that he was very, very nervous all week beforehand but the night before he assured me that he would do it. Then on the morning he said "I've changed my mind, I'm not going on the pitch." I was gutted but I left it at that. An hour before I left the house he approached me again. 'I'm going to do it for you Daddy, really I am'. I thanked him and looked away so he didn't see me fill up.

We walked up the steps and stopped at the top, waiting for my cue to walk through the guard of honour. That cue was the Z-Cars drum roll. The tension was huge.

As I stood there waiting to go out, I glanced along our line. Hibbo, Bainesy, Jags, Gaz Barry, Ross Barkley, Aiden McGeady. So much had changed since that Wolves game in 2004. I started recalling the players I lined up with at Molineux. Nigel Martyn, Davie Weir, James McFadden, Lee Carsley, Wayne Rooney, Kev Campbell...I had some good friends in that team.

Come on Z-Cars, come on! I really wanted to get things done now. I could see Hibbo and Jags grinning at me as if they were clearly enjoying my discomfort. If Hibbo had repeated his 'are you nervous?' question, the answer would now be a resounding 'yes!'.

I still hope that I can decorate my Everton career with some silverware but even if I don't I will still be so proud of the fact that I have walked out onto the Goodison Park pitch as part of an Everton team. Reaching the last step and walking out into the cauldron of noise that always greets the players is a unique feeling that I wish I had the words to describe here.

There is nothing like it.

On this afternoon, it was a cocktail of emotions the likes of which I had never experienced before. Pride, gratitude, humility, exhilaration and yes, a touch of embarrassment.

"Ladies and gentlemen, testimonial games in the Premier League era are becoming increasingly rare. To achieve more than ten years with a single football club is a magnificent achievement and we are here at Goodison Park today to honour one of our very own who has done just that…"

'Get on with it Rossie' I thought. My grip on Deacon's hand tightened and so did the knots in my stomach. Kendall was rather oblivious. Cole was hopping up and down eager to get out there.

"…please welcome the man we've all come to see this after-noon. Goodison Park, make some noise for LEON OSMAN!"

The familiar drum-roll started, the crowd roared, the players clapped and I took my first steps into the sunshine. My hands were full so I couldn't wave or acknowledge the fans but they could see from the widest smile on my face that I appreciated everything. And not just for that day. For my whole Everton career.

Eventually I released the small hand of my brave boy, Deacon, and saluted all four sides of Goodison Park. I probably shook hands with a few players from both Everton and Porto...I honestly can't remember.

The Z-Cars tune faded away, but the applause continued and I turned when I reached the centre-circle. I waved towards the Main Stand looking for three people. My mum, my dad and my wife were with me that day and I owe them everything.

Then the whistle blew and it was time to concentrate on the game.

This is my story...

01

Skem

Despite having come up through the youth system at Everton, I'm not a 'proper' Scouser, although these days I could hopefully claim honorary status. I grew up in Skelmersdale, West Lancashire, which was designated a new town in 1961, 20 years before I was born, to house the overspill population of north Merseyside. Skem, as everyone calls it, is famous for having loads of roundabouts and no traffic lights, which may explain why I found it difficult to come to a halt as a child.

I was a little bundle of energy, always dashing around and running into things. To say I was accident-prone is an understatement. I am the eldest of three children and when Carl, my brother, was born, I managed to split my head open in hospital when I was visiting my mum, Carol.

My dad, Derek, had given me a couple of toy cars to keep me entertained at the hospital but I tripped on one of them and fell into the corner of a wall, banging my head. There was blood everywhere but as Billinge Hospital didn't have any accident and emergency facilities, we had to travel to Ormskirk so I could be stitched up. Dad drove me there with my poor mum left with no visitors and in a state of panic, waiting for a phone call. I've still got a scar from that one!

This would be a recurring theme throughout my childhood, and I split my head open on an almost annual basis. When I was three, I tripped and smacked my head on the television. There was blood everywhere and it ruined Carl's first birthday party. Another time I somehow ran into a parked car when I was playing hide and seek and took a big chunk out of my leg. The other kids were still looking for me when I was four miles away being treated by a doctor with whom I am now on familiar terms! I had more treatment between the age of five and eight than I've had as a professional footballer.

When I was a bit older, I was riding my bicycle and a car got too close to me. Unnerved, I lost my balance and shot over the handlebars splitting open my hand and banging my head. I walked home but had to wake up Dad, who was sleeping before his night shift. He then had to drive me to hospital again. The bike was in a bad way too…and it wasn't even mine!

On another occasion, mum lifted me up on to the kitchen worktop while she was wiping me down. She turned away for a split-second and I fell off, landing on my forehead. It came up like a massive egg.

As Dad was at work it was her turn to do the hospital run but as Dad had the car, she phoned an ambulance. I was screaming at the top of my voice, even scaring the paramedics, until five minutes into the hospital journey I spotted my dad out of the back of the ambulance trailing us. I then proceeded to tell everyone "that's my dad" and then spent the rest of the journey to the hospital waving out of the ambulance window not realising nobody could see me through the blacked-out windows!

I'm sure that these days my parents would be called in to answer some questions – I was bashed up that often!

When I wasn't injuring myself and worrying the life out of Mum and Dad, I found time to behave like a normal kid and football was a big part of my childhood. I was always kicking a ball around and if it was too cold or wet to go outside, I'd kick a balloon or sometimes even a plastic cup around the house. Nowadays with Xboxes, PlayStations and the like, it's hard work getting kids outside, but when I was growing up only a few of us had video games. I did have a ZX Spectrum computer but it took 10 minutes to turn on and 15 minutes to load the game. I didn't always have the patience to wait for it to clunk into action, so I would get a ball, go outside and kick it around.

Our first house was in Lowcroft in the Ashurst area of Skem. There was a field behind it on which we played football. There were loads of kids, between three and eight years older than me, who used to play out. They didn't want me to play at first but when they saw I was decent at football I was allowed to join in. Mum had to check with the big kids that they'd look after me, which given my track record for injuries was probably a wise move.

I don't know if my ability was obvious straight away but I suppose I had to be good to hold my own against bigger and older kids. I was simply happy to be out there running, dribbling and taking people on. I had fun and I always wanted my team to win. Playing with bigger lads helped me develop. I could never out-muscle or out-run anyone, so I had to find a way to beat them using my brain, whether that was skill or a quick one-two. The field we played on is still there and it looks so tiny now. As a kid, though, it seemed massive and we got so many lads on there that finding space was very difficult. Again though, a handy learning curve.

When I was about 21, I went round to a family friend's house and she had her own mates around who were about four or five years older than me. One of them mentioned 'Ossie' and another guy said: "Ossie! I remember him! I used to play against him – dead small but really good. Whatever happened to him?" My friend took great pleasure in introducing me, although this was before I'd broken into the Everton first team.

We lived in Lowcroft until I was seven when we moved to an area called Merewood, which was also in Ashurst. Because it was nearby I was still able to play with the same group of kids. Then when I was 14 we moved to Parsonage Close in Uphol- land, where my mum and dad still live now. It was closer to my senior school and it was the first time I had my own bedroom. Before that, me and Carl shared.

Before we go any further I should point out that I also have a sister, Cheryl, who is four-and-a-half years younger than me. Carl is quite well known locally, having played non-league football until quite recently, while Cheryl is the extra bit of the family that she claims nobody knows about. Apparently, I never mention her in any interviews and she goes mad about it all the time. We turn up at parties and people ask 'who's this?' Hope- fully this will pacify her!

We all had a very normal upbringing. Dad worked as a shift manager for Fibracan, a company that made polystyrene cups and plates on the industrial estate in West Pimbo. Mum looked after us at home until we were all school age when she started working part-time at the Co-op Bank. She's still working for them and is full-time now. When I was 16, dad took redundancy and now works at Asco in West Pimbo where he is much happier with a structured 8-4 day. Although he did different shifts, between him and mum, Carl and I never missed a training session or a match, even though we could be training four or five nights a week with two games at the weekend. It was the same for Cheryl and her dancing classes (another mention!). We never missed anything we wanted to go to and I am always thankful for that. I honestly don't know when they slept. As a kid you take things like that for granted and it's only when you're older that you realise the sacrifices that parents make and the time and effort they put in to help you along the way.

Dad was actually my very first footballing hero. He played in the Liverpool County Combination for a few teams, including Rainford North End. He also played Sunday League and from a very young age I'd go and watch, standing on the line in all kinds of weather. One time it really was lashing down so he sat me in the car. He left the heating on, turned on the windscreen wipers so I could see the game and told me to stay in the car. After about ten minutes he trotted over to take a throw-in and was shocked to see me standing on the line dripping wet through. I tried to explain that I couldn't see the match because the windows had steamed up but he was none too pleased and they had to hold the game up for him to cart me back to the car. The rain didn't matter to me, I just wanted to watch my dad, but

I can imagine he got some stick from his team-mates about it.

Dad, who is an inch smaller than me, could play right across the midfield. From what I remember, he was a similar player to me, although people tell me he had more pace. Sadly, that speed bypassed me on to Carl, who was a flying winger. Dad was always 'Ossie' and I was 'Little Ossie' and even now if I meet someone from back then they'll tell me 'he was a great player, your dad'. A lot of them also say that he was better than me… and when he's had a few drinks he agrees with them! Dad was once offered a two-day trial at Liverpool when he was 14 but only went on the first day, as there was nobody able to drive him there. Because of him and his willingness to make sacrifices, that was never a problem for me when I was the same age.

While I was taking any opportunity to kick a ball around on the local field, it was difficult to find an actual team to play for. My primary school, Dalton St Michael's, was really small, with only six kids in my year, four in the year below and eight in the year above. Half of them were girls so to even think about having a footy team we'd have needed to include the headmaster, the lollipop man and the caretaker. There was no impetus towards sport, which, given the numbers, is understandable. A few of us used to play football in the playground, but that was as far as it went.

That changed when a teacher called Mr Sharkey joined the school and saw how good we were on the playground. He entered us in a five-a-side competition, which we won. Then they sent us to another tournament involving five districts and we won that as well.

We ended up playing at Preston North End's Deepdale ground on their old plastic pitch against the best six schools in

Lancashire. Our tiny little school was one of them. We didn't win the tournament but it was incredible to get there – there was something like nine boys in the whole of the juniors. Carl was on the bench and he was in Reception.

One of my friends, Scott Davies, was from the year above and he told me his dad was thinking of starting a team and invited me to join. He told me to go to his house for a certain time before we would head to the Skem College field for a training session. I was dead excited and couldn't wait to get started.

My enthusiasm was dampened though when we were walking over to the field and I could hear Scott's dad, Tommy, complaining: "I've told you, Scott, we've got enough kids, we don't need any more." Scott's recruitment drive had obviously gone well because there were a load of kids on the field waiting to play. "Dad, honestly, he's really good," Scott pleaded. Tommy relented and put me in one of the teams. They couldn't get the ball off me and at the end of the session Tommy said to me "same time next week, don't be late".

Elmers Green was the name of our team and Tommy Davies had a real impact on me. He was the manager, took the training, washed the kit, provided the balls, instilled discipline, everything. We joined the Skem Junior League at under-11, which was the youngest age group you could have a league. I was still only seven, we had a few who were nine and a couple of lads who were 10, so we were a very young team. As a result, we got battered every single week. Scorelines like 15-0, 18-0, even 24-0 were not uncommon. Someone recently recalled that we'd once lost 36-0, but I don't remember that one. I may have been injured or suspended that day!

An 11-0 defeat was considered a decent result for us. There was one other team we played against, 'something' Villa, I can't recall now. We got beat 2-1 the first time we played them, which was a great result for us, and in our next meeting we drew 1-1 and I scored. The third time we won 2-1 and I scored again. It was party time and we celebrated like we'd won the World Cup. We lived for those games. I absolutely loved it…we all did. And that's why Tommy Davies kept the team going. He knew we'd lose far more than we'd win but as long as the kids were enjoying it, that was good enough for Tommy.

At the end of our first season we had the presentation in the Upholland Labour Club and I was announced as the Player of the Year for the whole league. It was a massive surprise – I was amazed.

There was a walkway leading to the stage but in my haste I missed it out – I ran and jumped up (it was a miracle that I didn't stumble, smash my head and ruin the night!). It was a great feeling though.

We would get some fantastic former players coming to those presentations. Men like Gordon West, Brian Labone, Duncan McKenzie and Alan Kennedy. To be up on the stage with names like that was a great thrill.

My first winners' medal came from a five-a-side competition with a group of lads who lived by us in Merewood. It was a tournament at Skem Sports Centre and we went on to win it twice on the run.

They were my first medals and I was dead proud of them. It was an Under-11s team and the second time we won it they allowed Carl to be the sub so he could get a medal too. He was four years old! Good job we didn't get any injuries.

After playing for Elmers Green on a Sunday, it wasn't long before I was representing Skem Boys on a Saturday. Dad was playing himself so didn't get to see me very much. Mum took me, with Carl and Cheryl dragged along. Dad and I would talk about my game afterwards but it bothered him that he was missing my matches. When he was about 29 or 30, he gave up his own football because he wanted to watch me. I didn't appreciate his sacrifice and what it meant until I reached the same age. He stopped playing the game he loved just so he could watch his son. He didn't even play for a pub team on a Sunday because I was playing on both days. It was an incredible thing he did for me.

I still have debriefs with Dad now where he'll give me his honest opinion about how I've played. When I was younger, I didn't like it. He'd drive me to games and on the way home we'd talk about the match. I was a typical child who had an answer for everything – I wasn't ready to listen. He might say: "Why did you take two people on? There was an easy pass for you there and your team-mate could have scored." He wouldn't be shouting at me but he would question why I made a particular decision, making me think about it myself. I'd disagree with him and tell him that he didn't know what he was talking about. The discussions could get quite heated because of my reluctance to accept that he may actually be right and they would usually end with Dad remarking "there's no point talking to you if you won't listen."

As time went by, I was able to listen without automatically assuming he was having a go. It became very educational. Our talks would encourage me to look back at the game and analyse my own decisions, the choices I'd made on the pitch and why

I'd made them. Even now, I'll ask his opinion after every game. Following the Newcastle match in March 2014, he sent me a text to say he was going to bed because it was late but we'd speak about it the following day. I may be pleased with how the game turned out, while he will say 'well done' but he'll also highlight the time I chose the wrong option, or things I need to work on. Conversely, if I feel my game hasn't gone to plan, he'll gee me up and speak about the positives.

Dad was always quiet on the sideline when he was watching me. My two boys now play of a weekend and when the game becomes competitive, parents can get far too emotional. There is a difference between encouraging your own child and their team and getting so wound up that you start putting the other team down. You don't want to see that in kids' football. Dad kept quiet and would never really shout anything. There would be a word of encouragement, or a kick up the backside at the right time, but even then it wouldn't be a shout across the pitch. He'd wait until I ran past him and then have a quiet word.

Dad is black and experienced a lot of racism when he was growing up. He lived through a much worse time than me. I suffered a little bit in primary school but I hated anyone seeing my emotions if I was upset, so I wouldn't react. I wouldn't tell Mum either. I'd just keep it to myself.

Our Carl came home from school one day and Mum asked him: "Anything up with Leon, he's seems very quiet?" Carl said: "No, I don't think so…Mum, what's a n*****?" Mum exploded: "WHAT? Where have you heard that?"

"Oh, some of the kids in school called Leon it." She came straight to me. I was six or seven and shrugged it off, saying: "It doesn't matter. I don't let them see it bothers me." She marched me back to the school and spoke to the headteacher, who was very apologetic. I just dealt with it. I walked through an estate when I was nine and two separate gangs of lads started calling me names. It didn't happen massively but I certainly experienced it.

Dad and I shared a lot of time together where football was concerned, much of it spent at Anfield. As a child, I was a mad Liverpool fan and we had a father and son season ticket on the Kop.

The first season I went properly was 1987/88, which wasn't a bad year to start. My main recollection is John Barnes running down the wing towards me every week. My first proper stand-out memory is the two goals he scored against QPR when Liverpool won 4-0 in October 1987. That was incredible. Watching him dribble from the halfway line, cutting inside, beating two or three players and stroking it in the bottom corner. From that point, he was my hero. I'd had the shirts for a few years but that was my first full season of going to watch football, and what an introduction. Barnes, Peter Beardsley and Ray Houghton were my favourites but I appreciated all of them – Whelan, McMahon, Nicol, Hansen, Staunton, Burrows, Spackman, Grobbelaar…great players. That was an incredible Liverpool team. I wonder how I'd have felt then if I'd been told that one day I would play in front of the Kop…and be given all sorts of abuse when I went to take a corner!

I was a season ticket holder from 1988-94. I only had five or six years of being a proper Liverpool fan but at that age it seemed like forever. We had the same 'spec' on the Kop. I would sit on the bar with my dad standing behind me. The same 10 people stood around us every week and we got to know them well, swapping sweets as we watched the game.

I had a great little view but I don't know how my dad saw anything because he was behind me, holding me in place. When the surge came, I'd fall off the bar because I couldn't hold on to the guy in front. I'd get up, run underneath the barrier without having to duck, and dad would pick me up and put me back on so I could carry on watching.

One of the fellas stood by us was Stephen Warnock's uncle, John, so on quite a few occasions Steve and I were sat on the barrier together watching Liverpool and sharing sweets. A few years later, we ended up playing for England Schoolboys together at Wembley before, later still, being on opposite sides in the Merseyside derby at Anfield. Not bad for a couple of sweet-munching lads from West Lancashire.

At the end of 1987/88, with Liverpool champions by a distance, they were hot favourites to complete the double in the FA Cup final against Wimbledon. Dad had promised to take me to Wembley and duly managed to get two tickets. I woke up at the crack of dawn. I struggled to get up for school but I didn't have any problems getting out of bed that morning. I was up, washed, dressed and desperate to get out the front door long before we were due to leave.

Off we went, father and son, in our matching adidas track-suits, which bizarrely were navy blue with yellow flashes across the chest and shoulders. We must have been quite a sight. It was the way we dressed in our family. Carl and I used to wear matching clothes, until we eventually convinced mum it wasn't a good idea. I think I was 25 at the time!

Dad had a couple of pints in a London pub beforehand and then we got to Wembley. It was a boiling hot day and, 15-20 minutes before kick-off, everyone was getting squashed. The police started shouting at the people in the queue: "Lift the kids over the top, you'll be able to collect them once you get in." I was getting squashed so Dad handed me over, telling me exactly where to wait, and I was carried towards the gate. I can still recall being passed over the heads of the fans, desperately holding on to my ticket and being brought down inside the gate.

A policeman then came along and instructed me to follow him. I protested that I'd been told to wait by the gate but he informed me that there was a holding pen for all the kids. He assured me that my dad would know where to find me. There were about 30 other kids in this pen so I wasn't unduly concerned…until with only a few minutes before kick-off there were only two of us left.

Time continued to pass and a steward who shared my concern eventually made the decision to take us from the pen and look for our parents. I wasn't sure that was the best idea inside Wembley on cup final day, but he walked us to the police office outside the stadium to see if my dad had not got in. He wasn't there so as a last resort we were taken to the gate that we'd come in through and, sure enough, in the distance I could see a man banging on the outside of the gate.

As we got closer I could see it was one of my dad's mates, Glen Maddox. Boy was he relieved to see me! He and my dad had split up to try to find me. Glen had popped his head out of the gate to see if I was still outside the stadium, someone pushed him out and locked the gate behind him. He was frantically trying to get back in when we found him.

I was relieved at being found and Glen was delighted to be back in! We found Dad – I spotted the tracksuit through the crowd – and all was well (although he was tearful with worry when we were finally reunited). We finally reached our seats just in time to hear the referee blow the half-time whistle. Liverpool were 1-0 down to Lawrie Sanchez's goal but I thought everything was going to be okay from that point. Early in the second half, Liverpool won a penalty, John Aldridge stepped up but Dave Beasant saved it and Wimbledon held on for one of the greatest cup upsets of all time. The day I had looked forward to for so long hadn't gone well at all…

A few weeks before that FA Cup final against Wimbledon in 1988, Nottingham Forest had been Liverpool's opponents in the semi-final at Hillsborough. I didn't go because I was too young (the cup final was a special exception), but Dad went with his mates and they were in the Leppings Lane end. As they entered the ground, one of the stewards stopped them and said: "Don't go down to the front. Go up and to your right and you'll have a fantastic view looking out from above the corner flag. It's unbelievable, trust me. Go and watch from up there."

They followed the steward's instructions, enjoyed the view and the game and then, 12 months later, they were back at Hillsborough for another Liverpool v Nottingham Forest semi-final. As they entered the ground on April 15, 1989, Dad remembered what the steward had said and he suggested that they watch the game from the same spec – top right-hand corner. It was a decision that probably saved his life…

I was in my nan's house that afternoon. Everton were playing Norwich in the other semi at Villa Park and I was listening to both games on two radios. I had Radio City on one and BBC Radio Merseyside on the other. Liverpool had hit the bar, Everton were attacking and it was all really exciting. But then the Liverpool commentary stopped. I had been listening to the Everton game for a couple of minutes and when I returned to the Liverpool game, there was no football. They were talking about 'crowd problems' and the fact that there were some fans on the pitch. I hoped my dad was okay but I wasn't unduly worried as I knew he could handle himself. It was only when the reporter said that there rumours that people were dying that I went cold.

I ran into the room where my nan was shouting 'fans have died at Hillsborough' and there was absolute panic amongst us. My mum was working at the time. When she came, she was worried sick, but she probably tried not to show it. This was in the days before mobile phones don't forget and so all we could do was wait. It was agonising. I will never forget that feeling an hour or so later when the telephone rang. It was my dad in someone's house by the ground and he was letting us know he was safe. He had watched in sheer horror as the tragedy unfolded before his eyes and he told us that there were queues of people outside the houses so he couldn't stay on the line long.

I can't begin to imagine how the people who didn't get a phone call must have felt…

The following week we visited the shrine that was Anfield, and laid a scarf and flowers. The shrine reached halfway between the Kop and the centre circle by the time I was there. It's hard to describe my emotions of that day. I was only four weeks short of my eighth birthday but I recall there was a lot of sadness, a lot of grief and a lot of tension in the air. It was eerie. It was like the feeling you get during a minute's silence before a game, but magnified a hundred times. The only sound was that of people shuffling forward to lay their flowers or the occasional mourner crying. I remember being torn between being thankful that my dad wasn't one of those who lost their lives, but sad for those fans who never came home. For a child, it was hard to distinguish those feelings.

That the people who lost loved ones at Hillsborough are still fighting for justice is an absolute disgrace.

After going back to Wembley with Dad for the emotional FA Cup final against Everton which Liverpool edged 3-2, I was back on the Kop six days later for the Arsenal league title decider. Even a 1-0 defeat would have been enough for Liverpool but it was another surreal night at Anfield. I can still remember the feeling of absolute disbelief when Michael Thomas scored his last-minute winner. I kept thinking that the referee would rule it out or the linesman would flag for offside because it was just so unreal to lose the title with a minute of the whole season to go. I stayed behind to clap Arsenal because, like so many others, I thought it was the right thing to do, but I was very upset. I actually think everyone would have been a lot more disappointed had it not happened so soon after Hillsborough. You can't compare not winning a silver trophy with the loss of a life.

I was beginning to realise that the game of football tampered with your emotions like nothing else.

02

Once A Blue

When I wasn't watching football, I was playing it. When I was eight, I was selected for Skem Boys, which was run by a guy called Nick Corless, a schoolteacher. At the time, my usual position was right-wing, but I played the whole of the first season for Skem Boys as a sweeper. Mr Corless (I still call him that whenever I see him, even though I'm in my 30s now!) set up in an old fashioned way: one centre-half, a sweeper, two full-backs, a centre-mid, an inside-left, inside-right, outside-left, outside-right and centre-forward.

I always played with a smile on my face but after the games I would complain to my dad: "I'm not a sweeper, I want to play right-wing." Eventually, Mum spoke to Mr Corless who explained he was happy the way it was because we had a good left-winger called Kevin Leadbetter and a good right-winger called Darren Kellet, who was the captain, and the pair of them were scoring loads of goals.

In one match at St Helens we were losing 1-0 with five minutes to go and Mr Corless made a tactical change and put me up front. In the time left I scored one and set one up as we came back to win 2-1. I thought that would be my sweeping days over…but I was wrong. Despite my game-winning contribution, the next week I was put back to sweeper for Skem Boys and I couldn't understand why.

I found out later that Mr Corless had told Dad I was his secret weapon and he was holding me back until a semi-final against Blackpool in three weeks time because "they won't know what's hit them". Blackpool had battered us every game for years but this year would be different. I was put on the right-wing, we won 5-3 and I scored a hat-trick. The smile on Mr Corless' face was priceless that day as he shook hands with the Blackpool manager. We went on to beat a team called Darwen 5-0 in the final and we had some serious celebrations afterwards in the Skem youth club. We put away some Chewits, flying saucers and cola cubes that night, I can tell you!

The following season, as a newly-installed right-winger, we won pretty much everything in the Lancashire league. By this point, though, I was in Mr Corless' ear, telling him: "I am a central midfielder now, I don't play on the wing anymore!" In my last season (I got to play three seasons because I joined so young) I got my wish and was given the captaincy as well.

At the end of that game against St Helens (the one I turned around with five minutes left), a scout from Oldham Athletic had approached Mum about me. She was a bit flustered and wasn't sure what to do, but telephone numbers were exchanged and me and another lad called John Potter were invited to go to train at their ground.

We spent the whole of the following season travelling to Boundary Park, training on their old plastic pitch once a week. They gave me a pair of brand new trainers and a Mitre Delta football to practise with. When I was playing footy with my mates, I'd insist on using my Mitre because it was 'from Oldham Athletic'. I was really proud of it. But when we reported back to Oldham after the summer we were told to bring our ball back with us. I was worried because mine was wrecked after being used every day. The coach was really pleased with me though. He addressed the group: "Every ball should be like Leon's. He's obviously been using it all the time and that's why we gave you a ball."

Academy kids no longer get given a ball each to go away and practise with and I think that's a shame. To be given something as simple as a ball to look after and take pride in can be a big thing for a young kid, and you can't practise enough when you're a youngster.

Oldham was a long way to travel, 50 minutes there, 50 minutes back and an hour's training. I enjoyed it but after 18 months, Everton came along through the late Arthur Stephens. I was nine years old and turned down the first offer because I was happy at Oldham. Everything was going okay and Everton wasn't my team, Liverpool was. Despite my tender years, it was absolutely my decision. My dad weighed up the pros and cons with me but he said: "If you are happy at Oldham, stay there."

My attitude changed when my friend Scott of Elmers Green was picked up by Everton. It meant I knew someone there then and that was always a big thing for me, making that first step. I agreed to go down to Everton to see what it was like and after a little while it was a case of 'I'm really sorry Oldham, but I'm signing for Everton'.

Back at Elmers Green, I was loving it. After getting battered every week, as we got older we improved and for two seasons we won every trophy that was going in the Skem league. We needed a new challenge and Tommy decided we should join the Bootle league where we played our matches at Buckley Hill. We were under-13s by then and still naïve young kids from Skem. But we were about to grow up.

It was nice in the Skem league, very pleasant and well-mannered, but when we got to Bootle it was totally different. People were effing and blinding at us from the touchline and some of the play was rougher than anything we'd ever experienced before.

We were in an under-13s league but some of the opposition players were already shaving! I remember smelling cigarette smoke on one player marking me closely and I was shocked. A lot of our opponents were much bigger than us and I would have liked to have checked a few birth certificates. However, despite coming up for the first time against players who were trying to hurt us, we adapted quite quickly and in our first season we won one of the cups.

We were a game lot, the boys from Skem. I remember beating one of the established teams and they weren't happy at all, calling us all sorts of names and warning us that they were going to cut all our gear up in the changing rooms after the game. When the final whistle went they legged it to the Portakabin changing rooms and wouldn't let us in. One of our coaches,

Lenny, booted the door open, hung one of their players on a peg and the issue passed quite quickly.

Most of the aggressors in the Bootle league were kids of our own age (allegedly!) but some parents were a bit nasty as well and that's another reason why I have vowed never to get involved with players, coaches or officials when I am watching my own sons now. I have seen it happen and it is disgusting, simple as that.

You had to learn how to ride a tackle in that league. Some of the challenges were proper old-fashioned 'get the ball and the man' type tackles. That was a new experience for me. My dad always taught me not to pull out of anything and I had to stand up to some rough treatment. If there was a tackle, I had to be ready to win it. The Skem league had been hard because I was playing against kids older than me and I had to develop my skills, but the Bootle league really toughened me up. I had to learn to look after myself on the pitch, when I was never the strongest or the quickest.

Even though we were learning all the time in Bootle, we actually couldn't wait to get out of that league. We did one season and then moved to the Walton and Kirkdale league. It was under-14s by this point and I was 12. I think we finished third but the quality of opposition was much improved and they weren't out to hurt you. The league played representative matches and I was called up for the under-12s, as I was tech-nically eligible. I played alongside Franny Jeffers, along with other lads who were at Everton and Liverpool, and we ended up winning the tournament. I scored in the final at Melwood, Liverpool's training ground, which was nice.

The following season, when I was 13, Elmers Green folded

because the kids, as they tend to do, dropped their commitment levels, so I went to play for Denburn United, who had a fairly decent kid called Steven Gerrard playing for them at the time. I was with him and the team for a tournament at Anfield but didn't really get a game. And three weeks into the season, that team folded as well. Suddenly I was without a team and didn't know what I was going to do. I was available on a free transfer at the age of 13!

Thankfully I had a phone call from the manager of St Philomena's in the Walton and Kirkdale league. He remembered me from Elmers Green and invited me to join them for the season. I did so and it was the first time that I ever played at my own age group, under-13s. It was a really good, competitive league.

We played against Tony Hibbert's team, Kirkby-Knowsley. During the game there was a bit of argy-bargy on the side and our manager and their manager had a full-scale fight on the touchline – fists and kicks were flying and the game was stopped. Hibbo and I were playing together for Everton by this point so we were talking to each other on the pitch while all of this craziness was going on, each one of us claiming that our own manager was getting the better of it.

The match resumed, I was playing well and their manager's son was brought on to mark me. He was scary. He wasn't much interested in playing football – he just wanted to end my participation in the game. He followed me everywhere and was in my ear, menacingly telling me: "I'm going to kill you." I had never experienced anything like it in my life and I ran up to the ref telling him what he'd said but got the reply: "Has he kicked you or hit you?" When I confirmed that he hadn't as yet inflicted any physical damage but that he was quite keen to do so, the ref shrugged and said: "Well...not much I can do about it until he does!" It wasn't quite the support from the match official that I was looking for! Hibbo and I still giggle about all the things that went on that day.

We got to a cup final that season and I scored one of the best goals of my life thus far (it was similar to Ross Barkley's for Everton against Newcastle in March 2014). It was 1-1 in extra-time and the manager put me up front. We cleared a corner and I controlled it with my knee on the edge of the centre circle in our half; I turned and set off, changing direction as I beat one, two, three defenders, going round the keeper and slotting it in with my left foot to win us the cup.

It was played on a pitch that was known as 'Little Wembley' because of the quality of the grass. It wasn't very often you got to play on a top-quality pitch back then so these were occasions I always relished. We had a pitch similar at Bellefield that was also known as 'Little Wembley' where most of five, six and seven-a-side games were played over the years.

For the first two or three seasons at Everton, I trained with the year above me at my request. Among the lads I was playing alongside were Michael Ball, Mick O'Brien and Carl Regan. I got to know them really well, although when it came to tournaments, I'd go back to the year below. It wasn't until under-13s that I started to train with my own age.

Dad or Tommy Davies would take Scott and me. To begin with, it was once a week, but it quickly developed into two sessions a week. My brother soon became part of Everton so my mum and dad were there four times a week, shivering in the freezing cold large Bellefield gym. Sometimes, while we trained, Dad, Hibbo's dad and a couple of the other parents would nip to the pub. He'd say: "I'm going to keep warm, son. I'll be back before it finishes."

Neil Dewsnip did a lot of the training and he was a really good coach. He was at Everton for a few years before he got a job with the FA. Ray Hall took over for a while and as I got to under-15s and under-16s, we ended up with Ted Sutton and John McMahon and they were both terrific coaches, John especially. He would join in with us and certainly wouldn't be shy about throwing tackles in. It was so competitive and the games always flowed – everybody loved playing for John.

When I joined Everton, I was still very much a Liverpool supporter. I probably turned up in my Liverpool kit at first, making that statement all kids feel they have to make, but it wasn't long before my allegiance started to shift. I made the gradual transformation from supporting Liverpool to Everton between the ages of 13 and 16.

I was spending time at Everton every week and, honestly, you can't help but fall in love with the place. People would say, "you can't change your colours" and I'd reply, "I'm a Liverpool fan, but I really like Everton."

As soon as I started full-time at Everton, aged 16, and I was seeing the players every day, that was it. I officially let Liverpool go at that point. For two or three seasons before that, I was probably a fan of both, but I wouldn't have admitted that to anyone at Bellefield. I was sucked in to the feel of the place and the surroundings. I became an Evertonian and once it's in you, that's it.

I signed my schoolboy forms in the week leading up to the 1995 FA Cup final, so there was a lot of hustle and bustle at Bellefield and I was the least of anyone's worries. Joe Royle was great though and didn't give the impression that he had more important things to do when he joined me, Mum, Dad and Ray Hall in his office for the signing.

Mum has a picture of it on her wall at home. I'm wearing an awful leather jacket that she had bought me for the occasion, while Dad was sporting a Krusty the Clown haircut because he was in the process of going bald but still had a tuft on top. Ray Hall had the widest middle-part I've ever seen…so it's not the most flattering of photographs and I wish Mum would take it off the wall!

All schoolboys had free tickets to the FA Cup final provided for them and Everton asked for chaperones. So I got a ticket for free, Dad offered to be a chaperone and my brother was able to buy one as he was at the club as well at the time. At Wembley, I was sat next to two lads from my year, Eddie O'Brien and David Knowles, and we had big Everton hats and giant foam hands. We thought we might get on the telly as we were right above the tunnel.

We looked a bit daft in those hats but it was a great day, the result was obviously fantastic and the atmosphere was incredible. Up the Blues!

For all the football I was playing, my schoolwork didn't really suffer until my GCSE year. I got good marks across the board in primary school and when I reached senior school, at Upholland High, I could get by without really trying. It wasn't until I played for England Schoolboys that my schoolwork began to be affected.

I was invited for national trials at the end of my Everton under-14 season, first in the North West and then progressing to

Lilleshall. They gave you your own little residence, sharing with someone. You had trials in the morning, followed by lunch, and played a game in the afternoon. I ended up getting down to the last 30 but later received a letter telling me that, unfortunately, I hadn't made it. I was a bit gutted but shrugged it off as one of those things and put it down to experience. My mum, however, was distraught – she gets very emotionally involved in things like that and she cried her eyes out.

But I hadn't actually been turned down by England because, unbeknown to me somehow, it turned out that those first trials were to see who was selected for the national school at Lilleshall and not for England Schoolboys. The likes of Franny Jeffers and Scott Parker got in and they went away to live there for two years.

Looking back now I can honestly tell you that I'm made up I didn't get into the national school. To have to move away from home at 14 years of age would have been of no benefit to me. To go to school with a big group of football lads would have had dire effects on my education and the amount of training those kids had to do every day would, I believe, have burned me out.

It's obviously hard to judge things like that but of the 16-20 graduates that went to Lilleshall each year, how many made it to become professional footballers? And of those that did, how many played on into their 30s? I'd be interested to find that out. However, I am certain that me going to Lilleshall would have brought my injury nightmare forward a few years and maybe would have stopped me even getting a contract with Everton.

At the time I didn't let the disappointment linger and was soon representing Lancashire Boys, which led to representing the North West. Shortly after, I was invited to trials for England Schoolboys. I got to the final 22 but received another letter to say I hadn't made it. Cue my mum getting upset all over again! I must admit I was a little bit down myself and I couldn't shake the feeling of what could have been for me. But it didn't last too long, it tends not to when you're a kid of 14 or 15, and I moved on pretty quickly.

It was during this period that the Schools FA changed the selection criteria from the school year to the calendar year of a boy's birth. I had always struggled because I'm a May birthday and wasn't as physically developed as some of the other lads in my school year who had been born six, seven or eight months earlier, which can make a big difference at a young age. I read a stat not long back when I was starting to do my coaching badges that 75-80% of footballers' birthdays are between September and December because they develop faster and are bigger and stronger.

Anyway, I kept plugging away (the desire not to let setbacks affect me too much was to be tested frequently before I kicked a ball in the Premier League) and I did well enough to be invited back for England Schoolboy trials a year later. I was shaking like a leaf when the letter dropped through the letter box and I held my breath as I tore open the envelope. This time I was in! I had made the national schools team. Mum was made up.

We had our first meet-up at Lytham St Annes. John Owens was the coach with Stuart Parnaby's dad, Dave, as the assistant manager. I was presented with my kit, an adidas strip with Walkers Crisps across the front.

Because of the adidas sponsorship, they gave us pairs of Predator boots, soon after they were first manufactured. The ones with the giant spikes all over them! We were told we had to wear them – but I wouldn't have dreamed of not doing so anyway. They were by far the best pair of footy boots I'd ever owned. They were like nothing we'd ever seen before.

Among my team-mates were two lads on Liverpool's books, Ian Armstrong, also from Skelmersdale, and Steve Warnock, from Ormskirk. All three of us were from West Lancs, which isn't exactly renowned as being a footballing hotbed. It was a great achievement for the area to have three lads playing for England Schoolboys in the same year. I don't know what was in the water in Skem back in 1981 but if they'd have bottled it, they'd have made a fortune!

Our first game of the 1996/97 Victory Shield was against Wales at Ninian Park. I started and it was the first time I experienced the 3-5-2 formation – I was used to 4-4-2 with me as the attacking of the two centre midfielders. Suddenly, I became the holding man of the three midfielders with Ian Armstrong and Joe Cole going ahead. We won 3-2 and I was buzzing. It was strange playing a holding role and it felt completely foreign, but I loved every minute of it. It was a brilliant experience, the whole thing. I didn't play in the second game against Northern Ireland but I did against Scotland, whom we went on to share the trophy with.

Following that they took us to France for the Montaigu tournament, which is contested by international under-16 teams. Now I really did feel like an international footballer! Travelling on a plane in an England tracksuit was a great feeling. In the first match I was in the holding role again and we won 2-0 against Greece. In the second game we played Israel. The Schools FA had scouted the Israelis and found they played the same system as us with a lad on the right who was their most creative player. We set up with two holding midfielders, with me on the left to man-mark him. I was like a man possessed and inspired by the Three Lions on my chest I tackled him, roughed him up and then managed to do what I do best – get forward and score a goal, with a header at the back stick. I think I surprised our coaches, but I'm not bad at jumping. We reached the quarter-finals and it was a wonderful experience.

Next up was the game I had dreamed about all my life – England v Germany at Wembley. What an iconic fixture that is and in June 1997 it was my turn to try and do what Banks, Moore, Charlton and Hurst had done 31 years earlier. If this sounds a bit comic-book then I make no apologies. I can't begin to describe on these pages just how thrilled and excited I was to be playing for England Schoolboys against Germany. At Wembley Stadium!

I can still clearly remember being in the dressing room beforehand then walking up the tunnel and out onto the pitch, trying to take it all in. I knew roughly where my parents were sitting and I waved in the general direction. It felt like a World Cup final for me. It got better when I scored the opening goal. I was fouled between the halfway line and the penalty area on the left side. Steve Warnock floated the free-kick across and I flicked my header over the keeper and into the top corner. The crowd roared…and so did I. I ran off like a madman screaming with unadulterated joy. What a moment.

Germany equalised but Ian Armstrong scored the winner, and we won 2-1. We spotted everyone from Skem in the crowd and celebrated with them. There weren't many people left in Skem that afternoon and burglars would have had a field day.

We had loads of pictures taken afterwards. It was a really, really good day.

It's interesting to consider the different paths the players within that squad have taken and where they all are now. Myself, Joe Cole and Steve Warnock have had careers in the Premier League and played for England. Michael Standing was at Aston Villa then and had a decent career with Bradford, Walsall and Oxford. I know he is still close friends with Gareth Barry. Ronnie Wright is a medical university scientist and is apparently working within the NHS. Ian Armstrong went to Port Vale from Liverpool but completely fell out of love with the game and didn't speak to anyone connected to football.

That's a shame because we were relatively close when we played together. I met him recently and we chatted about old times. He was, and still is, a nice lad. He just has no interest in football anymore. As bad as it sounds, I'd never really given most of these lads much thought until I started doing this book. I've just carried on with my life, which I suppose is what most of them have done. I tend to look forward rather than back.

I was given some interesting advice in the aftermath of one of those matches. My girlfriend at the time was Sarah Deehan, the daughter of John, who was then the manager of Wigan Athletic. She had moved to our school and we dated when we were 15 and 16. John watched the Wales game and told me: "Well done, you've got really good close control and your short passing is decent enough but you never play the ball long. You need to work on your long game."

It made me think and I realised he was right. For a year after that I really practised my long passing, going round the back of

Bellefield with Alan Harper, who was one of the club's coaches at the time. Before then I had never really done a long pass because I never had to. I had a short game. It took me about three years or more, because of my injury troubles, to really improve.

Funnily enough, the person who I've spent the most time with, working on my long passing, is Hibbo. I would ask him how he did it and he would laugh his head off as I screwed the ball left, and sliced it right. I had to master it because I wanted him to stop laughing at me. He showed me his foot placement and technique and gradually I picked it up.

Even now when I do a drilled pass in training which goes straight to him, we both cheer and make a big thing of it. I executed a difficult long pass in a game a few months back which went like an arrow and I whispered to him in the changing rooms afterwards: "Did you see that?" He responded: "After I got over my shock that it was you, I laughed my head off, mate. Love it, lad."

We still work together on long passing to this day. That man can strike a football better than anyone I've ever seen. It surprises me that he hasn't taken free-kicks on the edge of the box. I've been telling him for years that he should. He can't half whack it. If you challenged him in training to put the ball in a particular area of the goal, he'd get it in there or get it close every time. He won't step up in a game, though. He did it once in his testimonial in 2012 and scored. There was a massive pitch invasion, he trotted back to the halfway line and hasn't crossed it since!

Going back to 1997, although representing England was a fantastic experience, I suffered academically as I say.

Foolishly I thought 'so be it'. In hindsight it wasn't the correct thing to do and I wouldn't do the same again. I had missed a week of school for trials, four days for every game we played and another week to take part in the Montaigu tournament. I still got decent results though – two Bs, five Cs and two Ds in subjects I didn't like anyway. That was without trying and missing a lot of lessons.

Looking back, I really wish I'd have studied harder to improve my results. If things hadn't eventually gone my way I would have really needed them, and once you understand that they can have a massive significance on your life, you realise how naïve you've been to not give them your full commitment.

By this point I'd signed a four-year contract with Everton, taking me until I was 20. It was one year as a YTS and a three-year pro contract.

I wasn't being arrogant or cocky, I'm not that kind of person, but I was going to be a footballer. There were no ifs, buts or maybes. Even when I had my injuries, as far as I was concerned, it was just delaying my career.

Now you look back and I was one of the lucky ones, but my conviction was so strong. There was nothing else I was going to be.

I didn't think I'd need a back-up plan for how my life would pan out. I just wanted to be a footballer. I had a meeting with the careers advisor in school and, like everybody, I was asked: "What do you want to do when you leave school?"

I said: "I'm going to be a footballer."

The advisor sighed, grinned and said: "No, what's your path? What's your plan?"

"I'm going to be a footballer."

"Is this realistic?"

"Yes."

I knew that I was one of hundreds of kids who must say that to them, but I meant it. Really meant it…and nothing was going to stop me.

03

Make Or Break

Pre-season training for my first year full-time with Everton, in 1997/98, began in Florida with trips to McDonald's.

Mum had booked a two-week summer holiday to Disneyland 18 months previously, which meant I would be starting a week later than everybody else. It wasn't an ideal scenario but, I have to say, Disneyland was much better than I thought it would be.

I was aware that the rest of the lads were doing pre-season training and I needed to go back in decent shape, so I devised a routine. Every evening during the second week of the holiday, when the lads had started back home, I'd run from our hotel to the nearest McDonald's, which was about a mile away, buy a burger and run back before eating it. You won't find it in any training manuals, but it worked for me. I had to be focussed and disciplined and keep my pace at a good rate or the burger would have been cold by the time I got back to the hotel! So Ronald McDonald was my fitness coach for a week before I returned home and back to Everton.

My first day full-time at the club began very badly, thanks, ironically, to a food-related issue. Actually, it was a bit more than a hiccup. I'd had a big bowl of Frosties for my breakfast and Colin Harvey had us running backwards and forwards on the Bill Shankly Playing Fields over the road from Bellefield. It was very heavy going and it quickly became too much for me. I doubled up and ended up crouched into a ball before vomiting everywhere. There were undigested Frosties all over the grass. It was a traumatic experience and it must have been another 10 years before I had breakfast again before training. It really affected me and taught me a lesson.

Simply getting to Bellefield from Skem was something of an ordeal. A lad called Dave Knowles, who was also on Everton's books, lived with us for 18 months and we travelled in together. For the first week, we had to get up at 6am and catch the 6.40am bus which took us from Skem to Walton Vale. Then we had to catch another bus to West Derby and walk the last bit. The timings were against us because we'd arrive at 8.05am. We didn't need to be in until 9am but the next bus would have meant we'd be five minutes late.

We didn't finish until 5pm, after which we'd walk to the centre of West Derby, get a bus into Liverpool city centre and then catch a train from Lime Street to Wigan, followed by a bus from Wigan to where we lived in Upholland. It was a two-and-a-half-hour trip so we wouldn't get home until nearly 8pm. I almost always used to fall asleep on the train and people would laugh at me as I slobbered down my chin with my face stuck to the window. It was very tough for us and if we both fell asleep, we'd often miss our stop. They were long days for a 16-year-old kid.

Thankfully, after about a month, Ray Hall and Colin Harvey offered to take turns to pick us up at Kirkby train station. My mum or dad would drop us off at Upholland station and we'd catch the 8am service that would get us to Kirkby for 8.20 where Ray would meet us. It made a massive difference.

I loved the whole experience of being part of the club every day, although it wasn't always as professionally organised as you might imagine. Because I arrived a week after everybody else, most of the boots had already been allocated, so I was left swimming in a pair of nine-and-a-halfs, almost two sizes too big, given to me by our legendary kit man, Jimmy Martin. I was far too shy to argue over them because Jimmy would have roasted me! About 10 days in, Colin Harvey noticed I was running awkwardly and beckoned me over.

"Ossie, come here."

"Yes, Col, what's up?"

"What have you got on your feet?"

"Boots, Jimmy gave them to me."

"What size are they?"

"They're nine-and-a-half."

"What size are you?"

"Usually an eight."

"They're too big, why are you wearing boots like that?"

"Because I started late, Jimmy had no sevens, eights or nines left."

"They're massive on you. You can't play in them, lad. When training is finished, we'll go in and see Jimmy."

I was made up because I thought he was going to get me a pair of size eights. When we got inside, Colin called 'Gonzo' over and queried it with him.

Jimmy said: "It's all we've got left, Col."

Colin asked: "Have you not got anything else?"

"We've got nines, nine-and-a-halfs, tens or sixes."

Colin said: "Give us the sixes. 'Ere lad, get them on the stretcher and get your feet in them."

Every morning I used to soak them in boiling water and stretch them for 20 minutes, just to be able to get my feet into them. Eventually I managed to squash them inside but I ended up with ingrowing toenails that required a mini-operation.

I still wear tight boots to this day, a size seven, even though I'm an eight. Looking back now, it was crazy. I should have just gone and bought myself a pair that fitted properly but I was on £40.85 a week and it didn't go far. If you wanted to have a night out, that soon disappeared.

It went up by about £2 a year later, but that was when they changed to the Academy system, so the first-year scholars started on £180 a week. I was on that a month. We were supposed to be their seniors, but they were arriving in fancy cars, going shopping and buying new gear. Me and Hibbo were wondering, 'how has this happened?' I was supposed to sign a pro contract at the end of my first year but, because I was injured, there was a big delay and I ended up doing the first four months of the following season still on £42, while these kids were on nearly four times that.

Colin Harvey was brilliant for me, a really, really top guy. On the wall in my house I've only got one picture of me posing with someone else and it's with Colin. I saw him at a game a couple of years ago and I got a club photographer to take a picture. I'm really proud of it, first of all for who he is – his superb playing career, before going on to coach and manage Everton – and because he helped mould me. He'd work with the whole team, obviously, but would then take me aside and tell me to practise using a size two ball. I was decent at that. I'd have to volley it against the wall, control it, volley it against the next wall, control it and keep on doing that. He would drill me every day.

He was always trying to improve young players. He could do all of it, technical coaching and man-management. He could really shout at you if you needed it but he would usually have a smile on his face. Every time he opened his mouth, I was listening. His assistant, Andy Holden, known to all as 'Taff', was similar.

There was probably as much off the ball work as on it with Colin. He taught me defending, being in the right position, and the mental side of the game. He toughened you up. If you couldn't deal with that, you might have suffered, but our group were winners. Losing wasn't accepted. He really instilled a winning mentality into us all. We won the Youth Cup, we won the Youth Premier League, we won the Reserve League – pretty much everything we could over that four-year period. Colin Harvey didn't accept off-days.

At the end of last season I was informed that I had drawn level with Colin on the all-time Everton appearances list. If someone had told me when I was 16 years old that I would play more games for Everton Football Club than Colin Harvey, I would never have believed it. I still can't even now! It doesn't seem right!

I was definitely intimidated by the first-teamers when I started full-time. When you're growing up, there's a big divide between young kids and Premier League footballers. They seem out of reach.

My first year was the first time that the YTS lads didn't have to clean their boots and that actually created a barrier between the first team and the kids. There didn't need to be any interaction any more. David Unsworth was always great, though, speaking to you and making you feel good about yourself. Dave Watson intimidated me. He was club captain and I didn't want him to look me directly in the eye in case I'd done something wrong. Duncan Ferguson was such a big character and I was scared witless of him (I still am in fact!). Once you got to know him, though, he was such a nice, humble guy and quite a mellow character. He just happened to be very competitive, bad tempered and aggressive on a football pitch.

During those early days, Neville Southall was still at the club and on Fridays he wouldn't do any goalkeeper training because that was his day to be an outfield player. He'd train with the youth team and join in our match. He was very demanding and angry if things didn't go his way and would shout at us. He was so intimidating. I only got to play with him once or two twice and it was an experience, I can tell you.

In my first year full-time, I was still involved with England, playing for the under-16s. When you go up an age group, you expect the players to stay the same, but half were different. Joe Cole was still around but Gaz Barry was also now in and he was the main player.

We had an international in Poland and me and Gaz roomed together. One night, we went out to a cinema in Warsaw to watch the film Private Parts, about the American DJ Howard Stern. That's still probably the funniest film I've ever seen in my life. I was giggling away, trying to keep quiet, while there was delayed laughter from the Polish audience as they read the subtitles.

I wouldn't have laughed so much had I known then that I would not represent my country at any level for another 15 years. Come the end of that season, I picked up my injury and I wasn't selected again until 2012, when I won my first full senior cap. Missing out on the Under-21s was a blow, but it isn't a regret. It would have been nice if it could have happened, but it's just the way my career panned out. If it had happened, playing extra games might have burnt me out early. You just don't know. Look at Franny Jeffers, who was one of the best strikers I played with. It all happened very quickly for him, before his career gradually tailed off.

While the Everton first team had a terrible time in 1997/98, barely avoiding relegation on the final day of the season, it was a memorable one for us youngsters. We ended it by winning the FA Youth Cup, although there was a sting in the tail for me.

It was an incredible run. Our first game was away at Blackpool, which we won 1-0. I started as a sub in that first game before I came on to play. I played centre midfield alongside our captain, Mick O'Brien. Dean Delaney was in goal, Carl Regan right-back, Adam Eaton and Richard Dunne centre-half, Wayne McDermott left-back, Dave Poppleton on the right-wing, Jamie Milligan on the left, and we had Phil Jevons and Franny Jeffers up front.

After another 1-0 win at home to Stoke, we were drawn away

at Watford. The game should never have taken place because half the pitch was frozen solid. Possibly because we were a young team and there was a lot of travel involved, they let it go ahead. I'd only packed studs and everyone was wearing moulds except me. We went 2-0 down and it was looking bad. Colin made a tactical change at half-time and brought Hibbo on for Dave Poppleton, changing our system to the 4-3-1-2 system 16 years before its time! We ended up winning 3-2. I scored, Phil Jevons equalised and Mick O'Brien got the winner.

We then beat Ipswich 3-2 at Goodison to set up a two-legged semi-final against Leeds United, who had Jonathan Woodgate, Stephen McPhail and Paul Robinson among their team. We won 1-0 in the first leg at Elland Road when Mick O'Brien scored a whopping half-volley, right in the top corner. Leeds were holders and expected to win but we secured our place in the final with a 2-1 win in the second leg at Goodison.

Blackburn Rovers were the opposition in the final and Sky Sports screened both legs live. Martin Tyler, their main commentator, came to Bellefield before the game to introduce himself and do his research. We were all dead excited to meet him. I can't believe it was 16 years ago. I hope he doesn't mind me saying but them 16 years have been kinder to me than him! He'll kill me next time I see him now!

We won the first leg 3-1 at Ewood Park on May 1 and I scored the third, a volley. It wasn't a bad goal. The ball went up to Phil Jevons and although I don't know if he was trying to set me up, it fell perfectly and I instinctively volleyed it into the net. I've still got it on a DVD somewhere.

We were all elated but the course of my career was about to be altered in a big way. A Blackburn player came in for a run-of-the-mill tackle and wobbled my knee. I got up, thought it was fine and carried on, finishing the game with little problem. On the coach afterwards I put my leg up on the table and sat like that for the journey back to Bellefield. When I went to stand up, I just couldn't move. My knee was swollen and throbbing.

I didn't know what it was but I certainly wasn't prepared for the diagnosis. They told me it was cartilage damage and that I needed an operation. My world fell apart. I was absolutely devastated. I know I've indicated that I am not one for regrets, but I must admit I am still gutted about it even now.

The lads were gutted for me, but there wasn't time for them to show it too much because they had to prepare for the second leg. I was very low. I hated the feeling of helplessness and disappointment as I went under the knife and they cheerfully prepared for the biggest game of their lives. We won the second leg to take the trophy and there's a picture of the players and substitutes celebrating and cheering while they showed off the trophy to the crowd after the second leg at Goodison. I'm not on it because I was stood to the side, on my crutches, feeling really upset. I should have joined in and regret that I didn't. I wasn't mature enough to put my feelings to one side and be happy for the team and happy that I had made a big contribution before being injured.

I pulled myself together to join the boys in the Paradox nightclub in Aintree afterwards. I don't know how we all got in – I think the Paradox had a reputation for being a bit loose with the IDs. We had a great night, even though I was on my sticks.

It was a tremendous win for us but that first leg was the start of all my knee problems and it would be over three years before I came out the other side.

When that tackle was made, I had no way of knowing the long-term significance of that one moment. My knee was throbbing but I had nothing to compare it to so I had no idea of just how bad it was.

Within two or three weeks of the original injury, in May 1998, I'd had my first op to shave the cartilage. I was told I'd be fine in six weeks but, as it was the end of the season, there was no rush. Three months later I was still feeling all sorts of pain, so I underwent another op in September. They found another bit of flapping cartilage and said afterwards it might have been missed in the first op or damaged during my rehab. So that was three wasted months for a start. It was frustrating for me and I was annoyed about it because I perceived it as being due to the negligence of the surgeon. I was virtually starting my rehab all over again and the first couple of weeks were mentally very tough for me.

With the original injury, I was out for about five months. I came back, played the rest of the 98/99 season, and we reached the semi-final of the Youth Cup where we lost to West Ham, Joe Cole's team. We should have definitely won it that year.

That run featured one of Hibbo's goals, easily the best of his career, at Gigg Lane when we played Man United in the fourth round. It finished 2-2 and he scored a half-volley like Barry Horne's goal against Wimbledon in 1994. It swerved away into the top corner with such power, we were lucky that the net caught it. He still likes to talk about that goal now, but that's not surprising as it was better than the other two he's ever scored in his entire life!

I did my ankle in that game but I was available for the replay, which we won 4-0 at Goodison. In the next round, against

Swindon, I rolled my ankle again and this time felt a snap. I was freaking out on the pitch but within two or three days I could move it and the swelling had gone. It wasn't until a while later that we realised I had completely lost the ligament. It hasn't been the same since and to this day I still wear strapping on my ankle in every game to support it.

Six months later my knee was causing trouble again so I had yet another operation. I was managing to play but I was repeatedly doing my cartilage. I'd turn and my knee wouldn't always come with me. I would come in and have a run of games here and there but I was repeatedly losing control of my knee, or I'd go over on my ankle. It was a very worrying time for me.

Thankfully I had a good support unit around me in my parents and family and they constantly kept me in a positive frame of mind. Well most of the time anyway. If it wasn't for their guidance at a difficult time for me mentally, I'm not sure I'd have had the strength to stay on the right path that eventually led me to where I wanted to go. I'm not saying that I was on the verge of seriously going off the rails. I really wasn't (my nights out have never been excessively crazy and I've never even been tempted to try any kind of illegal substance), but without the help that was always available to me from my family, I may have decided that all the pain, hassle and hard work just wasn't worth it. When you're that age and having a difficult time, it can be easy to take people for granted. I probably never told anyone in the family just how much I valued their constant support...so I'll do it now. Thanks guys!

I was very lucky to have that support mechanism to help see me through. Not everyone has that. I am very proud to be a Prince's Trust ambassador and the duties over the years have included meeting young adults who had nobody there for them when they needed support. Some have gone off the rails, but without someone to steer you through difficult times, I can imagine that it's easy to venture off track. I really enjoy meeting the ones who have turned themselves around and made something of their lives. They've had the tough times and they've suffered periods when they've had no guidance or support, but they've worked hard, and with the help of initiatives like the Prince's Trust, they've come out the other side. It's very rewarding for me to meet them and tell them to their faces just how proud they should be of themselves.

By January 2001, my injury was such that I was saying to people: "Look, I'm really struggling here." As the season was coming towards an end, I went for a run around Croxteth Park and I could really feel pain in my knee. After another assessment, I was told I'd need another cartilage op, which would have been my fifth in three years. I felt really low and was thinking things like 'I'll never be a player if I have to have an op every year' and 'how much cartilage can I even have left?' All the operations were done at Crank, the hospital on the Rainford by-pass (I often drive past it and although it's an excellent place, I have to say I cannot stand it!).

I remember coming round after the fifth op, expecting the usual: "yes, we've been in and shaved a little bit off." But this time there was really bad news and it shook me to the core. Instead of the familiar message, the doctor told me: "The cartilage op went well but your anterior cruciate ligament has been hanging by a thread for a while now and that's why you have had no control over your knee. That's probably why you keep on doing your cartilage, because there is too much give and it shears away at your cartilage. Unfortunately we're going to have to give you an anterior cruciate ligament op and it will take about nine months to recover from that."

I choked up immediately and experienced hot flushes, which I'd never had before. I managed to hold it together but as soon as he left the room, I grabbed the bedpan and vomited. The initial shock was horrendous. My head was spinning as I had to come to terms with a whole year out injured. I even started to convince myself that my football career was over as I only had a year left on my contract. I started wondering what I could do instead. Thinking that your hopes and dreams are all dashed is a dreadful experience and I have never forgotten the feeling of absolute panic and fear.

I even began to wish I'd paid more attention in my classes rather than use my exercise books to select my Best World XI during lessons!

It must have just been a little nick at first before it gradually wore away, but if it had been discovered initially, it could have saved me three years. Every time I was turning, I was shearing my cartilage away.

I felt bitter and angry about it at first, but that didn't last long. What good would feeling bitter do for me? I needed all my focus to be on getting right again and I needed positive not negative energy to do that.

Of course I would have liked it to have been sorted much sooner but who's to say my career would have panned out as it has if I'd recovered faster? Maybe I would have suffered a different injury. Maybe I would have got in the first team sooner but not been ready for it. Who knows what would have happened? I think sometimes things happen for a reason and in life you have to take the roll of the dice in your stride...even when you don't like the way it rolls.

Les Helm was our physio at the time. He was very good, a former first-team physio, but really old school. The type who, if you asked for a rub, would say: "A rub? A rub? Where d'yer think yer are lad...a fuckin' massage parlour? I bet you want me to go topless don't ye lad!"

Both him and Peter Beirne, a physiotherapist at Alder Hey who is still associated with the club, were telling me I'd have to make the most of the next few years because of the state of my knee. Despite trying so hard to keep positive I was taken aback and people have said since they thought my football career was doomed or that at best I'd only play until my early 20s.

I don't know if it was naivety or just blind youthful determination but I just didn't see it myself. To me, (after I got over the initial five-minute panic attack in the hospital) it was just a hurdle. It was a big hurdle – eventually more than a three-and-a-half-year hurdle – but at the time it was a three-month hurdle, followed by another three-month hurdle and then a nine-month hurdle. I always saw light at the end of the tunnel. If I'd known how long it would actually take, it would have overwhelmed me. It was done in stages, and I'd manage to play for a few months before something else would go wrong.

Once I had the ACL, I felt a lot better. My knee is not perfect and it never will be, but it's been good enough to play professional football and I'm thankful for that. I haven't missed many games because of it and although it won't be much use to anyone when my number's finally up, it hasn't been too bad.

My knee problems have been well documented but I have another physical issue which is not so well known. My left leg is longer than my right and this wasn't discovered until I was with England Schoolboys. When I was in the Everton under-15s, I kept on pulling my thigh muscle all the time, mostly my right. It was frustrating.

I made it into the England squad and the first time we met up for the match at Ninian Park against Wales, I felt the muscle the day before the game. I tried to keep it quiet but eventually mentioned it to Mark Eales, the physio. In the hotel, the day before my first appearance for England Schoolboys, he had me walking up and down the corridor, studying my gait.

He then asked me to lie down and got a tape measure out, which is how he discovered that my left leg is longer than the right by a good three or four centimetres. This was a shock to me and I wondered how I'd managed to walk without a limp.

Although now I knew about the leg issue, I didn't do anything about it. I spoke to my dad and, being naïve, we thought if Everton found out, they wouldn't sign me full-time, so we decided to keep it quiet. Looking back, this was incredibly stupid because Everton could have helped me right from the start. I still laugh about it with a doctor who still works for the club, Dr Irving. The day I had my medical at Everton, he was assessing my gait and said: "I think you might have curvature of the spine. I'll send you for X-rays."

I knew it was probably my left leg length but I still didn't say anything. Obviously when I was lying flat everything in my back was straight so there was no problem there. The doc saw the X-ray and signed it off. I was in. I played through the whole of that '97/98 season with the secret still intact.

Of course, I eventually broke down in the Youth Cup final. It is now thought that all my knee problems stemmed from my leg length and my alignment. I'd lived with it for the first 17 years of my life but as I grew up and played more football, issues began to develop. In that first season at Everton, I was training every day and putting so much force into the right leg that my knee suffered. If I'd have gone to Lilleshall and been training every day since I was 14, I'd have broken down sooner. Maybe things do happen for a reason.

After I had the second operation, I finally mentioned it to the club and Les Helm's response was: "Bloody hell, lad. Why didn't you just say something? You bleeding idiot."

They took me to Salford to see an orthopaedic guy and over the course of a month they moulded me a shoe and told me that I had to wear an inner sole in my right boot. I was wearing the size six boots that Colin had given me, so putting something else in my boot would have been ridiculous and impossible. I ended up going up to a size 7, which was great for both feet, and I got my mould in my boot.

My back, hip and muscles felt strange for the first two or three months as my body adjusted. Initially, my foot was sticking out the boot and there was no real grab around my ankle. That's why I kept going over on the ankle, snapping the ligament at one point. Even with strapping I was struggling for a year until it was suggested that we should do the build on the outside of the boot. They ripped the sole off my boot, put the heel-raise on the outside and closed it. I could then get my foot fully in the boot, which was encasing my ankle. I felt a lot more secure.

After the cruciate operation on July 4, 2001, as I say, I have generally been okay. It's not perfect and it never will be. At times it is sore and swells up but we finally figured out a way of getting by. It took a long time to get all my issues sorted, with some trial and error, as my body readapted. Once I did, I managed to go out on loan and eventually get in our first team. My left hip is particularly 'muscley' because for 16 years of my life that leg was doing a lot more work than my right one. That's probably where all my issues came from, my leg length. It's a massive part of my story.

I hurt my knee against Bolton in January 2012, the night before my daughter was born, which caused me to miss two months, and I had another issue in the Goodison derby in 2011 where my ankle went. They were just two little bumps along the road which, considering what I went through between 1998 and 2001, isn't bad going.

While all these things were happening to me, I did feel I was being left behind a bit but, like I've said, I think that things happen for a reason. Despite the setbacks, I never stopped believing that I was going to be a professional footballer.

Franny got in the first team at 16 and I'd been playing with him for years, setting up his goals. I played alongside Gaz Barry for England Under-16s and he had five years in the Premier League before I managed to get in the Everton first team. There was Joe Cole too, but he was a special talent. Even the likes of Kevin McLeod, Phil Jevons and Jamie Milligan had all had games in the first team.

There were times when I thought, 'why hasn't it happened for me yet?' But I never felt as though it was never going to happen. I knew that all I needed was a chance.

04

Starting Over

As I grew up on the books at Everton, the first team struggled for most of the time, apart from two years under Joe Royle in the mid-1990s. The club was so nearly relegated on the last day in 1994 and 1998, and I was in the stands both times.

For the Wimbledon game in 1994, I was with Scott Davies, my mate from Elmers Green. We had four tickets, two in the Joe Mercer Suite and two in the Main Stand. The dads took the posh seats. Before the game, I remember a large guy with a ponytail standing up and screaming at all the fans sitting around him: "Fucking get on your feet! Every fucking one of you...we can't afford to lose this! Fucking get up! Come on! Come on!" We were scared, so we did as we were told...as did everyone else around us!

The atmosphere was like nothing I had ever experienced before. There was genuine fear amongst the fans and I did wonder what it must have been like for the players to play in front of such a vocal and partisan crowd.

Everton went 2-0 down and 'ponytail man' was going absolutely berserk. He'd lost it completely and I really thought that we were going to be relegated. As everyone knows, of course, Everton came back to win 3-2. That has got to be the greatest and most important comeback in the history of the club. I'm not sure I've ever felt such emotion. I was drained at the end of the game, so goodness knows what the players felt like. David Unsworth became my team-mate of course, and he has since told me that he would have never recovered from being part of an Everton team relegated from the top flight. There were people all around me crying at different points of the afternoon, and the fact that there were only three sides to Goodison that day (the Park End had been demolished and not yet rebuilt) just added to the surreal atmosphere.

I was at the FA Cup final a year later and that was a joy, but it was a day out that went well. In 1994 there was so much tension. The ecstasy and the sheer relief at the end was something I don't think I've experienced since. Any Evertonian who was there will tell you what an incredible day that was.

I was sitting in the Main Stand, towards the Park End, in 1998 against Coventry, and when we scored first, the place erupted, but when they equalised late on you could hear a pin drop and there was fear and shock again until the final whistle. We could have won the game and still been relegated if Bolton had got a result at Chelsea that same day. Chelsea had a European Cup Winners' Cup final four days later but they still put a shift in and beat Bolton, so our 1-1 draw was enough. I've always liked Gianluca Vialli...

We shouldn't have been at risk of dropping out of the division and just because we're a big club, if we had gone down, there's no guarantee we'd have come straight back. Look at Leeds. Look at Portsmouth. Look at Wolves. The memory of it still makes me shudder.

I was still a Liverpool fan at the time of the Wimbledon game but the changeover period was already in process. From 1993/94 to maybe 1995/96-1996/97 – it was a two-to-three-year period where it just snuck up on me. I definitely went to Goodison that day cheering like the maddest Blue you've ever known. The change had already started to happen.

We've come a long way since then. It took a few years but now we're constantly fighting at the top end, where we should be, thanks largely to David Moyes. Joe Royle had a good go and he definitely left too soon, towards the end of 1996/97. We had experienced a bad few months but considering what he'd achieved before then, he deserved to see the season out and start the next one.

When Howard Kendall came back for the third time, we struggled badly. He did well to keep us up in the end but lost his job shortly afterwards. Walter Smith came in with a great pedigree but we couldn't seem to escape relegation battles.

We were training at Bellefield for my first year but, shortly after Walter arrived, it was decided that there wasn't enough room there for the YTS lads like me. They bought a place in Netherton and we were all sent down there. It was a real downer for us. We were training miles away and had nothing to do with the first team any more, only getting to see them occasionally. It was a shame because we could learn things by watching them train and play, and we missed out on a big development tool.

Netherton wasn't the greatest facility either, certainly not for the preparation of young footballers. In fact, after training there for the best part of a year, the building we were using was declared unsafe and the club was ordered to pull it down! We had to use the Civil Service Club in Thornton for getting changed. For a short time, we would get changed at the Civil Service, drive to Netherton, drive back to eat our dinner and head to Netherton for the afternoon session. After a while, we decided to train at the Civil Service as well to save all the hassle.

When Walter took over, he didn't fancy any of the lads Howard had brought in. Gareth Farrelly, John Oster and John O'Kane trained with us and played for the reserves. Slaven Bilic was also out of favour so he became a Netherton regular too. It was tough for him because when you've recently played in a World Cup semi-final, I guess Netherton and the Civil Service Club in Thornton are something of a comedown. It must have been like an actor playing Sydney Opera House one day and the Hope Theatre in Skelmersdale the next but, despite that, Slaven was a nice guy.

So even though we weren't based with the first team, being with these players was pretty good for our development. We were 17 and playing alongside six or seven first-team standard players every day for three or four months.

Colin Harvey and Andy 'Taff' Holden were ordered to bring them into our session. They would tell us: "Make sure you don't end up like these. Look at them," trying to point out all the negatives. A young lad needs that but on the other hand we had some very experienced players doing some very experienced things in training every day. You can't help but pick up a few things along the way.

Slaven was good to us, although I doubt he'd remember me. After our dinner at the Civil Service, he would go outside for a smoke on the steps.

He'd be turning to us asking, "does anyone want a ciggy?" We'd say, "no, Colin will kill us" and point out that Col was watching him. He'd drawl, "ah, no, I don't care about that. I need a ciggy." He would tell us stories from his career and I'd be hanging on every word.

One of my best mates was, and still is, Matt McKay. Howard signed him from Chester for about £250,000. He was barely 17 and they gave him a seat in the first-team dressing room. I was thinking 'he must be a whizz-kid. That's going to make it even harder for us'. He seemed like a first-teamer straight away. Then he started training and playing with us and we ended up becoming quite close.

In fact, it was inadvertently through Matt McKay that I met my future wife, Jenny. He's getting the blame anyway!

The Civil Service groundsman was a fella called Jimmy Tomlinson and Matt became friendly with him. Jimmy set Matt up with his daughter, Michelle, and they started dating and became close. Michelle fell pregnant and they had a son, Jordan, and it was at his christening that I met Jenny.

It was September 2001. I was 20 and still recovering from my ACL operation and had to wear a leg brace. I went to the church and celebration afterwards with Mum and Dad because I didn't know anyone else there and they'd been invited. Jenny was invited by Matt's partner, Michelle, but had been out the night before and didn't make the church.

At the do, Matt's mates were all in couples and knew each other. Matt was obviously busy so I was sat with Mum and Dad. It was a bit uncomfortable. About two hours in, Jenny turned up after her mum forced her to go.

She didn't really know anyone else, so I gravitated towards her. "Hello, how are you? Are you on your own as well?" I bought her a drink, we started chatting and the pair of us got on quite well. It went from there.

Our first date was on September 12 and obviously part of our conversation was about what had happened the day before in New York. As the evening wore on, she told me she didn't like the idea of footballers because of their reputation for being flash and wasn't really interested.

I had to woo her. I really did as well, being an old-fashioned gentleman by opening the car door and buying some flowers, which I gave to her when I dropped her off at home. I consider it smooth but she reckons I was dead corny. She said I was like that for about a month, but once I got her interested, I stopped making such an effort!

Mum called her 'Jenny Eye Shadow' for the first few months of our relationship, as she wore distinctive white eye shadow at the christening. Mum was a bit wary at first and protective of her son. It took her about six months to realise that Jenny was a nice girl and wasn't trying to take advantage of me.

Anyway, we'd go on double dates with Matt and Michelle and me and Matt have been close ever since (actually, sometimes I think it's a bit too close because he does my head in at times... he has a habit of removing his clothes in public when we're on a night out, he treats every pool table like a dancing podium and I don't ever open his Snapchats unless I'm on my own!).

Matt played about five or six times for Chester's first team, and in the youth team and reserves for us before he developed serious ankle problems. He had some sort of growth on the bottom of his shin bone and it was causing him pain in the ankle. He had two or three operations over an 18-month period but sadly nothing worked and he ended up retiring because of it. He was just 21 years old. I was very upset by it, but that turned to anger when Matt tried to claim his insurance money but ended up receiving only 30% of what he should have been entitled to.

Within a week of leaving Everton he was working as a drayman, lugging barrels up and down ladders into pub cellars. He had his girlfriend, a baby, a mortgage and bills to pay, but when his football career finished, he had nothing to show for it. It showed me the other side of football and I didn't like it one bit. It's to his eternal credit, and sums up what a great character he is, that Matt has never appeared bitter by his experience. I'm not sure I'd be the same and he should be very proud of himself.

My brother, Carl, made a massive career decision when he was 16. He was offered youth forms at Everton having been on the club's books as a schoolboy. In his final year at school, he came in on day release and trained with us to see what it was like.

As he got older, he started to dislike the experience. He felt he was shouted at too much and wasn't enjoying his football. It was the pressure and the huge demands placed on you, and expected of you, which affected him. He was a winger, he wasn't the guy in the middle of the park who gets around and makes tackles. As a winger, you might have one brilliant game followed by two stinkers. Wingers do that. The pressure to perform every week was maybe too much. Also, he had seen kids let go after two years and not have anything to show for it. He didn't want that to happen to him. He didn't want to be left with a job that offered no real career progression.

Straight from school, Carl had the option of an apprenticeship in joinery and, after weighing it up, he decided to take it and turn down Everton's offer. He has done joinery ever since, getting a full-time job at the completion of his course and making his career in the building trade.

I told him recently that I felt it was an incredible decision to make at 16. I asked him if he regretted it and he said no. He's got a trade behind him, he's got a job, he's happy. He has to work hard but he didn't want to be stuck in a job with no real career path. I told him I respected what he did and that he had the guts to make that decision. Whether it was right or wrong is not the point. What a massive decision to make at 16 about what direction you want your life to go in. Most people would choose to try to be a footballer. For whatever reason, he decided the gamble was too much. He wanted a job for life. Wow. That's the type of guy he is. He's cheeky, he's funny but he's stubborn, and when a decision needs to be made, he'll make it and stick by it. It seems to have been a good one for him.

Carl was still able to play football at non-league level for Cammell Lairds, Vauxhall Motors, Kendal Town and Skelmersdale United. He only gave it up about a year ago to spend more time with his son. Now he plays Sunday league for a team called Lancashire Ice.

Things are better now for youngsters who are released by clubs after their academy programme is complete. Because of the education programme that now operates, for those who don't make it at Everton, 95% of the lads go on to another club or forge some sort of footballing career. The percentage wasn't that high years ago and quite a few drifted out. They left Everton and had nothing to show for it, not knowing what they were going to do next. I know some who ended up going down bad avenues.

Players just consider the next two years. It seems like a really long time at 16 and many don't think 'what if I don't get kept on? What next?' Our Carl asked that 'what if?' question right from the start and made up his mind what he wanted to do.

While Carl went in a different direction, I concentrated on making it as a footballer. We had a good spirit within the youth squad but issues did crop up.

One of them was very unpleasant indeed.

For a three-month period, minimum, when we were at the Civil Service, things were going missing. A phone, a watch, a bracelet...not every day but every so often this kept happening. It was reported to Colin Harvey who said: "If it gets to a certain level and the club has to deal with it, it's going to be big. Try and deal with it yourselves."

We let it be for a while. One player, John Lester, got a brand new, state-of-the-art phone. It wasn't even available properly. He'd had it about three days before it went missing. About two days later another player, who I won't name but he knows who he is, went up to John Lester, in front of everyone, and said: "John, you know that phone you had. It went missing, didn't it? Did you have a charger for it?"

"Yes."

"Are you using it now?"

"No."

"Can I have it? One of my mates has got one and he's lost his charger."

"Yes, I'll bring it in tomorrow."

The penny dropped with the rest of us but John didn't realise.

Then my chain went missing during a game against Liverpool at their academy. What can you do? You can't go around accusing people, but eventually it came to a head. After a watch went missing, we collectively said: "That's it. Stop right now. Everyone empty their pockets. We're not leaving here until this gets found." We searched from top to bottom but nothing. Then we decided cars had to be searched, but the player who I still won't name said: "No chance, we're not doing that." He ran to his car, jumped in and drove off. The watch was never found.

Within the squad the accusation was that he was stealing the lads' gear. It was only an accusation because we never actually had any concrete proof, but it created a rift in the squad. The trust had gone. Thankfully, it was towards the end of the season and a few were getting let go, so it didn't last much longer. Needless to say, the suspected thief was one of those let go.

Among the other players from those years I still speak to is Keith Southern. He's had a great career and is currently at Huddersfield. I went to his wedding recently. Jamie Milligan texts me from time to time...usually when he wants tickets! I've not seen Dave Knowles since he left Everton, even though he lived in our house for a while. Carl Howarth nearly got a job at Everton as a physio a couple of months back. He was quite intelligent when we did our day release at college, getting loads of grade As. He went back to school and became a physio. He's worked at Wolves, as the Head of Academy Physiotherapy.

Joe McAlpine was sacked from Everton while we were at Netherton. He was a good lad, who lived with Hibbo. We were training one day and Joe wasn't in. We were told he had been to his nan's funeral and thought nothing more of it. The next day Colin Harvey called him over and there was an argument. Colin made him do laps of the field for the whole of our training session. I was wondering what was going on and at the end of it Colin pulled him over and told him he was sacked.

Apparently, a few months earlier Joe had been in Scotland with his mates and they had been caught stealing hub caps/ wheel trims. When he faced his day in the dock, he was recognised going into the courthouse by a member of the press, probably because he was playing for Scotland Under-16s at the time. The Liverpool Echo picked up on it and carried the story. I think he'd had a couple of warnings before that and he was sacked there and then. He was a decent player, Joe, but I think he went off the rails a bit after that.

As you'd expect with a group of lads in their late teens, there were a few fights. In Southport College one lunchtime, Kevin McLeod and Franny Jeffers were messing around, giving each other stick. It quickly got out of hand and they started throwing soup at each other. Kev got the worst of it and chased Franny up the stairs. We all followed. They started fighting and our teacher, Marilyn, was trying to get between them. She was shouting for help while we were all watching. Eventually, Knowlesy, who was the biggest, split them up.

One time, a few of us young players accompanied the first team to Marbella. We behaved ourselves impeccably until our centre-half Sean O'Hanlon had a bit too much to drink. Sean was a very quiet lad and Les Helm nicknamed him 'Chief' after the character in 'One Flew Over The Cuckoo's Nest' who never said a word. Anyway, he staggered into a bar where Davie Weir, Alan Stubbs, Gary Naysmith and Steve Watson were having a quiet beer.

Chief told the senior players that he wanted to learn from them and he turned to each one.

"I want to be able to strike the ball like you," he said to Stubbsy.

"I love your positional sense and your composure," he said to Davie Weir.

We were all giggling by now because it was so unlike Chief.

"I love your energy and enthusiasm," he said to Gaz.

Then he turned to Steve Watson. "Watto…Watto," he slurred. "I don't want anything from you whatsoever."

We were too stunned to laugh but Stubbsy, Davie and Gaz were in fits. Five minutes later, Chief was face down in the sand. I still don't know if he fell over or if Watto helped him!

At Netherton, as you drove in, there was a brick shed straight ahead where the groundstaff equipment was stored. On the right, there was a building that was something to do with Littlewoods. We used it for getting changed, but it was far from state-of-the-art. In fact, it was in a shocking state. The floor was made up of dirty wooden planks, there was no lighting, and you had to step over all kinds of random items to get from one side to the other. It was like an obstacle course and these days health and safety would kick you right out of there.

On the level above was a gym that, again, was very basic to say the least. It was effectively a dingy loft with one or two dim lights. It was more akin to Rising Damp than Premier League football!

Les Helm wasn't just the physio, he was fitness coach, strength and conditioning coach, nutritionist – the lot. He had amassed a group of weights that had seen better days. We used to ask him to thank his father for smuggling them out of France during the war!

He took a soldering iron and soldered the weights together. That was our training – a derelict building with weights that had been soldered together. When we left Netherton I don't know what happened to the weights because a scrap merchant would have turned his nose up at them.

During our circuit training one day, Franny was doing shoulder raises. I was watching him and as he lifted the weights above his head, the bit that had been soldered broke away and the weights fell on his head.

We couldn't move for laughing but Franny went absolutely berserk, effing and blinding. "This is a joke. Look where we are. We are supposed to be footballers. It's a disgrace. I'm not coming in this place again."

He stormed out. It was one of the funniest things I've ever seen.

It's a shame Franny's career tailed off after such a bright start. He was a very naturally gifted striker and he could finish. As a midfielder looking to supply him, his runs were incredible. I would look up and I just had to slip it through and he would score. He was getting compared to Ian Rush and it was under-standable. He made the same runs, he was fast and he was clinical.

The ability he showed at Everton got him his move to Arsenal. I'm not quite sure what happened after that. I don't think he ever really wanted to leave.

Maybe it was because of that, maybe it was being in the big city with lots to do, maybe it was being away from his parents. He would have only been 20, living on his own in London, probably bored.

If he'd stayed at Everton a bit longer, I think he'd have been fine.

05

Walter's Way

With Franny already in the first team, I made my reserve-team debut against Manchester United at Old Trafford in March 1999. It was an international weekend and quite a few faces were away with their under-21s or under-18s. The likes of myself, Hibbo and Peter Clarke were called up to be on the bench. Those in the Youth Cup team who had been substitutes regularly – the likes of Mick O'Brien, Jamie Milligan, Phil Jevons, Dave Poppleton – were starting. John O'Shea was in the United team and scored the opening goal. We've had careers spanning similar periods.

I remember walking around Old Trafford, thinking 'wow'. I was amazed by the size of the pitch – it was massive. On a really sunny day, we were 3-0 down at half-time and me and

Hibbo were told by Taff that we were going on for the second half. We played really well. It finished 3-0 but we looked the more likely to score.

I thoroughly enjoyed it and thought I'd played really well. I felt it was easier than youth-team football because you got more time on the ball, people didn't close down as quickly. It seemed less frenetic.

I was among the last players to come though the old system of the 'A' and 'B' leagues, which led to reserve-team football. I felt I had the best education. I was playing against men when I was 16 and I had to toughen up so much. My skill set was developing too.

In my opinion, academy football – under-18s and under-21s football – is a bit of a waste of time. Nowadays they are playing against their own age-group and to suddenly go from that into a first team is too big a jump, unless you're a Ross Barkley or Wayne Rooney and you're physically more developed than the other kids. It's nearly impossible to do. You get pushed off the ball too easily because you've never played open-aged football in your life. When a kid's first ever game of football against adults is in the Premier League, it's always going to be tough.

I remember Burnley were in our 'A' league. We played them at Bellefield and drew 3-3. I don't know the names but they had six first-teamers that day. I scored, chipping the keeper, and it felt such an achievement. Every goal and game meant something because you were playing against men not boys.

Another time we played Liverpool in the 'A' league and Jamie Redknapp needed a game. I must have been 16 or 17 and I played against Jamie Redknapp. For me, that's going to educate you a lot more than constantly playing against your own age group. Now the kids sign full-time and are still playing against under-17s and under-18s. Then they get to under-21s, which is basically academy players anyway. It's just not bringing the kids on as much and, for me, it's not rocket science to work out why.

We're not teaching our kids to win either. Some school sports days don't have proper competitions because they don't want any losers. We're teaching our kids not to be bothered about results. Academies don't play competitively at all until under-18s.

Kids are coming off the pitch and you might ask "how did you get on?" and they'll say "we got beat 5-0 but you should have seen this pass or bit of skill I did." Yes, but you got beat 5-0.

When they reach under-18s or under-21s, they've got no real winning mentality. They come into the first team and they say they want to win, but I'm not sure they know how. I'm not sure there is proper desire. There is no putting your body on the line to block a shot with your face. That was always expected of us in the youth teams. Too many times now I hear coaches saying that results don't matter because it's all about development. I don't agree with that at all. We're developing good players who don't know what it takes to win football matches. How can that be right?

A prime example, for me, was Jack Rodwell. He was talked up all the way through the academy. Technically and physically, he was really, really good. He could pass with both feet, he could do tricks, he could dribble past you. He was physically strong, quick and tall, but being upset at losing football matches just hadn't been instilled into him from a young age. Jack would come off the pitch after a defeat and be told how well he had played. There is no real match-winning mentality with a lot of kids these days. It wasn't Jack's fault, it's just the way he'd been brought up through the system. After playing a season or so in the first team at Everton, Jack learned that mentality, but for me, all young kids should have it from a very early age. It should hurt them to lose football matches. Jack still has the ability to get back into the England squad and I hope he does because I've got a lot of time for him.

In my time, up until under-16s we had leagues and we won it nearly every year, and we cared. It hurt us if we didn't win games. When we joined full-time we had the likes of Colin Harvey and Taff and they taught us a winning mentality. The result was important every time we went on the pitch. It was important to do your best to make sure your team won. For me, this new breed of footballer, I think they're more concerned with looking good (performance not appearance. In fact, maybe both) and they'd rather play well and the team lose. The team needs to win. That's what I was taught. The team comes before any player.

Another general issue within football, among players coming through, is a reluctance to play out of their usual position. I don't think the youngsters have got the desire to be flexible. Again, it's putting themselves before the needs of the team.

It's not just Academy youngsters either...

We played away at Wigan in November 2008 and lost 1-0. We didn't start well and the manager wanted to change our shape. He tried to play three across the middle with Marouane Fellaini out to the left (this was before we realised No. 10 was his best position and we were using him as a deep-lying midfielder). Felli gave it the thumbs-up and the nod twice but he wouldn't go out to the left. I was shouting at him but he told me to 'do one'…or whatever the Flemish equivalent is!

That stuck in my mind. With many players these days, the team is secondary to personal agenda. You might not agree with the manager but you have to accept that he is trying to get the team to win and you've got to do what he says. You have to make personal sacrifices – that's what I was always taught. You do what the manager tells you for the sake of the team. Felli opened my eyes that night and I realised that not every player had the same ethic as me.

They're not all like that because we've got some great young players – the likes of Seamus Coleman and James McCarthy – but I think quite a lot of the new breed are suffering because of a lack of competitive football. When Howard Wilkinson changed the academy system, I think it was bad news.

Throughout my career I have been well accustomed to being moved around the pitch. My versatility has worked for and against me. Sometimes I've got in the team because I can play a number of positions, and it's been good. On other occasions, I could be playing in the middle and be in the best form, but if there is a gap to fill on one of the wings, I'll be the one who is moved because no-one else knows how to do it. Sometimes it's because I'm the one who won't moan about it and the others will spit out the dummy. I'll be sacrificed even though I'm the one playing the best in a certain position.

I was taught that's what you do for the team. Not everyone does that these days.

I've always said to both David Moyes and Roberto Martinez that I'll play wherever they want. I'm happy whenever I'm in the team. If I was asked to play in goal, I'd do it. Sometimes that's been great for me but at others it's been tough. I'd never moan about it, though. I don't think I've ever been to a manager and told him I wasn't happy playing in a certain position for the first team. I'll play where I'm told.

Back then I was a proper box-to-box midfielder. We pretty much always played 4-4-2. One striker would come short for the ball, one would run the channel and a midfielder would get up and support and I was always that midfielder. I was the one who got in the box and I could finish. I knew where the goal was.

When I was part of the reserves, I particularly enjoyed it when we played at first-team stadiums. For us, it was so much more real and exciting when you were playing at a major ground. A lot of the young lads miss out on that these days. It helps with the step up to the first team if they have played at a proper stadium.

I recall playing Aston Villa at Villa Park in October 2000. We won 4-2 and I scored two 25-yard strikes, which wasn't my normal goal. I usually chipped the keeper, went round him or passed the ball into the net. These were absolute whoppers. All my memories are from when we played at proper stadiums. I always felt I played better; it seemed like more of a game.

In May 2000 we took on Sheffield Wednesday at Hillsborough. Chris Waddle was their reserve-team coach and played in the game, aged 39. We had a reasonably young team. They had Waddle and another lad who I had played against before. He was massive, 6ft 6ins, and half the time he played up front because he was so big. He could run as well. I remember thinking it would be tough against the big lad but 'Waddle's coming to the end, I'll be able to get round him and run off him'.

It was quite the opposite. It was a big learning curve that night. Every time I went close to Waddle, he would lay off a one-touch pass. After you've closed him down three or four times, and every time he has played a one-touch pass, you approach him more cautiously. When I didn't get close to him, he'd take two or three touches and play someone in with an inch-perfect pass. Nobody laid a finger on him all night. It was really good to see how an experienced player like that operated. He didn't run very far but he didn't need to. He was so good. I've never forgotten it. I ran rings around the big lad but I couldn't get near Waddle. That was a real big experience, and one I still try to use on occasions. When I'm playing certain games, it'll pop into my head. There are certain times for one-touch and on other occasions, you can try something else.

Unfortunately, though, Walter Smith and Archie Knox didn't really give any young kids a chance. Franny got in under Walter but that was a case of needs must, I don't think he had any other options. We had Steve Watson up front for a while under Walter.

We had just won the Youth Cup in 1998 when Walter came in. In 1999 West Ham won it with Joe Cole, Michael Carrick and Jermain Defoe and they all got in the first team over the next couple of years. When Liverpool and Middlesbrough won it, their players were given chances in the first team over the next two or three years.

When we won it, Danny Cad, Michael Ball and Richard Dunne were already in the first team under the previous manager, Howard Kendall. I didn't get a chance, Milligan didn't get a chance, Poppleton, Regan, Jevons…I was convinced that some of us deserved an opportunity.

Walter was bringing in people like David Ginola and Paul Gascoigne. Good players and great characters who had been legends in the game that you could only learn from, but they were well past their primes. We brought in Richard Gough who was nearly 40 and Mark Hughes, who'd been an unbelievable player but again was well past his best. Walter was bringing in temporary players rather than having faith in the young talent at the club. I think maybe he was afraid to give youngsters the chance. We were always struggling and, as the manager, he was in the firing line when things went wrong. Perhaps he felt as though he couldn't afford to risk young players because the stakes were too high. I also believe that Walter didn't realise how poor a side he had inherited so he was always going to be fire-fighting and he didn't trust the youngsters to get the team out of trouble.

I didn't have many dealings with Walter or Archie. Walter was a really nice guy, while Archie was the disciplinarian. He just seemed to shout at the young lads all the time. That was my opinion of him. No matter what we did, it didn't meet up with his expectations and he was roaring at us. There just seemed no way I would get in the first team under them.

One time, in 1999/2000, I asked to go out on loan and Archie said no because we had six "very important" reserve games coming up. I pointed out that I needed first-team football but he said I was their player and they needed me to play in the reserves. I didn't get angry – I try to find the positives in every-thing so I thought 'he wants me to stay, maybe there's a positive in that'. There wasn't. I saw a loan move as a way of showing them I could play in the first team. That was always my motive. It wasn't a case of forging a career elsewhere.

Once, Archie told me to go on the exercise bike because he said I wasn't strong enough and needed to strengthen my legs. I was put on at level 10, which was ridiculous. Chris Hoy would have struggled to cycle at that level. He told me to cycle for 10 kilometres but I couldn't even turn the wheel. I didn't even get to 10 metres and it made me doubt myself.

On the bike next to me was Richard Dunne who used to have to come in an hour before anyone else. They'd put a bin bag on him and make him do the bike and treadmill, sweating him like crazy. They thought he was too heavy but that's just Dunney's build, which someone should have known. He could still cover the ground quickly and was strong. Our management appeared to think he was overweight and they seemed to punish him every single day. He must have been knackered before training. We should have been working on his passing or the technical side of his game.

The lads who won the Youth Cup were a really close bunch. After we were shipped off to Netherton and the Civil Service Club, we called ourselves the 'Bindies' because we'd been binned. I don't know why but it developed into the 'Chicken Bindies' and we used to go round doing impressions of chickens. It was ridiculous.

There was always good banter with team-mates in the youth sides. It was mostly criticising each other. It was one of my favourite times and it set the tone for the rest of my career. It wasn't as personal as when you older with the first-teamers, but I've tried to carry on the light-hearted spirit in every Everton dressing room. I'm lucky that we've had the right characters to be able to do that.

In November 2000, the Bindies were actually training at

Bellefield. The first team had played Arsenal at Goodison on the Saturday and Danny Cadamarteri and Kev Campbell scored in a 2-0 win. We were that short of players that I got on the bench. Injuries and suspensions must have hit hard and big Norman on the gate at Bellefield must have been unavailable so I got the nod! It was brilliantly exciting and I loved every second. Every time I was asked to warm-up, I did so with real gusto. I ran up and down that touchline like an Olympic athlete thinking that the crowd would spot my enthusiasm and scream for me to be brought on. They never did, of course, but the illusion was nice while it lasted. I also resisted the unbelievable temptation to wave at my family while I was stretching at the side of the pitch. I'd have never lived it down!

Unfortunately, this would be my one and only time on the bench under Walter, but it served to whet my appetite and fuel my desire to make the breakthrough.

This was the first time that my mates and I would go out on what we called 'in the squad bonus nights'. Whenever I was selected as one of the 17 or 18 players for a first-team fixture, I used to get a bonus even if I never got on the bench or the pitch. I'd use that extra few quid to treat my mates to a night out in Wigan and we'd raise our glasses and salute the 'in the squad bonus'.

Now at this early stage it would usually only stretch to a few pints or two each unless we could find a happy hour, but it was definitely appreciated by my friends…who used to moan like mad when Peter Degn was preferred in the squad to me!

Despite being on the bench on the Saturday, I still had to train separately from the first team. The 11 first-team players and three senior subs trained in one group, while five or six of us from the youth team had to form our own group.

It was the Tuesday after the Arsenal game and we warmed up and went for a run. We came to a stop and were told to stretch. I put my left leg out to stretch my hamstring and bent over to touch my toes. At the same time, Peter Clarke went to stretch his right thigh and whipped his heel up. He stuck his studs into my eye at speed and I fell to the floor in agony.

The whole of the Bindies were laughing. I was crying out and it was only after a few seconds when I moved my hand away from my eye that the laughter stopped. I think it was Hibbo who said "oh, shit".

By now there were panicked shouts for physios and doctors. Kev Kewn was the reserve physio and he came running over. I had my hand over my eye again, so he asked me to take it away. When I did, he also said "oh, shit".

None of this was making me feel any better!

I went inside and held a pack of ice to my face. Within seconds of Clarkey catching me, the eye swelled up so badly I had no vision from it. An ambulance was called and I was taken to hospital. They had to use a machine to pull my eye apart. Thankfully the actual eyeball was undamaged but I ended up having five stitches in my lower eyelid.

I missed our home match against Chelsea the following Saturday because of my eye injury and Kev McLeod actually got on the pitch for the last five minutes. That could have been me if it wasn't for the freak eye injury.

At the time all I could think was 'bad luck strikes again' but, as I have already stated, I really believe things happen for a reason. We beat Bradford 3-1 to lift the Premier Reserve League in

May 2001 but I'd broken down with my knee just before the game. Keith Southern snapped his cruciate that night and we ended up doing our rehab together.

Nick Chadwick scored a hat-trick and we went into town that night to celebrate, although it was difficult to dance on crutches. It shouldn't be for me because I've had enough practice, but you just can't do the moves justice! That was two major honours for me now and both times I received my medal on crutches.

Soon after that, we had a family barbecue. We used to have barbecues in the Osman household every year to coincide with my birthday – May 17 – and, usually, FA Cup final day. We used to start at 2pm and finish in the early hours of the next day with the match in between. They were always great days and the 2001 final party was particularly memorable.

It was just before my 20th birthday and family and friends came together on the scorching afternoon when Liverpool came from behind to beat Arsenal in Cardiff. My loyalty to the red half of the city had vanished completely by now and I was disappointed at the result and annoyed that Arsenal had let the lead slip.

We started a drinking game involving a long Tupperware container used for storing dry spaghetti. We filled it to the brim with vodka, JD – all sorts. It was horrible. To make it worse, we added pork ribs and a chicken wing. The loser had to eat both. Now they'd been marinating in this vile liquid for about half an hour when my friend, Colin Sambrooks, was the unfortunate loser who had to eat them. He did it manfully but he had to be collected by his wife an hour later as he was in such a state!

At about midnight somebody suggested we all cut our hair. We all thought it was a terrific idea and so the clippers came out and we got 'number ones'. Then it was a shout of "let's do number zeroes – it will be even cooler" (a sensible adult should have intervened at this point!). So a razor came out and we all 'bicced' our heads. It sounds stupid now but we were young and foolish. A few of the reserve team were in my house that night and we all went for it.

What we'd forgotten about was the fact that we were all due on the pitch at Goodison seven days later to parade the Reserve League trophy in front of the fans at half time in the last Premier League game of the season. Because I'd been in the sun, I had a pretty decent tan but my head was white. I looked like a pint of bitter! For years there was a picture of us on the wall of one of the lounges at Goodison and I'd cringe every time I walked past it.

That impromptu haircut had unintended, and rather more serious, consequences six days later, helping to secure me a few hours in a police cell.

A few mates and I had decided we'd go and watch England play Mexico in a friendly at Derby's Pride Park. We jumped a bus to Wigan and caught the train to Derby. The plan was to watch the match, go out in Derby, stay the night in a hotel and catch a train back the following day.

It was an evening game so once we got to Derby, we went into a really busy bar with an outdoor balcony, and enjoyed a few lagers in the sunshine. There were loads of police about but no hint of any trouble.

I'd never been to an England game and we were all excited. We were wearing England shirts with England flags around our waists. We were singing "Eng-er-lund" with a pint in one hand

and punching the air with the other. To be honest I'd forgotten that I was technically a skinhead and in hindsight it probably didn't look the best.

Anyway, as we were leaving to walk to the stadium, the police jumped on us. Our arms were pinned behind our backs and we were arrested. One of my mates burst out crying, saying "you can't arrest me; my girlfriend's going to kill me." It worked for him and I don't exactly know how or why, but they let him go. The other five of us ended up in the back of a police van. The next thing I know I'm in a police cell for about four hours. Eventually, they brought me out for a formal interview. I was asking "what's going on?" They told me: "You were rowdy, you're football hooligans and we also feel you were being racist." I was dumbfounded.

"Racist to who? Racist? Why?"

"Because of the way you had one arm up in the air when you were singing. You were making Nazi salutes."

"What? Behave yourself. I just had a pint in my hand and anyway, my dad's black. I'm not racist."

They told me they were looking to charge me with section four or five of the Football Riot Act/Public Order Act. I asked what that meant and they said if they saw it through, I wouldn't be allowed to set foot inside a football stadium for 10 years. I was thinking, 'what? Hang on a minute. You can't do that'. I was stunned at first. As I sat in the cell, and during the interview, it began to dawn on me that this was a serious situation.

I was given a court date for a month later and told I could leave. I went back to our hotel for about 10.30pm and over the next three hours the lads all gradually came back. We were asking ourselves "what happened there?" They were told we could be charged with various offences but could accept a lesser offence of drunk and disorderly. My response was: "But I didn't do anything wrong."

We slept the night and made our way home the next day. I was thinking, 'oh my God, I can't not go to a football stadium for the next 10 years. What am I going to do?' I was really worried what Everton would make of it. I got my mum to phone and she spoke to Dave Harrison, the club secretary. He said they would look into it, but I was panicking, thinking 'they're going to sack me'. Dave got the club solicitor involved, who got in touch with the police. Both Dave and the solicitor were really good.

The police claimed they had video evidence from the bar. It was sent to the solicitor and he showed it to me. Honestly, there was nothing on it. You hardly saw us but when you did, we were just having a laugh and a chat. There were some guys at the bar who were a bit rowdy but we weren't doing a thing. The solicitor had watched it for six hours, we were in it for three-and-a-half hours and in that time we did absolutely nothing wrong.

It went to court. My mates turned up on their own, while I had the solicitor with me. My friends were told they would just be given a warning if they pleaded guilty to drunk and disorderly, so three of them did that. I stood up and pleaded not guilty to this football riot act charge. The solicitor did his bit, pointing out that there was no evidence, and they acknowledged they had nothing on me, so I was cleared. Another lad was cleared too.

Luckily for me, it was not picked up by the media. Incidents like that can give you a reputation, whether you are guilty or not. This all happened during the summer when we were off so maybe that had something to do with no-one finding out.

For a while I was very nervous. I think it was all down to us biccing our heads and then travelling to an England game as skinheads. It was simply naivety of 19 and 20-year-old lads.

When I went to Derby on loan less than three years later, I was thinking, 'will the police recognise me?' My mum and dad came down one weekend with Jenny, my then girlfriend and now wife. We went in that same bar and I still couldn't believe what had happened. What an experience...and what a lesson learned with regards to drinking games!

06

People's Club

The appointment of David Moyes as Everton manager changed the course of my football career.

Following my ACL operation, it was a tough road to recovery to have eight months rehabilitation on top of everything I'd already experienced. But I had to get my head down and work hard.

During that period me and my mates would attend all the Everton games, home and away, including the March 2002 trip to Middlesbrough in the quarter-final of the FA Cup. Around this time, I was pretty much getting back to full fitness.

We were well beaten by Boro, 3-0, and the next thing, the manager, Walter Smith, was gone. It was my first experience of a managerial change. Howard Kendall had left in 1998 but

I was having my own issues then with my knee. Walter leaving was a shock to me, even though we were once again struggling near the bottom of the Premier League. Questions swirled around my head. Who are we going to bring in? How would that affect me? Will the new man rate me? My contract was up at the end of the season and I was turning 21 that May so I was worried that they would simply let me go.

Within days, David Moyes came in from Preston North End. I didn't know much about him and my first impression was how intimidating he seemed. That was everyone's first impression. He wasn't unfriendly or unpleasant but he looked the sort who had a black belt in facial expressions. He was scary, but he was my manager and I needed to impress him. And impress him quick.

I was in the Upper Gwladys for his first game against Fulham when he let Taff pick the team. Moyes came out to the roar of the crowd and within 30 seconds of the start we were a goal up. Moyes was up and away and he did a great job of solving his first problem, which was staying in the Premier League.

At the end of the season he called me into his office and I was very nervous about whether I was going to be kept on or let go. I'd played for the reserves in the last two months of that season and Moyes had watched the games, but it wasn't much to go on. Going into that office, I was scared for my future. Am I going to get kept on or will I have to make a career for myself somewhere else?

It proved to be the first of many confusing conversations with David Moyes.

It began well enough: "Right, you'll be happy to know we're going to offer you another year's contract."

Initially I was thinking 'great, get in there', a feeling of massive relief because I could look forward to the next season. However, I could also sense that the conversation was a long way from over.

"But we're going to lower your wages. There is a really big wage bill at the club at the moment and I need to lower it."

I was looking at him, incredulous, thinking 'and you're starting with me? How much is Ginola on?'. I didn't know him at all well then so I was wondering if he was going to start laughing and tell me it was a joke.

But he carried on: "You're going to go from £900 a week to £700 a week. The offer is there if you want it but you don't have to take it."

My head was spinning. I have never, ever been motivated by money and I accept that £900 a week is quite a lot of money, considering I wasn't in the first team, but I couldn't believe my wage had been cut, after all I'd been through.

I considered it an insult. Okay, I'd been offered a contract, which is what I desperately wanted, but it came with a slap in the face. How could they consider that reducing a kid's salary by a couple of hundred quid a week was going to help solve Everton Football Club's debt?

Despite this, I never for a moment considered leaving. I just didn't know how to react. I kept my thoughts to myself and said: "Okay, no problem, I'm going to sign." I decided to take it on the chin, come back the following season and prove myself.

With regards to my physical issues, I was hoping that they had been overcome. I was feeling good about my knee but I'd just spent three years on the treatment table. After a bad injury, in the back of your mind you're a little bit worried that you'll break down again. Overall, though, I was optimistic about the following season. At least I had another year to make the next step, even if I had taken a pay cut.

I started 2002/03 in excellent form, scoring the winners in reserve games against Manchester United and Manchester City in September. In the middle of that month I was called into Moyes' office again.

He said: "You've had a great pre-season. You worked your nuts off and you've started this season like I knew you would. We're going to reward you because you've done so well. We're offering you a new contract to take you to the end of this season and next season. As a reward, we're going to put you back on the money you were earning last year."

I was incredulous again, 'as a reward? I'm going back to what I was on three months ago? That's my next step up the ladder?'.

I try to be like Marlon Brando's character in the Godfather, Vito Corleone, and not show any emotion, either way, good or bad. I don't like to give anything away. Again, I just said: "Okay, great, no problem. Thanks very much."

I stepped outside his office into the corridor and thought 'what just happened there?'. It felt exactly like the previous season. I'd had a pat on the back, been given the reward of a new contract but there was a sting at the end of it.

This was a trait I found with Moyes a lot. He could give with one hand and take away with the other. 'Well done, you've done well, but don't get too far ahead of yourself'. It was his way of keeping you striving for more and I got to see it a lot over the next 12 years.

I had to focus on the positives. My wages had gone 'back up' (to what they were a year ago!) and I now had nearly two years on my contract, which was a big thing as it gave me a bit more security.

Within days, David Moyes approached me after training again and asked what I thought about going on loan to Carlisle United. I was made up about the prospect of any kind of first-team football and I thought that maybe the gaffer had seen something in me that he wanted to nurture and test out in league football. My reaction was 'yes, I'll have some of that'.

I was excited at the prospect of a senior debut but also a bit nervous as I drove up the M6 to Carlisle. It was a step into the unknown and my first experience of living away from home.

I didn't realise how big a club Carlisle is and I was really impressed by the whole set-up. It's the only Football League club in the whole of Cumbria and the fans are extremely passionate, home and away. Even on a Tuesday night at Cambridge, Carlisle were well followed.

They put me up in a bed and breakfast. I would head up at 7am on a Monday morning to beat the traffic, stay that night, come back Tuesday afternoon if there was no midweek game as we usually had Wednesday off, travel back up Thursday, and stay that evening and Friday night, before the game on Saturday.

I shared a room at the B&B with a lad called Craig Farrell for a while. The one aspect I found difficult was that I didn't have my own space. You were sharing a bedroom and eating in a communal room. There wasn't any personal time and I hadn't been expecting that. On the whole, they were a good bunch of lads and I liked spending time with them. I enjoyed playing for the club. I just didn't like being in that B&B.

My debut was at Brunton Park against Torquay. I was nervous but at the same time excited because it was a new team, in front of a good crowd. I don't think I was nervous because it was my first experience of league football, it was more about being at a new team and the unknown of what was going to happen. In their side was Lee Canoville, who had been selected for the national school ahead of me all those years ago. We lost 2-1 and I was really, really upset. I was actually surprised at how much the defeat hurt me. It was my first game at a club I didn't know with team-mates I had hardly met before, but I was truly gutted. But then that was me, that was how I'd treated my football all my life. I have never been a good loser, nor do I ever want to be.

After another 2-1 home defeat, to Shrewsbury, we travelled to Macclesfield. It was October 19; the day Wayne Rooney scored his famous last-minute winner against Arsenal at Goodison. I was playing in front of 2,400 at Moss Rose but it was a big day for me as well.

My dad was there, and I'm pretty sure that Jenny, my mum and brother would have been there as well. Two minutes into the game I scored my first league goal.

A cross came in, someone had a shot, the ball hit the post, came back out and I put the rebound in from about eight yards. What a feeling! I was absolutely buzzing and it gave me loads of confidence for the rest of that game. It was probably one of the best games I've ever had in terms of being involved in everything.

We drew 2-2 and I made our second, an equaliser with 10 minutes to go. I felt we should have won. It was great coming off, having played and scored my first league goal. I'd been doing it in the ressies at Everton but this was different. I was just a bit miffed that Wayne's goal on the same day pushed mine off the back pages of all the national newspapers!

When I went back to Macclesfield with Everton in the FA Cup in 2009, it was the same. I played well again and scored the winner, a half-volley at the other end of the pitch. I love Moss Rose.

Doing well for Carlisle confirmed my view that I should have been out on loan years before, under Walter and Archie.

Our next game was at Oldham in the LDV Vans Trophy. We were bottom of League Two and they were mid-League One. We won 4-3 and I scored two. For the second, I cut inside, beat two men and whacked it low in the corner. I was ripping it up there. I don't want to put it down but it seemed the same standard as reserves football and I was thriving.

A couple of days later, Moyes' assistant, Alan Irvine, called to say he had been at the game and told me I had played fantastically. The message was: "Well done, keep it up, keep going." It was a Thursday afternoon and I was sat in a McDonalds when Alan rang me, having a bite to eat. I was willing the restaurant to stay quiet so Alan wouldn't ask where I was.

Next we played Swansea (which shows how far they've come) and we drew 2-2. Three days later we went to Cambridge and I remember it was a cold night, miserable and bleak. They had hardly any fans and the wind was howling. That was proper League Two football. When I try to compare top-flight football to League Two football, that's the match that comes to mind. I try not to be disrespectful but I knew that I really didn't want to play at that standard. I wanted to play in the Premier League.

On November 9, we won 2-1 at Kidderminster Harriers. I played really well and created both goals. My dad drove me home after every game and as we were listening to Radio 5 Live in the car, they mentioned how well I'd played. I was dead excited. To be involved in Saturday league football and to be spoken about on national radio, it was just brilliant for me. I loved it. It was a chest-out moment. I was 21, which is older than most people make their debuts, but still relatively young in football terms.

For my last two games, despite playing really well, the manager, Roddy Collins, surprised me by dropping me to the substitutes' bench. I couldn't understand why. I spoke to him during half-time of my penultimate match, against Rushden, and he told me he had to prepare his team for life without me! Roddy was brilliant but he could make some strange decisions.

I played really well at Carlisle and I thoroughly enjoyed my time at the club. I understand the fans appreciated what I did for the club and it's really touching to hear they thought a lot of me and still do after all this time.

The whole experience was great for me. When you're young, you're full of confidence, you try anything and you're not bothered if things don't work out. You have no fear. I believed I was good enough to be in the Everton first team then and Carlisle gave me something to back that up. I had demonstrated that I could do it. That loan spell gave me a platform. It was one of two rungs on the ladder I needed to step on.

Carlisle was also an eye-opener. I'd experienced the Civil Service Club and had to change in a derelict building but, once you were near the Everton first team, the standard really went up. In the first team at Carlisle, you washed your own kit (unless you stayed in the B&B thankfully) and you had to pay for your own food at dinner time.

Managers may organise training but not take part all the time. Roddy Collins wasn't like that. He acted like he was playing with his mates. He wanted to join in as much as he could. The day before a match, we had four teams taking part in a three-touch game. Roddy would kick lumps out of you. He was always desperate for his team to win so he could claim the bragging rights for the day. At times I think the next day's game was forgotten about. There was no "mind your tackles" with Roddy. He was so competitive, but I loved it. It was a lot of fun.

If I went into management, I wouldn't necessarily train with the first team every day but he did it with such enjoyment and a big smile on his face. If I do ever go down that path, the enjoyment is something I'd try to take with me.

He was under a lot of pressure from the club and fans because they were at the bottom of League Two, but he always seemed happy. He enjoyed every day and every training session.

Roddy is the brother of Steve Collins, the former world champion boxer. He looked the same, was built the same and his hands were massive. I suppose it's a bit easier to enjoy life when you are secure in the knowledge that you and your brother could take on and bash up anybody who crossed you! You wouldn't want to mess with Roddy, that's for sure, but I liked him and his approach.

Being Carlisle, the weather was often cold. If the training pitch was frozen, Roddy had a variety of alternative strategies. Sometimes we'd go for a walk, some days we'd go to a hotel for a swim or a Jacuzzi. Once or twice, we just went to the pub for a Guinness.

Pretty much after every home game, he'd say: "Anyone fancy a pint? We'll be in the Beehive. I'll buy the first round." My dad used to race him there. Jenny came up a few times and we'd been together for just over a year at this point. We became close to Roddy and we went out together a few times in Carlisle. He was a good man with a nice family.

Roddy was happy to mingle with the players. There was no divide at all. Once the game was finished, we were all mates. No other manager, in my experience, has done that. With other managers, there always seems to be a distance between them and the players.

On one occasion Brunton Park was frozen, Roddy drove us to a local hotel in a minibus. After our swim, he told us he had to leave with the assistant manager, John Cunningham.

He handed the minibus keys to our captain, a Scouse centre-half called Michael Taylor, from Blackburn Rovers, who was only 19. Roddy said: "Here you are, skipper. Make sure all the lads get home okay." We all piled in the minibus, Mike started it up but before he even got out of the car park, he went: "Lads, there is no way I can do this. I'm shitting myself. Does anyone else want to drive it?"

The bus was quiet until I found myself saying: "Go 'ed, I'll do it." I felt like the leader but before I knew it, I was doing 95mph down the outside lane of the M6. When I realised what speed I was going, my heart started racing almost as quickly. Imagine if something had happened. I could have wiped out the whole squad. Now I'd be sensible enough to drive 70mph but back then I got carried away with the situation.

I enjoyed it so much there that I went back up for the end-of-season do. I might even have won something. I kept in touch and had another night out with Roddy and his family, too. I have a lot of happy memories of Carlisle.

When I returned to Everton at the turn of the year, we were facing an FA Cup third-round tie at Shrewsbury. I travelled with the squad as the 17th man. We all know how that turned out – a demoralising 2-1 defeat. A week later we played Spurs at White Hart Lane and again I was the 17th man. Me and Kev McLeod were the two extras. Kev roomed with Ibrahim Said, who would get up at 5am to go through his prayer ritual. Kev wasn't too thrilled about it. They were certainly a bizarre pair. Ibrahim was from Egypt, Kev was from Garston. Ibrahim was very religious whereas the only time Kev went to church was for confession!

When we got to the ground, I was told I wasn't involved, but during the warm-up our goalkeeper, Richard Wright, hurt his ankle. The Norwegian goalkeeper Espen Baardsen, who was with us on loan, took over and that freed up a place on the bench. Moyes trotted across to where Kev and I were standing watching the warm-up and said: "Ossie, go and get changed, you're on the bench." Again, Kev was none too thrilled.

I was stunned. I went inside and quickly changed, but by the time I was ready the players were back in, so I didn't get the chance to step on the pitch and warm up. It wasn't until I took my seat in the dug-out that I realised I hadn't had time to even phone my dad. It was just as well really because he would have tried to hire a plane to get from Skem to London in time for the second half.

It was a brilliant game. Another loan player for us, Brian McBride, made his debut and scored after two minutes but Spurs came back and led 4-3 as time was running out. Moyes turned to me and said: "Ossie, get ready, you're going on." There was only about three minutes left so I frantically ripped off my tracksuit and managed to get on with 90 seconds left, replacing Li Tie. There was a kick from Baardsen that I managed to flick on with my head and that was the only time I touched the ball. It was over very quickly but I was on the pitch and thrilled. I'd made my debut. I'd played for Everton's first team. I hadn't actually kicked a ball in the Premier League yet but that didn't matter. I got my shirt signed by all the team and they left messages saying 'well done'.

I was in and around the team a couple of times until the penultimate home game of the season against Aston Villa when I got on for the last few minutes. It was 1-1 when I came on and Wayne Rooney scored an injury-time winner. I was ecstatic. Surely the fans would give me the credit for turning the game our way! They obviously didn't but back then I got more for a first-team win bonus than my wage, so I was happy enough. My first time in the first team at Goodison, a win, and I was absolutely delighted.

Davie Moyes had taken us right back up the table in his first full season, similar to what happened to Everton under Joe Royle. We finished seventh and were desperately unlucky not to qualify for Europe, fighting until the last game of the season. The club was on the up, we were doing well and I was part of the first-team squad. Life was good.

By then I'd experienced some of the quirkier traits of the first-team squad. Our Welsh midfielder, Mark Pembridge, would judge people's clothes.

"Alright, boyo. What are you wearing today?"

You'd come in after training and one player's clothes would be hung up from a hole in the ceiling. It could be one item or a whole outfit, and whatever Pembs deemed the worst gear of the day would be hung up for ridicule. I used to dread going inside incase it was mine.

I used to give Davie Weir stick about his clothes because he dressed like a teenage student. He went to university in America and came straight from campus into football and dressed accordingly. I'd tell him he was 36 and still dressing like a student. "Keeps you young, lad," he'd tell me.

As 2003/04 began, I continued to perform for the reserves and had scored eight goals by the end of November, including both our goals in a 2-1 win at Wolves.

Seven days later the first team played Middlesbrough in the Carling Cup and the outcome was very different for me. I was on the bench again and chomping at the bit for the whole game. Twenty minutes to go... ten minutes to go... five minutes to go... final whistle. It finished 0-0 and we were into extra-time. Now I was thinking 'another half-hour, everyone will be shattered, I'll get on here'. The first half went by and I began to lose hope before, with 12 minutes left, I replaced Franny Jeffers, who was back at the club on loan from Arsenal. I did alright, I felt comfortable, sharp and passed it around well. There were still no goals so it went to penalties.

This was my third game for the club. I had played 90 seconds, five minutes and 12 minutes. There was a discussion about who was going to take the pens and I put myself forward. 'This is it', I thought. 'This is a chance to make a name for myself. This could be my route in. You have to take these gambles'.

I was third and every penalty had been scored prior to me stepping forward. My intention was to slam the ball into the top right-hand corner. I'm not making an excuse here but as I ran up, when I planted my standing foot, the pitch gave way and I slipped a little. Instead of going top right, I screwed the ball straight down the middle. Mark Schwarzer was heading in the opposite direction to where I intended to hit it but he saved it with his legs. My heart sank. I felt sick. It was a long and lonely walk back to the halfway line. I was praying a Middlesbrough player would miss, but nobody did. We lost 5-4 and I was the only person not to score. That was one of the lowest moments I've ever felt on a football pitch.

On the bus afterwards people were commiserating with me. Unsy said: "Ossie, don't worry about it. Stay strong." No one blamed me but it was a real tough moment.

It's been a standing joke for 11 years with Jimmy Comer, our masseur. He still ribs me about it. "Penalty, Ossie? Ooohh, remember Boro?" The only one I've taken since was against Juventus in pre-season 2013 and I missed that one too. The Boro episode really did scar me because before that I had taken pens in all of my age groups...and scored most of them.

I wasn't involved in the first team after that and I felt I had set myself back. I couldn't help thinking that if I'd kept my mouth shut and not taken a penalty then I would have continued to get on as a sub. I thought it had all gone wrong down at the Riverside.

In late January, I noticed George Burley, the Derby manager, watching one of our reserve games, away to Manchester United, and not long after I was asked if I wanted to go on loan there. Again, I didn't hesitate to say yes. Derby was a big club, and had been in the Premier League less then two years previously. It was a good thing for me.

I drove to the training ground and was immediately impressed with the facilities. In the first session, we had an 11 v 11 match on a full-size pitch. Nobody really knew who I was. Near the end of the game, I ran through, beat a couple and from the corner of the 18-yard box, I lobbed the keeper. I could sense people thinking 'hang on, what have we got here?'. A few came up to say well done afterwards. It went really well from that moment.

I had a similar routine to Carlisle. Monday, Tuesday I'd be in Derby; Wednesday, I'd be home; Thursday, Friday, Saturday, back to Derby, with Sundays usually at home…or in the Stanley in Skem!

Derby put me in a lovely apartment. It was open-plan with two bedrooms. The wardrobe in the bigger one opened into a big wet room. It was so exciting. It had a sauna, shower and bath. I liked the privacy of my own apartment, which I didn't have in Carlisle. I enjoy people's company but I also like my own time, my own space.

Growing up, my dad always made us deep-fat fried chips and I got hooked on them, so I had to visit the Asda in Derby to buy a deep-fat fryer. I made chips nearly every night to begin with and over the four-month period, my cooking came on a lot. I was doing more than chips by the way. I could boil pasta and I could pop a chicken in the oven. At Carlisle I was cooked for in the B&B.

My first game was at Pride Park on January 28, a Wednesday night, against a Sheffield United side that included a certain Phil Jagielka. Jags and I have spoken about it since. The game was nearly called off because of ice and snow. My mum, dad, brother and Jenny (considering she hates football, she went absolutely everywhere!) nearly missed it because of traffic issues. Me and Tom Huddlestone were the centre-mids. He was barely 17 and massive. What a player he was, even back then. Two-footed with a superb passing range. We won 2-0 and I did okay, a good solid debut. It was an important win because Derby had been struggling.

In my third match, at home to Cardiff, Burley moved me up front for a period, but for the last 20 minutes he put me on the left of midfield. I scored a 90th minute equaliser, a header at the back stick. I turned to the fans to celebrate only to realise I was looking at a lot of angry Welshmen, so I quickly ran off in another direction.

Burley surprised me in terms of his managerial style. He didn't take training and we didn't have many meetings either. When we did, he would write out the opposition team and there would be a lot of arrows, but it was basic information. Compared to nowadays, it wasn't enough. But I quite liked how simplified it all was. He told you your opponents' favourite moves and let you get on with the rest, giving you licence to express yourself without several different jobs to be thinking about. Burley could read a game 10 minutes in, better than most managers. Other managers may have a clear plan but might not be good at adjusting once the game has started – I'm not talking about anyone in particular there, incidentally. Burley would start with a plan but he could see things better once the game was in progress. He wasn't afraid of changing methods and making tactical switches.

Derby v Crystal Palace, on February 21, was a big one for me. Up to that point I'd done okay, without lighting up the place. I hadn't shown enough, simple as that but the Palace game was the start of a run of form. I scored the winning goal. I closed down a midfielder; then set off after the left centre-half; then the right centre-half. He tried to knock it past me, but I got a foot in, picked up the ball and placed it over the advancing keeper with my left foot. I went absolutely mad with aggression that had obviously built up during all that chasing and I'm afraid I went a bit berserk. I think I kicked an advertising hoarding during my celebrations. I saw it back later on Central TV, when I was making my tea in my apartment (cooked chicken and home-made chips). I was horrified at my reaction and told myself that I needed to calm down.

The next big game was Derby v Nottingham Forest on March 20. My first senior derby. The Rams were generally getting between 15-20,000 a game but that day Pride Park was nearly full, with over 32,000 fans. The atmosphere was incredible and the game will always be remembered for the 'coffee cup goal'.

It was an awful, very windy day and when there was a back-pass to Forest's keeper, Barry Roche, a big gust blew this plastic coffee cup into the line of the ball. As Roche was about to kick, the cup hit the ball, which Roche then shanked to the side, allowing Paul Peschisolido to smash it into the net. The place erupted. Not only was it a goal against your derby rivals, but it was the coffee cup comedy goal, or the 'coffee horror show' as some headlines had it. I was right in line with the incident. It was brilliant! We won 4-2 and it possibly could have been more.

Next we played Sheffield United again, this time at Bramall Lane. They were going for the play-offs while we were still down near the bottom. We drew 1-1, which was a good result for us, but their manager, Neil Warnock, was not happy and he decided to take it out on me.

Our goal came from a free-kick awarded for a foul on me by Nick Montgomery, a good mate of Jags. After the game

Warnock accused me of diving. Every interview he gave, he said "that Osman kid dived". I absolutely hadn't. I wouldn't know how to dive. I was disappointed that an experienced manager was using me as an excuse for his team not winning. I was listening to the radio in the car with my dad on the way home when I heard Warnock say it again. I was incensed and wanted to phone the radio station to say that he was wrong and out of order. Thankfully, my dad calmed me down so it didn't distract me for long, but I was riled by what he was alleging. As you get older, you do get used to criticism or the occasional bit of abuse. I was fuming at the time but I would laugh it off now.

Our main match after that was against Bradford City at Pride Park on Easter Monday. It was between us and them as to who went down. We desperately needed to win and we did, 3-2. I scored one, set up the other two and played really well. That was the most pressured match I played at Derby.

We hammered Preston 5-1 the following week and with just two weeks to go before my return to Everton, I was really hoping that Moyesy would have noticed that one against his former club. We stayed up comfortably and a trip to Burnley on April 24 was my last game for the club.

It was a brilliant experience for me. I loved Pride Park and I loved the fans. I hate bigging myself up but I knew I was one of the better players. I was confident of playing well every week, and relished going out there and enjoying it.

When I went back to Pride Park with Everton in October 2007, the fans gave me a really nice reception. Lee Carsley was in our team that day and he was a former Derby player. Cars didn't get much reaction from the Rams lot and he wasn't happy. "Are you fucking messing? See that stand over there –

they built that with the money they got from selling me. And it's you that's getting a clap?" That was a funny moment.

Just before I left Derby, Murdo MacKay, who became their Director of Football, approached me in the canteen and said they wanted to sign me, asking if I would be interested. I told him: "I've really enjoyed my time here but I want to play for Everton. If Everton say they are going to let me go then, yeah, I'll happily sign. If Everton say they want to keep me, I'm staying. I want to be an Everton player." He appreciated my honesty and we shook hands and wished each other the best of luck.

I returned to Everton in late April and I heard that Derby and their big rivals, Nottingham Forest, had both made bids for me. I think they initially offered £750,000. Moyes said no. One of the clubs asked how much Everton wanted and Moyes told them £1.5m. Straight away they said: "Okay, done, deal." Moyes then backtracked and said he'd changed his mind and that I wasn't for sale. I think he was shocked that they were prepared to double their offer straight away but it planted a seed in his mind.

On my return, I was training at Bellefield with the first team and Moyes called me over. He said: "Ossie, good to see you back. Well done, I've heard you played really well. Did you enjoy it?"

"Yeah, it went really well."

"Well, it's been good for us too, because if we do sell you, we know we can get a bit of money for you, so well done."

"Cheers."

I ran off and was thinking 'he's done it to me again'. Back

then, I just couldn't work him out at times.

Despite that, I honestly thought, fingers crossed, that I'd be on the bench for the Wolves game at Molineux at the end of my first week back. We only had three games to go. I went for a walk around a golf course and a couple of people were saying "you're going to start". I didn't really believe it. 'He's not going to start me, no chance', I thought to myself.

Because I'd been away, I didn't realise how much we were struggling. If we hadn't been safe by this point, I don't think Moyes would have played me. But when he announced the team at our hotel on the morning of the game I was starting on the right of midfield. I tried to play it cool, but inside I was elated. I'd played every game of the past three months for Derby but to do it for Everton in the Premier League was a different level. I rang my mum and dad to tell them and they were out of the front door and in their car before I'd put the phone down.

There wasn't really anything riding on it for Everton but I did feel the pressure and I was nervous warming up. Kevin Kilbane wished me luck and Hibbo told me to go out and enjoy it – I'm glad he was there as that settled me down.

Within two minutes of the game starting, Wayne knocked a long ball forward, I won a header, James McFadden dribbled round his marker and as I ran into the box the cross came over. I headed it and it went in.

'Oh my God! I've scored! Yeeeees! Yeeeees! Yeeeees!' Hibbo and Faddy were jumping on me. It was at the end where the Everton fans were situated and they were all going mad. I remember it vividly. Next thing someone said "you've cut your nose".

As I'd headed it, a Wolves player put his foot up to block it and took a chunk out of my hooter but I didn't feel it and I didn't care one jot. He could have kicked my nose down the back of my throat and then bit my ears off for all I cared. I had just scored a Premier League goal for Everton.

Despite that early goal, we went on to lose the game 2-1. I had mixed feelings in the dressing room afterwards. I was gutted that we'd lost in my first start, but inside I was like a kid. I wanted to tell everyone: "I've just scored for Everton!"

My family and friends were delighted too because they had put money on me to score the first goal at decent odds. My mum, dad and a few mates were sat next to Derek Mountfield among the Wolves fans and some of the lads were chucked out for celebrating the goal and causing a commotion. Mum, Dad and Derek kept their heads down and were allowed to stay.

That loss to Wolves was one of many disappointing defeats that season. In 2003/04 Moyes just couldn't get us going. We were around the relegation spots for much of the campaign and we were only safe with about five games to go. A week after Wolves, we played Bolton at home and they had an excellent team – Jay-Jay Okocha, Youri Djorkaeff and Ivan Campo among them. I started again and we lost 2-1 again.

The last game of the season was Manchester City away, at their new stadium. We were battered 5-1 and it could, and should, have been more. That was a tough day. It was red-hot and I rolled my ankle after 15 minutes. I didn't want to come off but I was limping and struggled after that. I wasn't the worst player though, not by a long way. It was a dreadful way to end a shocking season and Moyes hammered us in the dressing room afterwards. He went absolutely bonkers. "This is fucking embarrassing. This isn't fucking good enough. We can't continue to represent the club like this. This club shouldn't be finishing 17th."

Effectively, three games into my Everton career, I was witnessing an absolute tirade from the manager. But it was all true and he was right to say it. There was an extremely critical article in the Liverpool Echo afterwards by their main sportswriter, David Prentice, which upset some of the players. He claimed that some of the players weren't putting a shift in and that they were trying to get Moyes sacked. When it came to pre-season, we weren't allowed to speak to the Echo. I was too young to have any say on that, though, and the Echo didn't want to speak to me anyway!

There was plenty of turmoil around the club in that summer of 2004, not least of it surrounding Wayne Rooney. But 2004/05 was a season when a team tipped by many for relegation sold their best player and still qualified for the Champions League.

And a lot of it was to do with a pre-season trip to Texas.

07

Goodbye Wayne

The summer of 2004 was a momentous one for Everton, with apparent arguments in the boardroom and the club's best player seeking a transfer. With the team having just finished fourth from bottom, it did not look good.

It was a summer of speculation regarding Wayne Rooney. He was linked with a move away with Newcastle United and Manchester United both mentioned. I remember watching Euro 2004 and Wayne was sensational for England. Even to me, it looked as clear as day that he would be leaving Everton sooner rather than later. But strangely enough, because Wayne broke a metatarsal in the Euro 2004 quarter-final against Portugal, we did not see him much during pre-season so although his transfer dragged on for weeks, it did not really affect us.

As players, we just couldn't afford to allow any of the off-the-field issues affect what is always a vitally important part of the season. We were working hard and concentrating fully on being match-fit for the new season and, although this backdrop of uncertainty was discussed amongst us, we never took it out onto the pitch.

We went to Austria first that summer and I do recall being on the pitch about to play a game when information was fed to us that our new Chief Executive Officer, Trevor Birch, had resigned after just six weeks at Everton. I was too young to understand all the repercussions of what was going on but I do recall that Moyes was in a chirpier mood after that particular bit of news.

The lads could sense the turmoil but we were concentrating on our business. I was new to the first team and needed to focus on my own game. This was a team that had finished fourth from bottom and was now likely to lose our star player. Off-the-field issues could look after themselves.

After Austria, we went to Houston and it was in Texas where we set the tone for the season that followed. That trip to America was fantastic and really brought us close together as a squad.

We'd been up from stupid o'clock in the morning for the journey across the Atlantic and there was no beer allowed on the plane. Moyes could be strict and often everything was uptight. No ale and no nights out. He would really control what we were and weren't allowed to do...but that was about to change!

We landed in Houston at about 4-5pm local time and it had already been a long day. When we arrived at the Weston Galleria Hotel the manager gathered us together and said: "It's five o'clock, I know you're tired but you need to stay up as late

Early memories: (Below left) Showing a turn of pace during a race at nursery – aged three – and (right) charm personified, at 10 months old

Starting out: A 'junior' member of Dalton School's football team (back row, third left), aged eight

Happy days: With my Skelmersdale League Player of the Season trophy in 1988 and lining up with Elmers Green JFC two years later. Dad is far right and my brother second left, back row

Model pupil: All smiles in Upholland High School uniform, and (above right) with Mum and Dad in more recent times

Wembley winner: A trophy winner with England Schoolboys at the old Wembley Stadium, against Germany in June 1997

Family ties: With Dad, brother Carl and son Cole on my wedding day

Smart-looking signing: Penning my first Everton contract – sporting my best jacket – in manager Joe Royle's office alongside Mum, Dad and Academy manager Ray Hall

Big influence: Everton legend and youth-team coach Colin Harvey inspired a winning mentality among all those who worked for him

Osman clan: The family, minus Dad, Jenny and Cole, watch me at Goodison during a first-team game in 2012/13

Under the skin of sport

Cup winners: My 1997/98 FA Youth Cup team-mates celebrate victory following the 2-2 draw with Blackburn, which meant we secured the trophy 5-3 on aggregate. My injury in the first leg meant I was unable to take part in the home leg, and I still regret not getting myself on the team photo

Making progress: (Left) Playing in the FA Youth Cup semi-final, second leg, the following season West Ham included future England players Joe Cole and Michael Carrick in their line-up.

Next step: (Below) Now a fully fledged 'Bindie', in the 1999/2000 team photo (front row, fifth left). Tony Hibbert is back row, far right; Nick Chadwick second row, second right and Matt McKay is front row, third left

Loan Blue: I enjoyed eventful spells at Carlisle United (above) and Derby County (right) in the early 2000s. My spell at Pride Park was deemed so successful that George Burley wanted to sign me

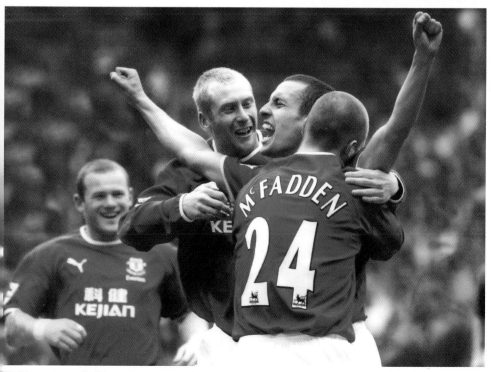

Making my mark: I was given a run of games at the back of the 2003/04 season – and I even scored my first goal, against Wolves (above) causing 'an incident' in the stands!

First-teamer: Sharing a laugh with David Moyes, a manager who always kept you on your toes; (below) celebrating my second goal of the game, the winner v West Brom, August 2004

Memorable moments: (Above) My good mate Tony Hibbert shows his delight after my late winner v Southampton; (right) a peck from Duncan Ferguson after my deflected effort had found the net against Bolton, a week before my first Merseyside derby (below), when Lee Carsley's winner sparked memorable celebrations

Pompey time: Being mobbed following my injury-time winner against Portsmouth at Goodison in January 2005. Below: A moody shot at local club Skelmersdale United the following month

Villa memories: Our 3-1 victory at Aston Villa was arguably our best performance of 2004/05. Here I celebrate after sweeping in the clinching third goal

as you can. Get yourselves out. Have a few drinks and relax. Go and enjoy yourselves. See you tomorrow for breakfast."

Because he was usually so uptight, it was totally out the blue. We looked at each other, dumbfounded. "Did Moyesy just say that?" someone asked. "Yes, but he's said it now, he can't take it back. Let's get out before he changes his mind!"

The lads scattered in no time.

The accommodation was situated next to a massive shopping mall. Some trips can be really aggravating if there is nothing to do but this hotel was attached to a mall that had everything – cinemas, an ice rink, a bowling alley, shops, coffee bars and a cheesecake factory. We were never bored at any time during the 10 days we were in Houston.

Like any club, the lads went out in their own groups of five and six. Myself, Nick Chadwick, Kev Kilbane, Steve Watson, Gary Naysmith, James McFadden and Davie Weir went to a sports bar that was attached to the hotel. We stayed there all night, eating, drinking and having a laugh. People came and went but we stayed put. At last orders we decided to go on the ice rink. It was probably Watto's suggestion. It seemed like a great idea at the time.

Somehow six or seven of us blagged our way on. I'm actually not a bad skater but I'd had a few beers which nulled my ability to gracefully move across the ice. I zipped aimlessly around, just managing to stay upright. Kev Kilbane managed one step before he went up in the air and landed on his elbow, cutting it quite badly. Sensibly he decided to quit at that point. Watto told Kev it was dead easy but when he stepped on the rink himself, he was Bambi on ice. He had to grab the side and walk a circuit of the perimeter before trotting off.

Our current doctor, Jon Thomas, was on his first trip with us. He had been for a walk and was quite startled to find seven of the first-team squad on an ice rink at 11.30pm. The doc can be quite naïve and Gary Naysmith somehow convinced him we were all on drugs. The doc had warned us about random drug tests and Gary told him: "You'll have to do what the other doc did and fiddle it for us so we don't get caught." The doc was horrified: "I can't do that!" he gasped. We had him panicking for three days. If we walked into a room, he walked out and kept as far away from us as possible. He could see his fledgling Everton career ending almost as soon as it had started! To be fair to him he took it well when we told him the truth.

The next morning, after our ice-capades, the gaffer had another surprise for us over breakfast. "We're not going to train today lads," he announced. "We are going to play golf. We are teeing off at 11am. Enjoy yourselves again. Anyone who doesn't want to play, see you tomorrow. Training will be at 6pm." We were all stunned again. That was it. The lads were out again.

We were still learning all the time about Moyes at this point but he was brilliant on that trip. He was relaxed and that filtered through to the lads. I was so impressed with him in Houston because he pitched it just right.

We had done three weeks of running before this and it was actually just a day-and-a-half of golfing and relaxing but that day-and-a-half brought us together so much. For the rest of that season, every goal celebration, everything we did, we always referred back to Houston. Something as simple as "go and let your hair down" had such a positive effect, partly because it was such a surprise and also because Moyes was showing the trust he had in us.

I partnered Chaddy for the golf and we played against Gary and Faddy. Before we started we checked we'd hired everything we needed. The correct sets of clubs, plenty of golf balls, scorecards, two buggies…and a case of Bud. The cans soon came out. It was red-hot that day in Texas but it clouded over in an instant and a really heavy thunderstorm with lightning was unleashed on us. We forgot about the golf, dived for cover in the buggies and chucked out anything that we thought could get us electrocuted – clubs, tees, the lot. We kept a few cans back and took a chance with them. We sat in those buggies for two hours, scared to move. It was a fine storm I can tell you.

When it stopped, we carried on playing but the clubs were saturated. From one tee, Gaz and I both drove our balls towards a huge lake but, incredibly, because we'd both hit poor shots the ball travelled very low and skimmed off the water and back onto the fairway. We blamed the wet clubs for our lack of accuracy but it turned out well in the end. Chaddy's drive went straight down the middle…but so did his club. As he hit the ball, and he generally hits it well, his club shot out of his hand and flew through the air about fifty yards.

We had another team night out that evening when we got back to the hotel, with bar games and a sing-song. All new players and staff have to stand on a bar stool and sing a song in front of everyone else.

It can be very, very nerve-wracking and I've seen some dreadful performances over the years. The lads love to see a bit of terror in the eyes of the new singers and it's a bit annoying when one of them then goes on and 'nails it' with a very good performance. Once the new boys have done their bit, everyone else gives a song. I tend to stick to Motown but on that night in

Houston I joined our media guy, Darren Griffiths, for Summer Of 69. We were brilliant.

Those 48 hours were such a laugh and we bonded in a big way. I would even go as far to suggest that those two days made our season. Because the Americans are so dramatic and expressive, "woo-hoo" became our slogan. I still do it to Kev Kilbane now. It stuck with us all. Fifty per cent of the goals scored in 2004/05 were celebrated with a "woo-hoo" and a high-five.

Eventually, 48 hours after our arrival, we started our first training session at the NFL franchise Houston Texans' facility. We watched them practise too and it was incredible – there must have been 100 of them. They were as intrigued by us as we were by them. They probably couldn't believe how small some of us were. They had a 3G pitch with an air-conditioned bubble over the top. It was really cool inside, which we needed in the heat and humidity. Their stadium was adjacent and that was an awesome sight too.

Once we got started on the training, it was really tough and physical. We had a good six or seven days of hard, intense work with two matches towards the end of the trip. Because of what we'd been allowed to do at the start, we got our heads down and worked hard. We knew we'd been treated like responsible adults, we appreciated it and there was no way any one of us was going to let the gaffer down.

Before that flight to Houston, the club had told us there were only 18 business class seats between the 24 players and four senior staff. The non-senior staff were already in economy but it meant 10 of us needed to join them. It was decided the youngest players would be the ones. We accepted that but requested that we would be in business class on the way back. That was agreed, but it didn't stop the senior players from rubbing it in because they had creature comforts while we were squashed in our seats.

For our return flight back to the UK, we piped up at the airport to say we would be in business class. There was me, Chaddy, Faddy, Hibbo, Peter Clarke and a few others. I was seated in 1D while Tommy Gravesen and Kev Campbell were something like 39F. The senior players started saying: "If I'm not in business class, I'm not flying. I'm not getting on that plane, no chance."

We got our heads down and headed for our seats as quickly as we could. One-by-one the senior players wandered on. There must have been five or six of them moaning but I only remember Tommy and Kev. They flat out refused to accept it and told us to move. They said they'd pay for their own ticket the following day if we didn't. This went on for about five minutes. Faddy was hardcore. "Ossie, you're a first-teamer. Sit down."

Eventually Davie Moyes wandered over, asked what was going on and told Tommy and Kev they couldn't fly the following day. The complaining continued until he lost patience and snapped: "Here, have my seat." The gaffer and his assistant, Alan Irvine, sat in economy for 10 hours all the way back to the UK. I'm embarrassed by this now but we had a nice sleep and were all nice and fresh when we landed.

As we waited by the carousel, Alan was in front of us. Chaddy was dead chirpy and said: "Are these our bags, Al, grab them for us will you?" Alan, one of the nicest most placid men in football, snapped: "I haven't had any fucking sleep. My neck's killing. You know what, Chaddy? Fuck off."

Two days later we played Sheffield Wednesday at Hillsborough and won 6-3. I scored a half-volley in the top corner after two minutes. Alan mentioned to me that he told Moyes I had to be in the team for the first game of the season. That was good of him but I'm not sure I would have been as gracious it if I'd sat in economy for 10 hours.

Although I'd played the last three games of the previous season, and I'd had a good pre-season, I didn't expect to start the first league game at Goodison against Arsenal. It was a red-hot day, roasting, and humid too. Arsenal were coming off the back of their invincible season and they started as though they'd never been away, beating us 4-1. They were really good that afternoon. We were okay, but we didn't hit their heights. Dennis Bergkamp and Robert Pires scored while Lee Carsley got us off the mark after a good one-two with Tommy Gravesen.

Wayne Rooney was still an Everton player at this point but we knew it was only a matter of time before he'd be leaving. Wayne was hot property after the Euros but because he had broken his metatarsal, he wasn't travelling with us. We were away for quite a long time in Austria and America and when we came back, we started playing games straight away and the new season was upon us. When 2004/05 started, it didn't feel as though we were missing him. He wasn't part of our squad and he wasn't available anyway.

While Wayne was going, and David Unsworth and Tomasz Radzinski, among others, had already left, we made some really decent signings for very little money that summer in Marcus Bent and, most notably, Tim Cahill, although we hadn't met him yet because he was with Australia at the Athens Olympics.

Eventually, of course, Wayne's move to Manchester United was confirmed. The lads expected it as it had been rumbling on for a while now and I think it was only the injury that had prevented it happening earlier. He went with my best wishes – as if he needed them! – and I am delighted at the way his career has developed. Scoring a hat-trick in the Champions League on his debut was pure Wayne. Captaining England and a club like Manchester United is some achievement but it's nothing less than Wayne deserves after the career he's had.

After the season we'd had the year before, and the fact that we had no real money to spend and strengthen, there was no expectation on us. The mood all summer in the press was that David Moyes was likely to be the first Premier League manager out of the door. Despite this, during the whole of that pre-season, it was the most relaxed I ever saw Moyes in the whole time I knew him. He took the shackles off and let us enjoy ourselves a little bit. Okay, we lost the first game but we didn't play badly. It was against the Invincibles and no-one expected us to win.

Most people would have Arsenal on their opening day coupon but our next match, away at Crystal Palace, was absolutely vital. The feelgood factor that everyone had contributed to had taken a slight knock against Arsenal but it would have been crushed had we lost at Palace a week later.

Davie Moyes' usual mantra was to keep a winning team. It was very rare for him to change a side from the week before if we had won. I was made up to be in the team for the Arsenal game but we'd lost and so I was worried I might be vulnerable. But I was still in for the Palace game, keeping Steve Watson out.

We went 1-0 down at Selhurst Park and Wayne Routledge was giving Gary Naysmith a tough game. Gary ended up being sent off in the second half. The smallest margins can be massive in football. We were 1-0 down when Palace's new keeper, Julian

Speroni, tried to dribble around Kev Campbell. Kev threw his shoulder in, nudged him off the ball and Speroni brought him down. We were awarded a penalty; Tommy Gravesen stepped up and put it away quite comfortably, as he always did, and that was it. That one moment changed our season. We were up and running and from non-fancied outsiders, we made all the running in the race for Champions League football.

Into the second half, Tommy again, corner of the box, took a touch, turned and put it on a postage stamp into the top corner. What a goal! Gary was sent off at 2-1 up and we were on the back foot but Tommy slipped a pass through to Marcus Bent and, with his pace, he was away. That combination got us our third goal and we were off the mark.

Tommy was a real character, as you might imagine. He would try to blow people's boots up with fireworks. On one occasion he blew a massive hole in the Bellefield grass and did the same in the concrete floor of the main gym. He would also light them, hold the stick in his hand and aim them down the other end of the gym where people were playing head tennis. They would have to jump for cover. He was mad.

Another thing that made us laugh was the fact that Tommy became annoyed with the cost of car insurance in Britain. "It's crazy. No, I refuse to pay," he told us. We explained he had no choice. About three days later his big car disappeared and he arrived in a purple Nissan Micra. It was tiny. He was boasting about it because he secured free insurance for a year as part of the deal.

In the game against West Brom, on August 28, 2004 – I remember it well – I secured my place in the first-team. After just two minutes, I scored for the first time at Goodison. It came from a long Gravesen throw, which we used very effectively back then. As the throw was taken, I started trotting into the box, on my toes, and Kev Kilbane, who couldn't half jump, flicked it perfectly into my path. I headed it right back where it had come from and it looped over two defenders into the far corner. Wow. There is a great picture of me celebrating with the crowd in the Gwladys Street going mad behind me. It was a really good moment and, again, it was enhanced by the fact that I knew my family were watching me.

Confidence was up. We'd won away from home, we were 1-0 up at Goodison but West Brom then equalised with a freak goal. A corner was whipped into the near post, Lee Carsley went to clear but headed it into the back of Scott Dobie's head and it went in.

The previous season, we probably would have got a bit shaky at having been pegged back. But Duncan Ferguson won a free-kick with about 20 minutes to go. Cars was stood over it and I couldn't believe my luck because I was standing right in front of the keeper, expecting someone to mark me, but no-one did. I was waving to Cars and I don't know if he went for goal or intentionally whipped it at me, but I managed to get my body out the way while at the same time flicking it on with my head. I'd scored again – two at Goodison! Myself and Duncan Ferguson ran to the crowd, celebrating. That was a moment. My first three goals for Everton were all headers.

Two days later we went to Old Trafford on the Bank Holiday Monday. That was the first time we met Tim Cahill. He was expected to be on the bench but Tommy went down with a bug or strain a couple of hours before kick-off so Tim stepped in and immediately made a positive impression.

In the first two games we had played 4-4-2. It was me on the right, Carsley and Gravesen in the middle, Kilbane on the left, and Kev Campbell and Marcus Bent up front. We were a bit more defensive at Old Trafford. Tim came in and Steve Watson played too. We went with 4-1-4-1, for which we would become renowned. We got a good point and could even have won the game. We'd lost to Arsenal at home on the opening day but we won our next two and then got a positive 0-0 at Old Trafford. It was a case of 'hang on a minute, we're doing well here'. Results and a great spirit really breed confidence.

We went to Man City next and Tommy was back. We bossed the game, feeling very comfortable and I remember missing a sitter at 0-0 which I've never watched back. I was slightly to the side of the penalty box with David James to beat. I tried to give him the eyes and he read me. I couldn't believe it. You get certain moments in your career that you remember and would love to change. That was one of them.

In the second half Hibbo put in an unbelievable cross and Tim did what he does best by popping up at the back stick with a header, before running along the touchline to celebrate. His run eventually stopped in the dressing room because he had lifted his shirt above his head and that was deemed a second yellow card. He was devastated to be sent off and it proved once again what a ridiculous rule that is.

Tim had actually aimed his run to celebrate with the manager, which he got a lot of stick for later. 'The Gaffer's new pet' was certainly mentioned afterwards! Despite being down to 10, we managed to see the game out and, suddenly, we're on a roll here. We're flying.

Tim fitted in straight away. If you bring players in from top teams, they can have a bit of arrogance about them. They have a swagger in the way they walk. Sometimes that can be good on the pitch but it can be a bad thing in the dressing room if they are very arrogant or have too high an opinion of themselves.

Tim came from Millwall and had had a tough upbringing. I remember him saying a few times that he was just made up to be with us. The manager had given him an opportunity and he was grateful for it.

The difference between the player he came in as, to the player who left, was like chalk and cheese. When he arrived, he was little Tim Cahill who had scored the winner in the previous season's FA Cup semi-final. He had earned his chance. By the end he was Australia's golden boy. He was largely unknown when he first joined us. The world knew him by the time he left.

A lot of that was down to the way he played, but he also knew how to promote himself as a person. I really like Tim but, and I'm sure he'd agree, he was like David Beckham in the way he would market his potential. He was really good at it and hats off to him. Football is a short career. You have a little more than 10 years to make your life's money. Some people get their heads down and just play football and that's enough. Tim knows how to sell the brand Tim Cahill. He was probably the best I've ever known at it and to his great credit it never affected his ability on the pitch. Of all the players I've played with, he was the best at arriving in the box and scoring. He would appear from nowhere. He could do it for us in the big games too. He loved scoring against Manchester City and Liverpool.

The wins kept coming. I set Marcus Bent up for the winning goal against Middlesbrough. That was my first proper assist for Everton and I was made up with it.

We had a rare win in the League Cup next, beating Bristol City at Ashton Gate. I won a penalty but tweaked my groin as I was brought down for it. I lasted another couple of minutes but had to come off. We played Portsmouth a week later. I'm not the type to rule myself out of games even if I'm injured but it was one of only two fitness tests I've ever failed up until now. I must have had 15 tests with our former physio, 'Baz' Rathbone, and passed 13 of them.

Steve Watson came in for me. In the first half a cross came over, he made a great run inside the full-back, opened his foot up, side-footed it and it hit the outside of the post and went wide. If that goes in, I might not be getting back in the team. It was one of those fine lines in football that dictates what follows.

There have been a lot of fine lines in my career and that was certainly one. Even though I was injured, I wanted to leave it to the last possible moment to see if I could be fit. I hate missing games and I was still new to the team. My two nieces were being christened that day and I was meant to be a Godparent. I could have accepted I was injured and gone to the christening and been a Godparent, but I wanted to give myself every chance to play. In the second half Tim Cahill scored one of his trademark headers for a 1-0 win.

From the Crystal Palace win through to Portsmouth, we'd played six games, won five and drawn the other at Old Trafford. We were right up there, in second. We then lost to Spurs but if you have a good start to the season you can ride the odd setback.

The following season we had a poor start and we were down the bottom. To get out of it, you see that you need three or four wins. It quickly becomes a mountain to climb. When you're doing well, it only takes one game to get back on track. A positive start to the season can be massive.

Whenever we lost, we always managed to get ourselves back on track. We were so full of confidence and had so much fighting spirit. We didn't dominate teams possession-wise but we would pick our moment to strike. Football was different back then. Right now it is either complete possession, like ourselves, or complete counter-attack, like Real Madrid did to Bayern Munich in the 2014 Champions League semi-final. Back then, you went blow for blow.

We were so well set up defensively. Moyes had us very well organised and we all knew our jobs and we all helped each other. We were a proper team. Every time one of us was out of position, someone would cover. If someone ran 15 yards, we'd have three men backing him up. We worked together. That was the reason we were so defensively together.

Our goalkeeper, Nigel Martyn, and back four were fantastic but we defended well as a team, with Lee Carsley in front of them, sweeping up everything. Myself and Killa were the wide men, with Tommy and Tim in the middle. We were set up on the edge of our box with no space behind us, like a Jose Mourinho team.

Against Southampton at home it was boring, a bit of a stalemate, but we kept a clean sheet. Going into the last minute, a long throw came in from the right. I decided I should get in the box, had a look around, saw Fergie, and decided to stand a little bit behind him. He was the one who was going to go for it. He got a little flick, or made the defender miss the ball, and it fell into a little space between four Southampton defenders. It was waist-high but I managed to stick my leg out, bring it under control, shimmied to adjust my feet and hit in on the turn, right into the bottom corner. I couldn't believe it – a last-minute goal at the Gwladys Street end. The place erupted, I ran off and, as usual, Hibbo was the first to celebrate with me, jumping on my back. I don't want to say it was what dreams are made of but you desperately want to score a last-minute winner at the Gwladys.

We were 10 games in, we'd won seven of them and I'd scored three goals. I couldn't have asked for a better start to the season. We had finished 17th the year before and suddenly we were in a Champions League spot.

It was probably too soon for me to really appreciate what was happening at the time and how well things were going.

08

Go Fourth

It's such a good thing to have an excellent keeper behind you, especially experienced ones. I am so lucky to have played with two really top-quality keepers in Nige and Tim Howard.

Off the pitch, despite being nearly 40, Nige was a big kid. Whenever we were travelling away from home on the bus, as soon as Nige could see the stadium, he would ask the young lads, in all seriousness, how long we had until we got there. Someone would point to the stadium and say "we're here now!" and Nige would be cheering and congratulating himself that he'd 'got' another one! Every single time he would do that. We all loved him. He was such a great keeper. His ankle started to go the following season and he struggled kicking it but, in all other aspects, he was top-class.

Our trip to Norwich in October 2004, was a great game. We went 2-0 up with two really good goals from Kev Kilbane and Benty. We weren't possession-based but when we got on the ball, with the likes of Tommy Gravesen, Tim Cahill and me, and Benty making runs in behind, we had some quality and scored great goals.

Maybe we took our foot off the gas but Norwich came out at the start of the second half and scored two quick goals, which put us on the back foot and got the crowd going. That's when you need people like big Dunc to come off the bench and do what he does best. It was a great cross from Watto to the back stick, Dunc headed it in and we'd done it again, a 3-2 win. Who's going to stop us now? It was incredible what was happening.

We drew against Villa and were doing fine at Chelsea, pressing them well. We even thought we'd nick it but Arjen Robben, who was almost unstoppable at the time, showed a bit of skill and was away for the winner.

We had lost for the third time but, again, we got straight back on track at Birmingham City. It was a very tight game, but they didn't look like scoring. A corner came to the edge of the box and Lee Carsley hit a fantastic shot which Muzzy Izzet 'saved' on the line. Tommy did what he did best and put the penalty away in front of the Everton fans. We'd won another one. We kept keeping clean sheets and picking up wins. We always fancied ourselves to score so, as our defence was so tight, we knew we could win games.

A draw at Newcastle kept the momentum going before we faced Bolton. Davie Moyes didn't like being outsized by another team and they certainly had players with a physical presence.

Three or four times he told me I wasn't playing because he needed someone taller in the team, (that was something that Leighton Baines also had to contend with in his first 18 months at the club and so did Hibbo at times). It wasn't because of merit and it was tough to take for both of us. I often missed games against the likes of Bolton and Blackburn when they were managed by Sam Allardyce.

When Bainesy first came to the club in 2007, he found it difficult getting in the team. Moyes kept saying he needed someone bigger so Joleon Lescott would play left-back. It wasn't until we signed Marouane Fellaini that Joleon moved inside and Leighton got in. Bainesy and I had a couple of conversations about it and I told him: "Bazza, I've had the same thing."

It was winding up Bainesy. I wouldn't say he was about to leave but it might not have been far away. A player of his quality doesn't want to sit on the bench. It ended up working out – Felli came in, someone was injured, Bainesy got in the team and there was never any doubt what would happen after that.

Anyway, back to 2004/05. I was a substitute against Bolton and came on when we were 2-1 down. We equalised through Tommy Gravesen, while the winner came from a corner. I was stood at the back edge of the box, the ball came out and I volleyed it. I'd love to tell you it was flying in the top corner and it took a slight nick off Radhi Jaidi. It wasn't – it was going wide but his shin diverted it past Jussi Jaaskelainen for an own goal. We'd won another one and little me had made an impact against a tall team.

A week later it was my first Merseyside derby. I'd been left out the week before but thankfully I'd made an impact as a sub, so I started. Moyes would usually pick his team on a Friday and go through some set-pieces. Later on in my Everton career I could usually work it out by the Tuesday because of how he would line up certain players in training. I don't know if I could do that then, but I recall being confident about playing against Liverpool from the way he had organised his sessions.

Everyone must have great memories of that game, 'the Lee Carsley derby'. We hadn't beaten Liverpool for five years, and seven years at Goodison, so to nick it was a big deal and put us 12 points clear of them into second position in the Premier League.

After the game, the chairman bought us framed pictures of our celebratory mound with Tim Cahill on top. We all signed them for each other, but the only player you couldn't see was Carso because he was buried at the bottom! I'd grown up with Merseyside derbies and that win still gets talked about to this day. He may not have had the best welcome back to Derby County but Lee Carsley guaranteed himself a warm welcome at Goodison for life when he scored that goal. We deserved to win that day. I managed to touch it on to Cars for him to score, so it was nice to be a part of the goal.

I picked up an injury shortly afterwards and missed the games over Christmas and New Year. Successive defeats at Charlton and Spurs set us back a bit as it was the first time we had lost two on the trot in the league that season. I was back for our home game against Portsmouth and what a night that was, one of the best moments of my Everton career.

Stubbsy scored the first goal with a header at the back post. Later in the half they had a long throw, I tried to get up to it but only managed to flick it over Hibbo. It was no problem, though, as the ball was going to safety between the penalty box and the touchline, with no real danger. However, Yakubu took one touch and then whacked it right into the top of the net. It stunned everyone. What a goal that was.

From then on we pushed and we pushed and we pushed but we just couldn't get another goal. We were throwing everything at them. Injury time was running out when Stubbsy knocked a long ball forward. Kev Kilbane won the header, it took a ricochet off someone and it dropped towards me. I was actually facing the goal at the Park End but I swivelled and hit it on the half-volley right into the top corner. I couldn't have caught it any sweeter. I'd scored a last-minute winner at Goodison under the lights and that was the most electric feeling I've experienced for something I've ever done on a football pitch. Everyone was going mad. Davie Moyes was on the pitch, the fans were running on and we had two or three piles of players celebrating. I'm getting goose bumps just thinking about it now.

For me, that's one of the best feelings I've had in football. It was a brilliant moment, one of the top three I've had as an Everton player (Jag's penalty at Wembley in the '09 FA Cup semi-final and my debut goal against Wolves are the other two). The last-minute winner against Southampton was great but this was more intense, under the floodlights, and we'd been pushing so hard for a goal. It was off the back of two defeats, so regardless of the dramatic nature, it was a much-needed win.

We lost at home to Charlton in January. We didn't play badly but Matt Holland scored a stunner. I remember Davie Moyes told us afterwards: "It was a worldy goal, but, do you know what, that could have been a draw and the Portsmouth game could have been a draw and we'd have got two points so let's be positive about it and move on." I always remember that speech because I was impressed with it. He could have a go from time to time but he could also speak fantastically well and he put that defeat into perspective. I took that on board and I have used that strategy myself over the last 10 years, putting games together where we may have experienced different fortunes.

We had faced Plymouth in the third round of the FA Cup. It was the first time in a while Moyes had played me centre-mid. We had just signed James Beattie for a lot of money, about £6m. About 20 minutes in, Gary Naysmith whipped a ball in, I managed to stop it dead, played it to Beattie who knocked it back to me and I chipped the keeper from the edge of the box. Within four days I had scored two of my best goals. We destroyed Plymouth that night. My mate Chaddy scored our third goal. I gave him stick about him pointing to his name on his shirt when he celebrated – he used to do that a bit.

Paul Sturrock signed him for Plymouth later that month. Chaddy asked for my advice and I told him he should stay at Everton. He said: "But I want to be playing regularly."

When you're young, you don't appreciate your life and your career span. He was only 22. He had been in and around the first team for two-and-a-half years and said he needed to be playing. He thought he would score goals elsewhere and would return to the Prem. It was a long way to go and it didn't quite work as he intended. He picked up a few injuries and maybe lost a bit of form, but ended up having a decent career in the lower leagues. We're still close friends and I'm pretty sure he regrets leaving Everton when he did. If he'd had another two years and wasn't playing then, okay, but I felt he left too soon and probably shortened his career because of it.

I always felt that Chaddy suffered from the amazing break-through of Wayne Rooney. Chaddy had been the bright young thing and the new kid on the block but he didn't have long in the limelight before Wayne arrived on the first-team scene. Wayne was just on another level and nobody could blame Moyes for not wanting to play them together.

I tell the young lads now: "Don't be in such a rush to do everything. I got into the first team at virtually 23. It can still happen." Davie Weir gave me good advice: "The minute you step down, it's tough to come back up. Stay as high as you can for as long as you can." Football careers can be so short. I am hoping for another three years at least but I know my time is coming towards the end. It's amazing how quickly it's gone. I still feel like a kid but I know my receding hairline gives me away! The stuff that's still there is going grey but that process only started when I met Jenny. Before I met my beautiful wife I looked like Leo Sayer! (Google it if you don't know the name!)

Chaddy wasn't the only player to leave that January as we lost two big characters from the squad. As a fan and player, I was really sorry to see Kevin Campbell go. He had a great offer to go to West Brom and, as he wasn't getting many opportunities to play for us, it was too good to turn down, especially as he was approaching his 35th birthday. He helped keep them in the Premier League, as he'd done for us in 1999.

Kev was a fantastic player for us, both on and off the pitch. He scored some crucial goals at crucial times, including, as I write, what is still our last winner in a derby at Anfield.

Off the pitch, he was one of the biggest, if not *the* biggest, character in the squad for a number of years. Kev had a massive presence. He always had a smile on his face and always treated the staff well, frequently giving out thank-you gifts. There is a perception that the big personality footballers are ignorant and rude. He was one of many players who demonstrated that's most definitely not the case.

My family background has always instilled in me the importance of including people and being respectful. I'm talking about Kevin Campbell here but the club as a whole demands it. There are no real divas to have been through Everton because the club – the players, the staff – won't allow it. If you start to get a bit big-time, you'll probably last a season.

I don't like to be around people who are disrespectful. No matter what your role is, you treat everyone with respect. The young lads coming through the club now are another great breed. I don't know if we pick them because of attitudes, or if it's something you fall in line with once you join the club, but we've got a great set of players and pretty much always have done.

For me, Hibbo typifies an Everton player and character. He's fiery on the pitch, tough when he needs to be, but totally respectful off it…even though moaning is his main hobby! The fans know an Everton player when they see one. There are a few in the Premier League now who would fit the mould, and there are certainly some out there who wouldn't. Maybe we've signed some of them in the past and we've made them fit. It's a tough judgment for a manager to make, balancing the ability and character you want from a player.

At the same time as Kev left us, Tommy Gravesen signed for Real Madrid and I was also very sad to see him go. He was such an important player for us in the first half of that season. His contract was up at the end of 2004/05 and Real came knocking.

It was impossible to turn that down and it would have been bad for the club to make him honour those last few months, so it made sense to allow him to leave.

Madrid signed Tommy as a defensive midfielder and we used to joke that they got him mixed up with Lee Carsley. Cars had done all the work and Tommy got all the benefits. Maybe Real were confused. If you put their attributes together, you'd have an incredible player. Maybe one Real scout saw a great defensive midfield player who sniffs out all the danger, while the next guy saw a skilful player who creates and scores goals. They did look similar to be fair!

Tommy, on the ball, was certainly good enough for Real Madrid. He was incredibly skilful and a superb passer of the ball. I just wouldn't say he was a defensive midfielder.

He was a mad character and I mean 'eyeballs popping out' mad. He had this Scouse twang to his Danish accent which just made everything he said sound more funny. But he was so soft and caring too, despite the crazy exterior. He would pick out a person and give them a bear hug as he entered a room. He would squeeze you, get you on the bed and then to pretend to shag you! He was so strong that if you fought him, he would carry on doing it. We learned that the minute he picked you up, you had to go limp and play dead. If you pretended nothing was going on, he'd get bored and stop. The more you fought, the more he loved it. It was one of Tommy's many quirks. Apparently he's a multi-millionaire now, worth about £85m, living in Las Vegas with a supermodel. Where did it go wrong, Tommy?

As Tommy said goodbye, Mikel Arteta was brought in on loan from Real Sociedad. We didn't know anything about him. I don't remember Mikky's first couple of games but when we went to Aston Villa at the end of February, he certainly made an impression. He was really good that day. In fact, we all played well. It was probably our best performance of the season. Mikky was a different kind of player to Tommy, but he certainly turned out to be a great signing. He was such an intelligent player. We'd know what each other was thinking, and where we should run in relation to each other. I remember linking up with him a few times and thinking 'this is going really well'.

We scored on the counter-attack for the first goal at Villa. Killa passed it to Tim Cahill, who took it on a bit and whipped it in to the back post. I managed to head it in at the back stick and we did our American celebration – "woo-hoo" – with two arms up. We were so dominant that day and it should have been 3-0 at half-time. We came out for the second half and conceded almost immediately. It can knock the stuffing out of you but virtually straight away Tim put us back in front. For our third, Thomas Hitzlsperger stumbled over the ball, Marcus Bent gave it to Arteta, who played it inside to Tim and, as the central defenders came towards him, he popped it into my path inside the penalty box with just the keeper in front of me. I gave him the eyes and put it to my left. We were so good that afternoon and it was a day to remember.

For some reason, our best performance of the season was followed by our worst run as we lost three on the trot to Blackburn, Liverpool and West Brom in March and April. I don't know whether being on such a high suddenly affected us or maybe teams raised their games against us because we were so high in the table. Luckily, we managed to get back on track against Crystal Palace. Mikel scored his first goal for us with a free-kick, there were a couple of trademarks from Tim Cahill and a 16-year-old James Vaughan came on to turn in a Killa cross at pace, becoming the club's youngest ever goalscorer.

Vaughany was a good kid. He was fast, he was strong and he could finish. His problem was he was reckless. He was so brave and excited about getting on the pitch that he would spring and jump and throw his body all over the place. The body can't take what he was asking it to do. He was putting his body in such crazy positions because he was so into the game and so wound up.

Also, at that time, he didn't always work hard enough off the pitch to keep his body as well tuned as he could. He'd do his rehabilitation and think 'I'm fit now' and would never go in the gym again. You need to keep on top of these things by doing some leg weights, by walking up and down steps, whatever it might be. He probably needed to do double the amount of everyone else if he wanted to play as he did, or tone his style down a bit. He was quite unlucky with his injuries, though. It wasn't all about being reckless, but it was another lesson. I learned that you need to look after yourself. You've got to work in the gym, or if you don't, make sure you do something at home.

For example, wherever I am, I always go up stairs two at a time on my right side to try and keep my knee strengthened. It sounds silly but it's helped. I find the gym boring and it can be quite draining mentally. There is no ball in the gym but it's necessary and I understand that a lot more now. As I've got older, I've always done a little bit of something. Although Bellefield was brilliant, the gym wasn't the best. Finch Farm has fantastic facilities so it is easier to feel motivated in there.

In April 2005, it was tight between ourselves and Liverpool for fourth position when we played Manchester United at Goodison. That was a massive night. They had all their big guns out and were wound up, desperate to win. We kept another clean sheet and scored from a set-piece through Duncan Ferguson to get the win we deserved. The atmosphere was amazing. Dunc did what he'd done to United almost exactly ten years earlier, they had Gary Neville and Paul Scholes sent off and Goodison was like a bear-pit, at its most intimidating best, even for a team like United. I read it was Moyes' favourite memory from his time as Everton manager and I couldn't argue with that from his point of view. Beating United under the lights at home. It was crucial in securing us fourth.

We drew with Birmingham three days later and Big Dunc was again on target, scoring the equaliser at the Park End. He jumped over the hoardings and I nearly fell over trying to join him. I needed a ladder to get over it. Hibbo had a chance to win it right at the end but shot straight at the keeper. Had it gone in it would have eclipsed absolutely everything else that happened that season. A late Hibbo winner would have been the story of the decade never mind the story of the season!

I remember watching one of Hibbo's first derbies at Goodison under Walter Smith. Everton gave me two season tickets. I had two in the Upper Gwladys. Row C, seat 93 and Row D, seat 96. They were close but they couldn't manage to put them together for some reason. Anyway, as I watched, a cross came in from the left side and Hibbo ran in at the back stick. The whole stadium was up – we thought he'd scored – but it skimmed the post and went wide.

He nearly scored at Anfield in 2007. I cut it back from the left and Hibbo came running in from nowhere. He half-volleyed it so sweetly but Pepe Reina saved it. The other time was at Norwich a couple of years ago when his cross hit the bar. I watched that game on the internet at home because I was injured. I breathed deeply when it bounced back off the bar. I had told him years ago that if he ever scored, I had to be on the pitch. "Don't even bother if I'm not there because I've got to be able to celebrate with you." Honestly, as much as I am desperate for him to score, I'd have cried my eyes out if he'd done so without me being there!

It was crazy when he scored his testimonial goal in 2012. I'd told him for years: "You should take free-kicks." He can't half hit the ball. If I asked him to hit the bar with a shot he would get close every time, and probably hit it six out of 10 times. From 30 yards, that's good going. But when there's a free-kick, he always says "nah, I'll stay back". The one time he got involved, he scored against AEK Athens.

I picked up a lot of niggles in 2004/05. I'd never experienced a full season at first-team level and my body just wasn't used to the intensity. I suffered a few tweaks and strains because my body was so tired. I would finish a game and feel it afterwards. I picked up another niggle towards the end of that season and missed the games against Newcastle and Arsenal. One was dreadful to miss, the other was a Godsend!

I couldn't help it but I always regret missing the Newcastle match. It effectively clinched the top-four finish. Everyone was tense because it was our final home game. Davie Weir scored with a header just before half-time and we started to relax. Tim Cahill made it 2-0 in the second half and suddenly that was it.

That match was played on Saturday, May 7, and Jenny was due with our first child on May 8, when Liverpool were playing Arsenal and needed to win if they were to have any chance of overhauling us for fourth. Davie Moyes warned us that if Liverpool didn't win, we should expect a phone call. He had hired the Baby Blue Bar in the Albert Dock in case we ended the weekend in a guaranteed fourth spot. We did and the minute the final whistle went at Highbury, after Arsenal had won 3-1, we all got the phone call.

The gaffer was interviewed on Sky from his home after our fourth-place finish was confirmed, famously wearing a big cardigan and slippers. I can confirm the cardigan was also worn in Baby Blue but he'd had the presence of mind to pop on a pair of shoes before he left his house!

To this day I don't know why but when I got the call to head for the city centre, I decided not to tell Jenny about it. Maybe I didn't want to stress her with the baby imminent or maybe I thought she wouldn't stamp my pass and I'd miss the night out! Anyway, we were all at my mum's, so I knew Jenny wouldn't be on her own, and I asked Dad if he fancied a pint and we called a cab. Jenny was fine about us going 'for a couple' but once in the cab I asked the driver to take us to the Albert Dock and I put my dad in the picture

This was about 7pm and we came back about 11.30pm rather the worse for wear. Jenny, quite understandably, was fuming. "Why didn't you just tell me where you were going? I would have let you go but you had to lie to me. I've been sat at your mum's, waiting. You didn't even leave me the house keys. I can't believe you're doing this to me. You're supposed to be a dad this week and you're acting like this."

I knew I'd done wrong, I knew I'd get a rocket and I just had to take it. I think Dad sloped quietly off to bed while I took the full force of Jenny's anger.

She got her revenge though…she didn't give birth for another fortnight! So I could have stayed out all night with the rest of the lads instead of heading for home at half eleven just as it was really starting to get going.

Indeed, some partied too much and paid the penalty at Arsenal on the Wednesday night. We lost 7-0 and had Richard Wright not been in great form it would have been double figures. I was still injured so watched it on the television. It wasn't an enjoyable experience and David Moyes refused to speak to the press afterwards because he was so angry. But you couldn't take away what we achieved that season. We were one of the favourites for relegation at the start and we finished fourth at the end. Everyone was singing to us, "Champions League, you're having a laugh" but we did it.

It was a brilliant season. We had confounded the critics, we had stuck together and the camaraderie in the team was quite unbelievable. But even as the champagne was flowing at the Albert Dock, I began to wonder whether I was going to be at Everton Football Club for very much longer.

09

New Arrivals

As enjoyable as that 2004/05 season was from both a personal and team point of view, I couldn't help but feel an undercurrent of frustration as the club failed to offer me a reasonable contract.

I have already stated that I have never been motivated by money but I have never been afraid to speak out if I think I am being treated unfairly.

By the time I got into the first team at the start of the 2004/05 season, I was on a basic wage of £3,000 a week, with an appearance bonus of £3,000, which remained the same until 2013 when it was taken off me, plus a win bonus of an additional £3,000.

I was at least doubling my wage every time I played and if

we won, it was tripled so I was delighted. Some weeks I'd earn £9,000, some £6,000. But my basic wage was £3,000 a week. If you compare that now to someone like Raheem Sterling, two months into his first season as a Premier League player he was on £50,000 a week according to the papers (that's probably doubled following his impact last season). Everton's average wage back then was £35,000, I think. I played virtually every week on a basic of £3,000.

When I was loaned to Carlisle in late 2002 I was on £900 a week. They wanted to sign me but they probably thought my Premier League wages would be too much. They didn't realise that their top players were earning more than me.

I didn't lose sleep about being, by some distance, the lowest earner in the team, but Kev Campbell was probably on £40,000 a week and wasn't playing, while I was on £3,000 and starting most weeks.

My contract was up at the end of that season so I was going to be a free agent. I didn't want to leave, not for a moment, but I can't say I was thrilled by the new deal the club had put forward. David Moyes was offering to double my wages to £6,000 a week but I was going to lose my appearance money. So I was no better off and to me it just didn't make sense.

The first thing to understand here is that Moyes' control within the club was total. In my opinion he would get involved in issues that did not demand his intervention. I think his thoughts were, 'if I keep a player on a low wage, then I'll be able to sign someone else on a higher wage'. That's fair enough from a football business perspective but it meant he was involved in every deal and I don't think it was healthy or necessary.

I also understood that all clubs treat young home-grown

players differently to seasoned professionals and players they've paid a lot of money for. But it was still an unpleasant situation for me.

I decided not to accept Everton's offer and left it as the 2004/05 season progressed before it eventually came to a head. Portsmouth were really interested and offered me £12,000 a week, double Everton's figure. I went down to meet them in the final weeks of the season, speaking to the chief executive, Peter Storrie, and Alain Perrin, the Frenchman who had just become their manager. They spoke about their plan for the future and where I fitted in. At that time, Portsmouth were very much on the up.

I was very non-committal but it got pretty serious at one point. I wasn't asking Everton for the same wage that Portsmouth were offering, I just wanted a fair return for a young Premier League player. I felt Everton were taking advantage of me and I also didn't know why the club was prepared to let my contract run down because I could have stood firm and just moved for nothing.

If I'm being honest, I never ever wanted to go to Portsmouth, I really didn't. Going all the way down there? I suppose it was helping to get a better offer out of Everton. If I had to swap Goodison for Fratton Park it would have been with immense reluctance.

The season finished on May 15, away at Bolton, on a Sunday. My 24th birthday was on the 17th and, on the 18th, Jenny was admitted to Ormskirk Hospital because she was almost two weeks overdue with our first child. The contract situation was still far from resolved and I was facing the very real prospect of having a newborn baby and no football club to play for.

Jenny and I went in on the Wednesday morning with her due to be induced. They were so short-staffed that after starting the procedure, nobody came back to carry out the next step. When it got to 10pm they told me that I might as well go home. When I did, I looked at my phone and saw I had four voicemail messages. One of them was: "Hi, this is Davie Moyes. Will you get in touch?" I won't phone or text anyone past 9.30pm, or before 8.30am, so I didn't respond.

I was back in the hospital at 8am on the Thursday morning. The staff apologised but unbelievably the same thing happened again. I left the hospital late at night with still no baby but some more voicemails, including another one from Moyes. Again, it was too late to get back to him. I must point out here that I wasn't ignoring calls from anyone, it was just that there was no signal in the hospital and my main priority was my wife and unborn child.

On the Friday morning, I was back and the same thing happened for a third consecutive day. Although Jenny was having contractions, I was told every night: "Go home. She's not quite there yet. We'll call you if something happens." I must admit that I didn't feel as though this was right. There were alarm bells ringing and I was worrying myself sick thinking about worst-case scenarios.

I was 24, Jenny was 22, so we were still very young, it was our first child, we'd never experienced anything like it and we went along with what the doctors were telling us. Afterwards, Jenny's mum went mad because she felt I hadn't kept her informed properly and that she'd have done something about it. I hadn't deliberately kept anything from her mum, I just didn't want to worry anyone. I thought I could cope with it on my own.

I was back again on the Saturday morning to find Jenny absolutely shattered. It was FA Cup final day, Arsenal were playing Manchester United, and I was adamant that day that we were put in a room with a TV. I'd been there three days and quite frankly I was bored. I wanted to watch some footy to get some normality to the situation.

At 1pm Jenny was given an epidural, which relaxed her. They were monitoring the baby and the wait continued. We were taken into a proper delivery room but the TV was broken. I got Jenny wheeled into another room with a functioning set and I watched the match while she started to feel better as the epidural had alleviated her pain.

The match reached extra-time, still 0-0, when suddenly an alarm started beeping. The midwife ran in and looked at the monitor, scribbled something down and left.

Ten minutes later the alarm went off again, the midwife ran back and a surgeon followed. Within two minutes they had rushed Jenny out of the room.

I dashed after them, panicking like mad and asking: "What's going on?"

I was told the baby was in distress – the heartbeat had stopped – Jenny needed an emergency caesarean section and they asked for my consent. I spluttered: "Yeah, fine, whatever you need to do." They stopped me following and said: "You can't go any further, go back to the room and wait."

My head was spinning. Thirty seconds earlier we were sat relaxed, watching the match, and suddenly she was in theatre having a very serious procedure. Jenny and I had made a pact, on her insistence, that if anything was to go wrong then the baby should be the priority. "Don't worry about me, just make sure the baby is alright," she had said. I went along with it but never in my worst nightmare did I think I may actually need to do something like that.

It was the longest ten minutes of my life. The football was still on but I wasn't paying the slightest bit of attention to it. All I could think about was my wife and the situation she was in. When I heard the footsteps of the midwife approach the room, I went cold and braced myself.

She walked in, smiled and said: "Congratulations, you have a baby boy. He is fine and so is mum."

The combination of sheer relief and unbridled joy was too much for me…you can guess the rest.

Jenny had been put into a sleep and was in the recovery room. I couldn't go and see either her or the baby for a while, so I sat and watched the cup final penalty shoot-out.

I was called into the recovery room before I could watch the cup being presented but I had my own presentation ceremony to attend. I got to hold my son for the very first time. He was 20 minutes old and when Jenny came round I was sitting there feeding him a bottle.

"Is he okay?" she asked.

"He's great, he's brilliant. Look what you've done. It's the best."

Still very drowsy, Jenny fell back asleep and I went outside to phone people with the news. My mum and dad were beside themselves. Jenny's mum shouted at me again for not telling her earlier! So did her sister!

Jan and Lynsey were absolutely thrilled with the news but they were understandably concerned about Jenny and weren't happy with my lack of updates.

My dad was actually at Haydock Races with my brother so I arranged to meet them afterwards. The hospital asked me to leave at 8pm so I headed straight to the pub. All the tension and pressure came gushing out and I had a right good night that ended in the not-so-small hours in my mum's. It was great!

What wasn't so great was when I went to see Jenny the next morning. I didn't realise, because nobody thought to mention it, that the done thing was to buy your wife a gift when she gives birth. I breezed in, still tipsy from the night before, with a few magazines for her to read. "Is that it?" she asked. "Haven't you got me a present? Really?"

I honestly didn't think to buy anything and I was stuck for an excuse.

"Well you haven't got me one for me have you?" wasn't the cleverest response I've ever given! And for some inexplicable reason, Jenny wasn't cheered up by me showing her a video on my phone of me dancing and celebrating the night before…

She stills brings that up from time to time. She particularly enjoys mentioning it when we are in company.

While all this was going on I honestly hadn't given my contract much thought until I checked through a load more voicemails. Some things in life are more important than football contracts and this had been one of them. The contract was clearly still on my mind but my agents, Dave Lockwood and Peter McIntosh from the Stellar Management Group, said: "Don't worry about it. You concentrate on your baby." So I left it to them.

Jenny was in hospital for five days after the birth which made it nine days in total, with me there with her from morning until night. I hadn't been bothered about anything else, including phone calls about a contract.

It was finally sorted out through a chance meeting between the chairman of Stellar, Jonathan Barnett, and Bill Kenwright. I think they're in the same social club and they're good friends. Bill stopped him and told him: "One of your players is messing us about." Jonathan responded: "Bill, do you know what's happened?"

"Just what Davie's told me, that he's trying to strong-arm the club."

"He's been in hospital for a full week while his first child was born. There were a few complications along the way."

Bill apologised and after that conversation my contract was sorted out within three or four days. When Bill heard what I was asking for, he agreed to it straight away and I happily signed my contract. I can't help feeling, though, that the whole saga was totally unnecessary. Bill is terrific like that. He's a great chairman. He loves the lads, he gets on with all of us and yet I don't think I've ever seen him in the dressing room. He's not one of those chairmen who likes to mingle with the players on a matchday. He stays out of the way but he's always there if we need him.

There were more complications with Cole. We took our first baby home and followed the instruction manuals to the letter and did what our parents told us. (By the way, Jenny's mum and I get on fantastically well. She only lost her rag with me because of the pressure of the situation). Every time Cole had a bottle of milk, he vomited. I thought it was normal initially – acid reflux, every baby has it, according to the leaflet – but it kept on happening.

He had lost a little bit of weight after a week but the midwife also said it was normal and that we shouldn't worry.

Of a night, we'd have to sit up in bed while we fed him to help him digest. Even though we were doing that, 10 minutes later, with us having fallen asleep with him on our chests, he'd throw up all over us. The whole bottle, every single time. We started putting towels on top of the quilt when we went to bed.

After two-and-a-half weeks at home, we took him to the health visitor to be weighed and checked. He was born at 7lb, he was 6lb 13oz a week later and now he was 6lb 1oz. The midwife told us he shouldn't have lost so much weight and that we needed to take him to hospital.

We headed to Alder Hey, Jenny gave our details in at the desk and within 10 minutes we were called through. As they were going through Cole's details, they quoted his birth date as May 21, 2004 – they were very concerned at that point because they thought he was a year old and therefore exceptionally tiny. I pointed out that Jenny had given them the wrong year in her panic.

Cole was taken upstairs for a scan and it turned out he had a condition known as pyloric stenosis, which meant his stomach muscle was too big and food couldn't pass through the digestion system properly. He had to undergo an operation to relax it.

They had to put Cole to sleep, cutting him up open by his belly-button and going up towards his stomach. To have that done to your two-week-old son is very scary. Because he had been vomiting for so long, his body and blood sugar was all over the place. He was on a saline-sugar drip for four days to get him in condition to have the op. He had a dummy and by the end of the stay it dwarfed his head – he was skin and bone. Jenny slept there for five out of the six nights he was in and I stayed the other night. We were in Ronald McDonald House, where families can stay to look after their children while they are in hospital. They were brilliant in the way they looked after us. Thankfully after the op Cole showed he could take a bottle and started to put weight on again.

The whole saga was over and I went back for pre-season about three or four days later. What a summer that was – the most stressful of my entire life.

The team went to Austria and then Thailand for our pre-season in 2005, which was an incredible experience. When we go to America or Australia, we are quite anonymous. You can go for a walk, go to the cinema, go to a coffee house, and no-one will stop you. In Thailand it was superstar status. Our main sponsor, Chang Beer, is based in Bangkok and we hadn't realised that our pictures were on 100ft billboards all over the city.

Every time we trained, there were 2,000-3,000 people watching. The only real downtime was in your room and it was quite tough at times. Goodness knows how David Beckham copes! Or Tim Howard in the USA following the World Cup. Or Seamus Coleman when he goes back to Killybegs!

We'd flown out in the afternoon from Manchester and landed in the Thai morning. We hadn't really slept and by the time we landed, we were all ready for bed. Instead, to get our body clocks right, they made us train. I've never been so tired for training in my life, but with 2,000 people watching, we had to put a shift in.

We were taking part in the Premier League Asia Trophy and that tournament was crazy-intense. It was the year Joey Barton, then at Manchester City, stubbed the cigar in a team-mate's eye and had a fight with an Everton fan. But we were in a different hotel so didn't get caught up in any of that.

On the first night, at 8pm, the gaffer said: "I'm not setting a curfew but maybe get back for about midnight." I decided not to go out and just had a couple of drinks in the hotel bar with a couple of other players, while Moyes and other members of staff joined us. Jimmy Martin and Jimmy Comer had gone out and they got back pretty much bang on midnight and the gaffer offered to get them a drink. About 20 minutes later James Beattie, Tim Cahill and Marcus Bent came in and the gaffer suddenly changed and went mad at them for breaking his curfew. He told them he'd send them home. He also started having a go at the two Jimmys for setting a bad example! He really went to town on them. It was crazy and came out of nowhere. Jimmy Martin couldn't believe it and started arguing back before Jimmy Comer reined him in.

Moyes could do that sometimes. You'd see the eyes get wider and the change happening. There was a difference to Moyes on that trip compared to Houston twelve months earlier and I think the weight of expectation was now on his shoulders.

Sometimes he could be such a nice, considerate man. A very kind man. But at other times he would have a cob on and be nasty. Everyone can be like that, I suppose, especially football managers who are under constant pressure, but with Moyes, whatever his emotion was, it was more intense than everybody else. If he was happy, he was happier than anyone. If he was angry, he was angrier than anyone. He always wore his heart on his sleeve.

We played two games during a quick five-night stay in Bangkok so we were only allowed one night out, which was fair enough. We made the most of it though. We didn't set out to go mad, but for whatever reason, it was a crazy, crazy night. We got back to our private floor, the 17th, and there was a security guard with a gun protecting us. I remember walking back to my room and there was music blasting, drinks everywhere and people having races down the corridor. It was carnage.

There were no balconies on the rooms but a ledge that was maybe a yard wide. We were all congregated in a room when Faddy popped his head in the window from outside. We were shocked! He was 17 storeys up, standing on the ledge cheering and yelling. We were terrified at first because he would have been certainly killed if he had slipped. He'd edged his way from the room next door but when he climbed in through the window we all burst out laughing.

It was one of those nights when all we did was laugh…and drink! We paid for it the following morning though when we all had different social engagements. A few of the lads had a helicopter ride to Phuket with the gaffer to see an area affected by the tsunami which had hit the previous Boxing Day and some of us had to go and visit our sponsors at the Chang beer factory.

I was in a right state. That morning, Jimmy Comer had been banging on my door to wake me up but it had no effect. He had to go to reception and get a key to my room. I'm hardly ever late, maybe just three times in my whole career (including against Man City in May 2014, which you'll read about later). Luckily, I wasn't the only one and the senior staff weren't with us as they were on the helicopter trip.

The trip to the Chang headquarters included a visit to an elephant sanctuary and let me tell you, you don't want to ride an elephant hungover. I was sat on this gigantic elephant with Darren Griffiths and it wasn't pleasant! The smell, the way they sway when they walk...oh God, I regretted every beer I'd had the night before. We then went to the Chang factory and were given a tour. I managed to get my professional head on for the meet and greets and I was charm itself. Then we had a presentation film about the bond between Chang and Everton, and within a minute of the lights being flipped off, Faddy was fast asleep. He was sent back to the bus because his snoring was spoiling the video!

The Chang people were lovely, so courteous and welcoming. They even offered us a draught beer. We were trying to be respectful but there was no way on this earth any one of us could have stomached a beer, so we had to decline.

The matches over there, against Manchester City and the Thai XI, didn't go well. We lost one in normal time and lost the other on penalties. We were hopeless. Joseph Yobo is a very, very laid-back guy and used to tell everyone how good he was at everything. He swaggered forward to take a penalty in the shoot-out, missed it, and swaggered back to the halfway line giggling. Not much upset Joe!

We were also hammered 5-0 by Fenerbahce in a pre-season friendly at the Ataturk Stadium, just before playing Villarreal in the Champions League play-off. It was so intimidating. They were banging on the side of our bus, threatening us and lifting their fingers up as though it was a gun. I couldn't wait to get out of there.

Simon Davies was signed from Spurs that summer, a player in my position, right midfield. That seemed to be a recurring theme for the next three or four seasons. Wherever I'd just been playing, we strengthened. Fortunately I always managed to outdo the person who came in. Whether it helped me kick on, I don't know, but Simon's arrival had a major effect on me.

There was certainly no animosity towards Simon, who is a great lad, but we'd worked all season and I felt we all earned the right to play in the Champions League. I didn't play in the first leg of the play-off at Goodison, Simon took my spot. It was very hard to take and I was annoyed about it. Angry is a strong word but I'm still frustrated about it. I was the only regular starter from the previous season who didn't play against Villarreal. It's the one thing in my Everton career I'm still really unhappy with. I so wanted to play Champions League football at Goodison Park – I still do and I haven't given up hope, not by a long way.

I'd had a great breakthrough season, worked really hard, we'd finished fourth and we then signed a guy who played in my position which meant I didn't get to play in the home game, that we lost 2-1. In the away leg, Simon played again and I was sub. I got on for the last 30 minutes but we lost 2-1 again and were robbed that night – there was nothing wrong with Duncan's header that would have levelled the tie with five minutes to go. UEFA had brought the vastly experienced Pierluigi Collina out of retirement for the second leg and all I will say is that I don't think he had a very good game…

The only positive to take from our elimination was that we wouldn't have to wear the Champions League suits again! The club had provided us with navy blue blazers, pale blue shirts, beige slacks and a yellow tie. We were all calling 'Hi-Di-Hi' to each other at the airport. It was a dreadful outfit that I would never have dreamt about wearing in public. Later that season we had a trip away and the manager told us to report in normal clothes. However, someone (and I won't say who!) told Dave

Billows, the fitness coach, that we were all to report to Manchester Airport in the Champions League outfit. To say he stood out like a sore thumb goes nowhere near to describing how embarrassed he was.

I don't have any personal problem with Simon Davies but he didn't play for us in 2004/05 and left within 18 months. He still got to play in the Champions League against Villarreal, home and away, whereas I helped get the club into the competition in the first place but had to sit out those games. It frustrated me then and it still does now.

That was a massive disappointment. Having lost the play-off, we dropped into the UEFA Cup and were drawn against Dinamo Bucharest, this time going away for the first leg. Our lack of experience in European two-legged competitions was demonstrated that night. We went a goal down and equalised through a Joe Yobo header, although I am still adamant I tapped it in and it should have been mine.

We had the away goal, it was 1-1 at half-time and it should have been a case of 'great, no problem'. Early in the second half we conceded another goal to go 2-1 behind, which still wouldn't have been a bad result at all, in a hostile atmosphere. But we were instructed to chase another goal and in doing so we left ourselves exposed. That's fine if it's the second leg and we needed a goal, but we opened ourselves up and, instead of losing 2-1, the game got away from us and we lost 5-1. We were effectively out the competition.

That's also why we went out against Fiorentina in 2008. We kept it tight for almost 70 minutes in Florence and they scored to go 1-0 up. Almost immediately, Andy Johnson came on for Hibbo. Instead of losing 1-0, we lost 2-0. 1-0 would have been fine – 2-0 is a much more difficult scoreline to overturn. Of course, we went on to win 2-0 at Goodison but lost on penalties. I really believe that we could and should have got to the final that year.

Going back to Bucharest, that result really, really affected us. Villarreal shook us and wobbled us but we would have recovered a lot faster if it wasn't for the Bucharest game. That humiliated us. That's a strong word but it's the right one. On the plane back nobody said a word. We were shocked, stunned and embarrassed. Normally, we'd discuss it or have a sing-song, no matter what the result, to show that we were still a team. That time we didn't speak, it was virtually a silent flight back. There was such disappointment.

Things were going badly in the Premier League as well. We lost to Manchester United on the opening day, won at Bolton but then lost to Fulham and Portsmouth. At that point we always lost at Craven Cottage, so that wasn't unexpected, while Portsmouth were tough opponents.

Simon Davies came in and played all the time, while I was generally sub. When I got back in the team, our form improved. I don't think I deserved to be left out in the first place.

In our opening 12 games in all competitions, we lost 10. It was a terrible start. We had just three points towards the end of October. We'd won 1-0 in the second leg at Goodison against Bucharest and if we'd kept it to 2-1 over there, that would have been enough. Two years later, getting through against Metalist Kharkiv really kicked us on. Beating Bucharest might have had the same effect.

It was much later in the season before we started winning

games. The year before, we were set up to defend and keep it tight. When we had the ball, we were good with it but we were at our best when we were keeping it tight. The following season, teams started giving us respect. They wouldn't come on to us and we couldn't enforce our usual game. We were better when teams came at us. We stopped them and went, bang, goal. That's how we won games. In 2005/06 the opposition wouldn't open up. We would have to be more open ourselves to try to break them down and we would get sucker-punched. It took us four months to adjust.

On New Year's Eve 2005 we were down in 17th position and had lost 3-1 to Liverpool three days earlier. Confidence was low when we travelled to Sunderland, who were bottom of the table. That game was our most important of the season. It was a must-win six-pointer if ever there was one. If we'd have lost that, we would have been in serious trouble.

We had been under a lot of pressure that afternoon and hadn't looked like scoring, while they missed two sitters. We won a corner in the last minute of injury time and I was thinking, 'this is it. We're going to score here'.

Kev Kilbane was usually in the box because he was one of our big men, but he swung it in and Tim Cahill made a brilliant run, right along the six-yard line, and headed it home. It was the 94th minute and we went ballistic in front of our fans. We felt that was the turning point and it set us off on a tremendous run for the next two to three months.

We were given an away tie against Millwall in the third round of the FA Cup. It was a day when all the frustration I felt about spending so much time on the bench was finally let out.

I came on but we were 1-0 down with 10 minutes to go. Killa

put a cross in with his right foot, everyone missed it and I came in with a left-foot volley that was saved by Andy Marshall but I was able to head the rebound over him and into the net. I lost it a little, shouting "Come on! Have some of that, Moyes! Always sub I am. Come on!" Four months of emotion came out in one celebration!

I was very frustrated. It wasn't like I'd had a poor run of form, lost my place and was trying to get my confidence back. The manager had signed someone else in my position and because he signed him, he was playing him, even though results were poor. When I was in the team we finished fourth. I'm out the team and we're losing every week. There was a lot of confusion along with frustration at that point. As I look back on that spell I have to stress that I am certainly not suggesting that we weren't winning as many games because I wasn't in the team – it was the frustration of not being given a chance even when we were losing matches.

Our win against Blackburn Rovers in February was exceptionally good. Nige Martyn and Richard Wright were injured so Iain Turner played. Unfortunately, Iain was sent off for picking the ball up just outside the box from an Alan Stubbs back-pass; it was just a nervous mistake and I think it's a silly rule to have a keeper sent off in those circumstances.

John Ruddy, who was only 19, came on for his debut with 80 minutes still to play. 'Oh my God! 80 minutes with ten men and a debutant keeper!' But Beats scored at the Park End from a Mikel Arteta free-kick and we hung on. It was such a good team effort – it was just like the season before. We soaked up the pressure, defended like men, kept it tight and got our goal. We were such a good unit, spirit wise. We would cover for each other and look out for each other.

In the second half of the season our form picked up. I managed to get back in the team and we won eight out of 11 league games from December 31 to the middle of March. The Aston Villa match was the last in the run and I scored as we destroyed them, 4-1. Everything we tried came off – it was like the season before.

After such a good run, we fizzled out again before the final game of the season against West Brom, which was Duncan Ferguson's farewell. It was an emotional day, especially for him. I think he was half expecting it to be his last game but the crazy thing was that he hadn't been given official confirmation from Moyes either way. That was an incredible situation for such a massive servant of the club. If the manager didn't want to keep Dunc, he should have told him three months earlier. We were all called into Bellefield the day after the West Brom game and it was then that he was told that he wasn't being offered a new contract. Dunc was fuming that he had not been given proper notice and for a guy who served the club for so long, I think he was right.

Jamie Carragher went out with everyone understanding he was retiring, getting a wave and enjoying the last few months. Dunc didn't even know and that's what hurt him so much and why he left the country for a while – I think he needed to get away from it all. But football is such a big part of all our lives, it eventually seeped back in to him. He's back coaching with us and he's very good – he did excellent work with the kids and he's now part of the first-team set-up.

We were losing 2-0 to West Brom before Victor Anichebe came on and changed the game. In injury time we were awarded a penalty to bring it back to 2-2. The fans started screaming Dunc's name and Mikel Arteta gave him the ball. My position for penalties is always right behind the taker, on the edge of the 'D', so I can take a run-up for any rebounds. Dunc hit it down the middle, Tomasz Kuszack saved it and the ball came back towards him. I very nearly ruined what has become an iconic moment. I ran to the ball as Dunc was having another swing. I had to dodge out the way at the last minute and, thankfully, Dunc scored. He got the accolades and adulation that he deserved. That could have been the end of my Everton career if I'd ruined that.

Davie Moyes made some tremendous signings during his time as Everton manager but he had mixed results with the players recruited in the summer of 2005. The gaffer paid £5m for the Dane Per Kroldrup, which was a lot of money for a defender back then. He came in and passed it well but…

On his very first day of training, the gaffer took him to one side and started doing heading practice with him, like you would with a seven-year-old. It was a case of holding the ball, saying: "Are you ready? One, two, three – jump." Honestly, it was incredible. I don't know what happened, but he had obviously realised that heading wasn't Per's strong point. £5m for a centre-half who can't head the ball..!

You can be as talented as you like but in the Premier League you've got to be able to head it. Per came from Udinese in Serie A where the defenders were comfortable on the ball, good at positioning but not overly physical. Per didn't seem to want to head it, which was incredible for a centre-half. He went on to spend six years with Fiorentina, so he's obviously a good player but he wasn't set up for the Premier League. Per started one game, away to Villa on Boxing Day, and we lost 4-0. He was up against big John Carew, who just annihilated him.

I reckon if Per came back now he'd be a lot better. It can take people a while to adapt to the physicality of the Premier League and he simply wasn't ready. Overall the manager made some great signings, and you are always going to get a couple that don't work. He brought in Joleon Lescott and Phil Jagielka for £5m each and they both worked out incredibly well.

Andy van der Meyde's problems were very different. Gary Naysmith had been destroyed by him during a Scotland-Holland Euro 2004 play-off and told us how brilliant he was. He came with such pedigree and, occasionally, he showed it. I'm not saying he didn't always try to show it – he probably didn't if I'm honest – but sometimes he tried and it didn't work out. That's what wingers are like. Andy could really turn it on but he had so many problems off the field. It's nigh on impossible to put all that behind you and go out and play a game of football successfully, and have enthusiasm for it. I'm not going to go into his off-the-field issues – they've been well documented and I don't know his whole situation.

He had injury problems too, although I'm not sure how quickly he tried to get back because of his issues. He would hit the ball as hard as he could every time. On one occasion he literally ripped his thigh muscle off the bone at Goodison during an open training session. I can't believe he was with us for four years. He didn't play much during that time.

Overall, it was a very frustrating year, from a personal and team point of view. We lost play-offs in the Champions League and UEFA Cup and finished 11th.

It wasn't what was expected of us and another of the new arrivals in August 2005, Phil Neville clearly hadn't been used to this type of season either. Nev was a really bubbly character. He always led by example, in drills, the warm-up or during matches. He'd turn up an hour earlier than he'd need to.

I remember he came to me during the season and said: "Os, I need a chat with you." We went to one side and he asked: "Os, do you think we're going to get relegated? We're not, are we?" He was properly upset so I tried to reassure him.

"Nev, we've had a bad couple of months but we're not going to get relegated, don't worry. Behave yourself – I thought you were experienced." I guess he wasn't used to being bottom of the table at Man United.

Not counting 2003/04, when I came in for the last three games, it was the only time in my Everton career when I've not finished in the top half, so there's no getting away from the fact that it was a disappointing season.

In the summer of '06 we needed to strengthen the squad. We did just that and started the next campaign brilliantly.

10

Back In Europe

In the summer of 2006 our pre-season tour took us to Colombus and Salt Lake City. Colombus are now one of the top teams in the MLS but the facilities eight years ago weren't the best, probably no more than League Two standard in England, with all due respect.

That trip was an eye-opener into how much more low-key football is over there, compared to here. We went on a night out with some of the Dallas players after a game and they were telling us how most of them were on about $300 a week. A 'soccer' club over there might spend $5,000 wages for one player each week and $5,000 for the rest of the squad due to the salary cap. More than one of those Dallas lads told me he had a night job to make ends meet. It was crazy.

The town we stayed in was quite small and because Utah is a Mormon state, they don't really drink alcohol, but we were recommended a particular nightclub one Tuesday night and it was absolutely heaving. It took us totally by surprise. Ice Cube was performing and it was one of the best nights we ever had.

Apparently people came from all over Utah for that one night. We went back to the same nightclub two years later when we were back on tour and it was empty…on a Saturday night!

During that '06 trip, some of the club staff told me that they had a night out and were drinking bottled lager. They'd been in a nightclub for about three hours before somebody read the label on one of the bottles. The lager was alcohol-free! They'd been sitting there quaffing 0% lager for three hours without realising.

As anyone who has been to America will know, you have to take identification everywhere. A few of us went to New York a couple of years back for a social trip and one night I stayed in while the other lads went out (honestly Jenny!). Jack Rodwell must have been about 19 at the time so he borrowed my driving licence. Anyway, about two hours later I was bored so I decided to head out and meet them.

I turned up at the pub they were in and showed my passport. The security guy stared at it for ages before eventually saying "I'm sure you're already in here."

"I'm not mate, honestly. I'm on this step talking to you!"

"This ID is already in here. I remember the name."

I thought to myself 'remember the name?' Surely this huge security guy from New York wasn't at Moss Rose when I scored that goal for Carlisle United!

The big fella was as good as gold as it turned out and he let me in but he collared Jack and made sure he stayed on lemonade all night.

At the end of the previous season, Nigel Martyn had decided to hang his boots up. I was gutted to see him go because he'd been brilliant for us and he was such a popular guy in the dressing room. Moyes did brilliantly again, though, when he persuaded Tim Howard to come in on loan. I'll be honest, we wondered what we were getting but Tim very quickly showed what a fantastic keeper and person he is. Nigel's were big gloves to fill and we needed a quality goalie as well as a big, big character. 'T-How' ticks those boxes and more, and he's become a mainstay of the team as well as a great friend. And any mate of Barack Obama's is certainly a mate of mine!

The mood was really good going into 2006/07 and I'd worked hard all summer to get fit, but in the pre-season friendly at Goodison against Athletic Bilbao, I tweaked my groin which meant I wasn't fit for our opener against Watford.

I watched that match from the stands and saw our new signing, Andy Johnson, score the first goal. It was a left-foot half-volley that was going to hit the corner flag until it bounced off a Watford player and looped into the net. I thought, 'well done AJ, but that's an own goal'. It wasn't taken off him, though. I was made up for him but I couldn't believe it after the goals that had been taken off me the previous season.

We went to Blackburn in the midweek and Tim Cahill was on the bench, which was very unusual. He wasn't happy about it but came on to score a late equaliser and was shouting to the bench: "See, see, see, get in there – don't drop me."

He was like me at Millwall that time. If you accept being left out, you'll never get back in the team. I don't mind players letting their frustrations out as long as they do it in the correct manner.

On the Saturday, we went to Tottenham and won at White Hart Lane for the first time in 21 years. Players do know about stats like that, believe me. Even though you may have only played in a couple of those games, it can weigh on your mind. To break the hoodoo was absolutely massive.

We did well for the first 20 minutes and then within the space of five minutes Kev Kilbane picked up two needless bookings and was red carded. The nicest man in footy was sent off! The sad thing is, it was his last ever game for Everton because by the time he'd served his suspension, he'd left. Kev was back at Goodison before too long, playing for his new team Wigan. It was strange seeing him on the other side. I can't understate how nice a guy he is and how big a character he was in that dressing room. He's doing really well for himself now with the BBC and I often text him to hammer the gear he's wearing. Being on national television clearly hasn't stopped him rummaging through lost property boxes for his clobber.

We were really sad to see him go but, as always, you move on. Other characters come to the fore. AJ was a big character and he fitted in seamlessly, as did another new boy, Joleon Lescott.

Joleon came in for £5m and some people were worried that his knee, which caused him to miss the entire 2003/04 season, wouldn't stand up to the rigours of the Premier League.

In his first game he came on a substitute and the gaffer put him at left-back, where he'd never played before. I've told Joleon since that he was all over the place that day, but it didn't take long for him to settle down. Joleon was a really good player and so comfortable on the ball. He didn't like to knock it long – he liked to keep it short and play out from the back, which brought a new dimension to our play. He became one of the biggest characters in the dressing room.

Back to White Hart Lane and being down to 10 men, we shuffled the team around. Arteta was on the left, I was on the right, Carsley and Cahill were in the middle, and AJ was up front. It was 4-4-1 and a case of keeping them out until half-time, which we managed to do.

When the chips were down like that, Moyes was at his very best. He spoke to us all and organised us for the second half. He exuded calmness and we went out for the second half as if it was still 11 v 11. He was great at times like that, the gaffer.

We won a free-kick that Joleon tried to head but he missed and it hit Calum Davenport on the shin and went in for an own goal. We got on the ball from then on and you wouldn't have known we were a man down. For the second goal, I won the ball on the edge of our box, carried it forward and passed it to Arteta. I was exhausted, so I thought laying it off would be a good chance to get my breath back. However, Mikky must have been thinking the same thing because he passed it ahead for me to chase. Off I went for 20 yards, panting for breath, with Edgar Davids chasing me. I cut across him, turned inside and played it out to Phil Neville, who whipped in a great cross from the right and AJ got onto it to put us 2-0 up. It was unbelievable and we comfortably saw the game out. The gaffer was buzzing afterwards because it was one of our best wins.

In the News of the World player ratings the next day, I was given five out of 10 – 'needs to get involved and affect the game more'. We had just played for 60 minutes with 10 men and I'd been heavily involved but, apparently, I didn't affect the game.

I have since found out that, for some reason, the reporters who give marks out of ten file their stuff with about half an hour to go to save time. Jimmy Comer was laughing his head off. Every time I play well now he says: "Well done lad, that'll be a five at least."

If breaking the White Hart Lane hoodoo was good, beating Liverpool at Goodison was special. After winning at Spurs we had such confidence and it showed, as we enjoyed our biggest derby win since the 1960s.

For the first goal, a cross came in and Steve Finnan was about to clear it when I threw myself at him to barge him out the way and we fell over each other. I had fouled him but because he was trying to kick it away, it looked like he had fouled me. I did it deliberately because I knew Tim Cahill was running behind me. The ref waved play on and Cahill slid in to put us 1-0 up. Finnan was going berserk.

Within a few minutes, AJ did Carragher and we were 2-0 up and a great afternoon was crowned by Pepe Reina treating the ball like a hot potato from Lee Carsley's shot, which AJ followed up to make it 3-0 at the end. Absolute delirium. I remember the television camera panned to an Everton fan and Liverpool fan sat next to each other. The Evertonian was jumping up and down while the Liverpudlian sat there looking tearful. It summed up a day of which all Evertonians have very good memories.

Alan Stubbs had acquired a share in a wine bar in Formby and the official opening was that night. Needless to say it was a rather enjoyable evening!

We were still unbeaten in mid-October that season but we drew a few games we should have won, such as the home matches against Wigan and Man City, and results became inconsistent as injuries piled up.

We had a good win over West Ham at the start of December. That was a windy winter's afternoon and we were on our knees with the injuries going into that game. I played centre-mid, which was very rare at that point, and Andy van der Meyde was playing, which shows how bad it was!

The ball was swirling in the air, the conditions were really tough, but I managed to score one of my best ever goals early in the second half.

The ball was knocked down the right-hand channel and it looked like it was going out of play but James Beattie set off at full pelt and managed to hook it into the box. George McCartney headed it out, I chested it down and shaped to volley with my right foot. As it bounced, the defender came charging out at me and I realised that I didn't have time and needed to hit it with my left. I smacked it on the up, over the keeper and into the top corner. I look back at it with good feelings and a bit of pride.

Late in the game I tweaked a hamstring, which I'm also quite proud of because generally I'm not quick enough to do that! The average footballer will probably tweak his hamstring 10 times over the course of his career. I must have done it twice because of the pace at which I run.

I was injured for the game at Portsmouth the following weekend. James Beattie had organised our Christmas night out in Bournemouth after the match and so six of us, Tim Cahill, Gary Naysmith, myself and three members of staff, hired a minibus and got someone to drive us to the south coast on the Saturday morning.

The gaffer had agreed to let the lads stay down…as long as we didn't get battered at Fratton Park.

We all met at Bellefield and had a fried brekkie before we set off. We had a few drinks on the way down, listening to Radio 5 Live for score updates. Matty Taylor scored a whopping volley from 40 yards to put Portsmouth 1-0 up but we were still optimistic and it didn't spoil the mood too much. Ten minutes later it was 2-0. Trouble here. We were saying: "If this gets any worse, the Christmas do is going to be off."

I phoned Darren Griffiths and asked him: "How are we doing? What's happening?" He said: "We're not doing too well…don't drive too fast!"

There was a genuine fear that the gaffer would cancel the night out so we did tell the driver to slow down. Thankfully, the lads worked hard and played reasonably well even though we still lost 2-0 and it was game on. We had a very good night in Bournemouth. Beats could lay on a night out, that's for sure. We had VIP entry everywhere we went.

I was back the following weekend for a thrilling game against Chelsea which we were desperately unlucky to lose. Joe Yobo put us 2-1 up with a header and we were playing really well. With less than 10 minutes to go, there was a long ball which one of our central defenders headed out and Didier Drogba just banged it first time from 30 yards and it went in off the underside of the bar. Wow! What can you do about that? A great player can produce a moment like that and that's why you pay the big bucks for them. They can suddenly turn a game on its head. A few minutes later, Frank Lampard cut inside from the left and let one loose which was still picking up pace as it went in the top corner. We had played so well in that game and it took an own goal and two absolute worldies to beat us. That's football.

After that West Ham game I had stayed in the middle of the park and we went on a good little run, taking seven points out of nine in our last three matches of 2006. Then, after losing at Man City on New Year's Day, we were tonked 4-1 by Blackburn in the third round of the FA Cup.

That was a massive, massive disappointment. For about four seasons we let ourselves down in the FA Cup. When I first got in the team, we had spent the previous 10 seasons struggling to stay in the Premier League. I think there was a mentality of 'forget the cups; let's just stay in the league' and it took a couple of years to get over that.

Staying in the Premier League was hugely important, of course, but we were now at a point where we weren't fighting relegation any more. The FA Cup should have been vital at this point, but I'm not sure it was.

A lot of managers these days, and it certainly happened with us, use the FA Cup to make changes, freshen up the team and allow certain players the opportunity to get a game. But for me it's more important that you get through. It sends out the wrong signal to the team and the fans if you are making six changes for an FA Cup tie. I am a traditionalist when it comes to the FA Cup. I love it.

I understand why managers make changes – you have bigger squads these days and you want to keep everyone involved, but it's surely vital that you win the tie. Sometimes when a player comes into the team as one of these six or seven new faces, he will be concentrating on his own game, wanting to play well and try to get himself back in the team, rather than thinking 'this is a must-win cup tie and by hook or by crook we need to win it'.

I'm not just talking about Everton here, by the way. I'm talking across the board. People make far too many changes. We played Oldham at the same stage in 2008 when we were on a great run. The manager naturally thinks 'okay, we're playing Oldham, two divisions below us; I can play this player, this player and this player'. Theoretically, as a Premier League club, you should be able to do that but these players you are bringing in might not have featured for five or six weeks and they're not quite up to speed. If you win, great, these players have had a game, some regulars have had a breather and you've got through. But if you lose, you're out. We had a good team out against Oldham, one that should have won, but there were too many who hadn't played for a few weeks. Stefan Wessels was in goal; Tommy Gravesen came in having not played for ages. There were a lot of changes, too many in my opinion, and it cost us a chance of winning a trophy.

A week after suffering that knockout against Blackburn, we got to meet Rocky. Three months earlier, Robert Earl, the founder of Planet Hollywood, joined the Everton board and he invited Sylvester Stallone to Goodison when he was on a promotional tour for the Rocky Balboa movie. Big Sly only took him up on the offer and came to watch us play Reading!

It was a Premier League game and you need to concentrate fully on the game and not get sucked in to anything else that might be happening but Stallone caused a lot of excitement. He came into the dressing room before the game and was shaking hands with us all and we were like, 'Wow – that's Rocky'. We all had our picture taken with him and everyone was trying to get on the photos. That was one man having that effect on all these footballers. It was incredible.

He looked really old, I have to say. I said to Tim Howard: 'No wonder Apollo Creed took him the distance!' You could see he'd had a lot of plastic surgery done. I've seen him in films recently and he looks relatively young but that day I thought he looked really old. After we met him, he went out on to the pitch and waved to the fans. They gave him an Everton scarf and although I'm not sure he knew exactly what was going on, I would have loved to have been in the crowd shouting "Rocky! Rocky!"

Robert Earl always looks after us whenever we're in the States. I know Jags speaks to him and he's a great person to have associated with the club, a very nice guy.

The game itself was a bit of an anti-climax and Stallone was the highlight of the day. We were slow to get going and they went 1-0 up. But with true Balboa grit and determination, we came back to get something from the game through an Andy Johnson equaliser.

In early February we drew 0-0 with Liverpool at Anfield. We were set up not to lose that day and hope we could find a way to win. In a derby, that can sometimes work. Liverpool were a good side and Davie Moyes liked to be difficult to beat. As we had beaten them 3-0 at Goodison, we got four points out of six against Liverpool that season.

Rafael Benitez didn't like playing us and he resorted to shouting his mouth off a few times, calling us a "small club". I always remember the press conference where he kept saying "fact" when he was talking about Sir Alex Ferguson. He used to get really sucked in to mind games. He couldn't have been that good at it because he constantly lost his head. You're only good at mind games if you can take the emotion out of it and Benitez was far too emotional. I think he wanted to beat us 3-0 that day to even the score and he was really frustrated that they couldn't break us down. AJ had a great chance in the second half, so we could have nicked it ourselves.

Personally, I find that Benitez type of stuff really funny. It shows you've got to them. It shows that they're frustrated and wobbly. Benitez didn't win the league over here because he was competing against Sir Alex Ferguson and Jose Mourinho, who are brilliant at the mind games. Benitez wasn't. He had an excellent record in Europe because there is less emphasis on the mind games. I felt he really struggled with that side of things and it showed when he was coming out making foolish, ill-thought comments like 'small club'.

In our game at Wigan, for the only time in my career I played against David Unsworth. He was a good friend to Chaddy and I when we came through the youth team. He looked after us and was an older brother figure. To play against him was crazy. I was scared he was going to smash me, especially after he gave away the penalty for our first goal.

I'm glad to see him on the staff at Finch Farm now, working with the young lads. He's a true blue and he can teach these young lads the Everton way. I started my 'B' licence coaching badge 18 months ago and Davie Moyes suggested Scotland was a good place to do it. Faddy and I did the course together and Unsy was our teacher. He only lives up the road from me now, so I see quite a lot of him.

Unsy's got tremendous bottle. He scored something like 29 out of 30 penalties over the course of his career, including the one that kept Wigan up against Sheffield United at Bramall Lane in what was effectively a relegation play-off. I've spoken to Bainesy about that because he and Jags both played in that game, immediately before joining us. Bainesy was only 22 at the time and was on pens. Unsy came on after Ryan Taylor was injured and within five minutes there was a penalty awarded. Basically, Wigan needed it to go in to stay in the Premier League. Bainesy went to collect the ball but Unsy marched over, put his hand on Bainesy's chest and said "I've got this, son." Bainesy told me his reaction was "thank God for that!" And, of course, Unsy tucked it away.

At the end of February '07, I was sub for our game at Watford. We were 2-0 up when Moyes brought me on late in the game and I scored a great goal with my left foot. Beats laid it off for me and I whacked it on the angle. It flew in.

I had come on for Manuel Fernandes, the Portuguese mid-fielder who joined us on loan in that January. He returned for another loan spell the following season but he was definitely better the first time around. He was good on the ball, had a lot of skill and he could pick out a pass, but he just didn't suit our team. We worked as a unit and he didn't. We'd often have big holes in the unit because he wasn't there. No matter how pretty he looked, he didn't do the basic stuff.

Fernandes played in the centre of midfield. If you have someone in the 'number 10' role that does what he wants and is full of tricks, it's not a problem because you've usually got two banks of four behind him. Gerard Deulofeu didn't always do the unit stuff but he is one of those players who can bring you a touch of magic and win you a game. Because he is so high up the pitch, seven other players work as a unit to allow that. Manny Fernandes played right in the middle so if he did what he wanted, it messed the whole thing up. I thought he was a terrific technician but he didn't always want to work hard enough. On occasions he did but, for the most part, he was a hindrance rather than a help to the team.

I'm not sure he knew exactly where he needed to run, defensively. Tommy Gravesen was like that at the start. I remember watching him before I got into the first team and he would just run wherever he wanted. The crowd would clap as he sprinted all over the place but he might have been making the wrong runs in the wrong direction at the wrong time. He could leave our back four exposed when we needed to be operating as a unit. Lee Carsley was the only one who could play with Tommy because Cars didn't want to go anywhere. Manny Fernandes was a potential match-winner but he played in a position that requires a team man.

The win over Arsenal at Goodison in March was thrilling. It started sleeting heavily towards the end of the game and Andy Johnson's last-minute winner was one of those moments, like the semi-final against Man United or my Portsmouth winner a couple of years before. We had a corner, it ricocheted about, it came to AJ and he blasted it in with his left foot. We all ran over to celebrate with the crowd. Arsene Wenger wasn't happy but we were immense that day and earned that win. It was a great feeling – total elation with a tingle down the spine. You don't get that very often in football. You may be happy and cheer a goal but you know there is a lot of time left and it's not over. If you get the second, third or the fourth, each goal becomes less important and is celebrated with less intensity. That was a last-minute goal against a top side where you know there is no coming back. It was amazing.

My mate Faddy scored the goal of the season to beat Charlton in the middle of April. We were 1-0 up and comfortable until the 89th minute when Darren Bent equalised. We got extra men forward in injury time, the ball came to the edge of the box and everyone was screaming "hit it, Faddy, hit it." Instead he flicked it over the Charlton player, as calm as you like, and volleyed it into the bottom corner. Wow. What a goal. I was really close to Faddy so I was made up to see him do that. He had a tough time at Everton overall. He came in as this whizz-kid with a rat's tail hanging out the back of his head. He soon cut that off! Faddy could set the place alight at times but his career at Everton just didn't take off in the way it could have done.

Tim Howard picked up an injury and missed the Manchester United match so young Iain Turner was in goal. He really was knocking on the door and we felt like he earned that opportunity because he had been brilliant in training and reserve matches. The only issue he'd had was being sent off against Blackburn the previous season and I think that played on his mind a bit.

We were 2-0 up and cruising after a fantastic strike from Manny Fernandes when something happened that I believe unravelled Iain's Everton career. They took an inswinging corner and Iain didn't even have to jump to catch the ball because it was right in front of his face but inexplicably he dropped it. John O'Shea tapped in and it was 2-1. A few minutes later Phil Neville scored an own goal and it was 2-2. Our fans and our players felt the nerves, United sensed it and picked up momentum and we ended up losing 4-2. The manager decided it was too big a mistake and, after showing such promise, Iain never played for us again. He's played for a number of teams since, including Preston, Sheffield Wednesday and Dunfermline Athletic, and as I write, he's just joined Sheffield United. I felt sorry for him. I liked Iain, he was a good lad and he worked hard. He had John Ruddy underneath him and at that point I felt Iain was the better keeper. I hope things work out for Iain at Bramall Lane.

Before that United game, there was a minute's silence to mark the death of Alan Ball. On occasions such as that, you can feel the extra emotion in the stadium. You feel upset because you know what an icon he was for the club but you've got to keep yourself in the right place before the game, even though all that's going on.

When Brian Labone died a year earlier, that was harder for me because I knew Brian. Alan Ball was a huge figure for the club and the country but I didn't know him personally. When it came to Gary Speed, I'd played and trained with him. Both Gary and Brian were a lot more personal. I mourned those two men, their passing hit me hard.

For obvious reasons Gary's was a bigger shock. I found out about it from watching the television. It came on the news and I couldn't believe it…still can't. I had met him at an airport just the previous summer and we had a good chat. I was in the youth team when Gary was in the first team and you couldn't help but be impressed by his attitude. I used to watch him practise penalties and I had so much respect and admiration for him. His death was so difficult to comprehend.

It's tough to keep yourself in the right frame of mind when everybody, yourself included, is part of a pre-match memorial moment. You need to keep yourself in the right place. If you go into the game having just felt significant emotion, it might take you 20 minutes to properly get into it. It's very difficult when they bring families onto the pitch. Don't get me wrong, it is entirely the correct thing to do but it doesn't help you stay in the right place mentally for kicking off a game a couple of minutes later.

We rebounded from the Manchester United defeat by beating Portsmouth 3-0 in our final home game. Gary Naysmith scored a header with his last touch as an Everton player and we qualified for the UEFA Cup. It was a very joyful afternoon because we were going on a European tour again.

We finished off away at Chelsea and I put Vaughany through for our goal in a 1-1 draw. I was up front that day and John Terry was talking to me during the game, telling me: "The manager (then Jose Mourinho) likes you. I'll speak to him. Do you fancy coming to Chelsea?" It was quite funny. We had a corner at one point and I said to him: "Nah, you couldn't afford me!"

I married Jenny that summer. Although we didn't live in Ormskirk at the time, Jenny's nan did and she asked if we would have the ceremony in her local church as she is quite religious. After the service, we had a coach ride over to Thornton Manor in Wirral. The marquee was on a lake and we made our entrance on an old boat with the James Bond theme tune blasting out over a Tannoy. Everyone was expecting us to appear in a speedboat but it was more of a tugboat!

It was a fabulous day but the pre-amble didn't go to well. I'll start at the very beginning…with the actual proposal.

I put a lot of thought and effort into the process of asking

Jenny to be my wife. I planned to take her to a location that we both like (she wants it kept a secret), I had a bottle of champagne and I took an iPad on which I'd downloaded 'our' favourite song. She obviously had no idea and complained of a migraine that morning. I was gutted so I forced a few paracetamols down her throat and suggested going for a drive.

Anyway, it's all going well and I am on the brink of making the proposal when an elderly couple appeared from out of nowhere. It was a very secluded spot so goodness knows what they were doing there. I was still geared up to ask the question and didn't want to hang back, so I grabbed Jenny's hand and walked her a few yards across the grass.

I pressed play on the iPad, held Jenny close to me, looked straight into her eyes and prepared to ask her to be my wife.

She looked down, looked back up at me and said: "What are you doing? You've just dragged me through dog shit!"

Thankfully, we got there in the end and we set about making our plans for the big day. We brought in a wedding arranger and she started to put things into place. However, six weeks before the wedding we fell out with her because she wasn't doing what we wanted and we basically had to start from scratch ourselves.

It was great in the end and I still enjoy looking back at the pictures, particularly one of me, Faddy and Gaz Naysmith singing on stage. We had the Drifters do a set! Not a tribute band but the actual Drifters. I give Faddy stick about that because he had a tribute Proclaimers act at his wedding. They looked real enough and a lot of people thought it was them but it wasn't. It was two guys from Glasgow who Faddy knew!

My stag night (actually that should be nights!) was in Benidorm and Carl, my best man, dressed me as Borat in the green costume, what there was of it. Altogether, 29 of us went and it was a terrific four days.

When Carl got married, there were 34 of us on his stag weekend and when Chaddy had his I decided not to take any luggage. I challenged myself to just take my passport and the clothes I had on. I bought a toothbrush in Magaluf and kept the same gear on for four days. I wouldn't recommend it but having set myself the challenge I had to see it through.

I've never been bothered about material things. I turned up to training with a Lynx wash bag for two or three years. Everyone else would have Louis Vutton or Armani. It became such a joke that Andy Johnson and Tim Cahill stole it off me and gave me a Louis Vutton washbag about seven years ago. I still use the same one. Other players have a different bag every month.

I've had the pleasure of going to some great wedding parties over the years. James Beattie's was like a rock concert. There were different bands on this massive stage all night.

Chaddy and Hibbo got married on the same weekend. The only problem was that Chaddy's was in Nantwich and Hibbo's was in Marbella. Jenny and I went to Chaddy's and we booked into a hotel at Manchester Airport so we could fly out to Marbella the next day. We vowed to take it easy so we didn't spoil ourselves but I've known Chaddy for too long and I got carried away and we didn't get back to our hotel until 4am. We had an hour's sleep and then had to check in for the early flight.

When we checked into our hotel in Marbella Jenny realised she hadn't packed an adaptor for the plug so I offered to go and buy one. I got as far as the bar in the hotel where Hibbo's family were having a pre-wedding whisky. I joined them and got back to our room two hours later! Jenny wasn't amused.

Our pre-season trip in 2007 took us to Los Angeles where we trained hard and played hard. We always used to have a meal when new signings had to sing in front of everyone.

In 2007, one of them was Jags and he was quite nervous about it. He'd only just joined the club, he was rooming with Phil Neville and he'd printed the words to Eye Of The Tiger so he could learn them. We were making a really big thing of it and Jags was genuinely worried about it. He had a few drinks to try to calm his nerves but it didn't work, it just made him louder.

Unbeknown to him, Nev had tipped us off that he was going to sing Eye Of The Tiger and so, after the meal, Jimmy Comer called for order and began to MC the singing event. "First of all, please welcome…Ossie" and I sang Eye Of The Tiger!

Jags was absolutely horrified. He'd been practising for three days. When I finished, Jimmy shouted: 'Next up…Jags!'

We had a big plastic flower as a microphone and we all waited in anticipation of Jags making a right mess of it. He sang the Peter Andre song Mysterious Girl word-perfectly and even did some dance moves to accompany it. He was brilliant and it was the best entrance I've ever seen from an Everton player.

Later in the evening, even though he didn't need to, Jags got up again. He was fortified by a lot more alcohol and he started waving the flower in the gaffer's face urging him to "get up, come on! Your table's next, your table's next!"

It was hilarious and Chris Woods took one for his table when he agreed to get up and sing. It probably got him out of buying a round so he was pleased to do it! Phil Neville, who had initially thought the whole thing was funny, looked a bit concerned as he whispered to me: "Ossie, do you think we've signed a wrong 'un here?"

The night carried on at a nightclub that Joleon had sorted. Nev told Jags he'd be better off getting back to the hotel but Jags wasn't having it and he knew Nev had stitched him up with the song. "I'm not going anywhere with you, Nev. 59 caps? 59 caps? Shove them up yer arse. You shouldn't have fucking one, never mind 59. You stabbed me in the back. Captain? Captain? I'll never trust you again. I'm not following you anywhere, not to a hotel and not even onto a pitch."

We were wetting ourselves laughing at this 'tirade' because we knew he was winding Nev up and, to be fair, Nev took it well. He's a great lad, Jags. We all love him. He's Everton, club captain and we all follow him on the pitch. He's our leader.

We've had some decent singers over the years...and some poor ones. Kev Kilbane does a brilliant Vanilla Ice (Google it and watch him for yourself!). Alan Irvine would always sing Don't Look Back In Anger but I can tell you it sounds better with a Mancunian accent than it does with a Scottish twang.

Steven Pienaar also joined us that summer of 2007. He replaced me after about 75 minutes of our first game of the season against Wigan and he did about five tricks inside his first minute, rolling it under his feet and twisting and turning. We were well impressed. He was still quite frail back then but he's turned into a fantastic player.

There are not many left-side combinations like him and Leighton Baines, with the subconscious knowledge they have of each other's games. I think Bainesy really missed him when he went to Spurs for 12 months in January 2011.

We broke the transfer record to sign Yakubu a couple of weeks into the season. He came with a pedigree but you never know what you're getting.

Some teams have four strikers and they'll all play at different times, with each player peaking at different points. We've only ever had one playing the whole season. As good as Andy Johnson was at scoring goals, Davie Moyes likes more of a presence up front in his team. AJ was great at getting over the top but he wasn't a presence in regards to holding the ball up.

For his first 18 months with us, before he ruptured his Achilles tendon at Spurs, the Yak was incredible. Defenders would just bounce off him. He hit the ground running and finished with nearly 20 goals in his first season.

11

Bellefield Spirit

The 2007/08 season was the most enjoyable I experienced under David Moyes, from a personal and team point of view. It was the first time I established myself in the middle of midfield and we played some really good football. It was a lot more exciting than 2004/05, even though we made the top four that season. We were a lot more exciting to watch in '07/08.

We started with me playing out wide as David Moyes brought in Pienaar. We already had Mikel Arteta and the manager was trying to find a way to fit us all in the team. Thankfully, I slotted into the centre of the park. My recollection is that, for the most part, the midfield was Cars sitting, me and Tim Cahill ahead of him with Pienaar and Arteta out wide. At times it was me and Cars as a two with Tim pretty much right up front.

The season got off to the best possible start when I scored our first goal of the season in a 2-1 win over Wigan. Hibbo sent over a cross which bounced and came straight towards me, 18 yards out. What went through my head was 'that's too high to control, I'll head at goal'. I had to generate the power as it was a 90 degree change on the angle of the ball.

As it looped towards goal I thought 'that's got a chance' while Chris Kirkland back-pedalled. It went in off the underside of the bar to get us going. There is a picture of the celebration on the wall at Finch Farm featuring me, AJ and Victor Anichebe, who scored our second goal that day. The tan on me was ridiculous – I'd obviously had a good summer and I was glowing.

Steven Pienaar came on for the last 15 minutes to make his debut and my first impression was that he was skilful but a little bit weak. That's the case with many players when they come over, but it didn't take him long to adjust.

Steven's arrival provided extra competition for places in the midfield, which could have affected me. But as we had qualified for Europe, we needed to increase and strengthen because the existing squad would have struggled to maintain the standard of the previous season with the extra demands of potentially playing another 15 games.

Look at what happened in 2013/14. We thought we were covered in all positions and then Darron Gibson and Arouna Kone picked up season-ending injuries in September. James McCarthy and Gaz Barry had to play most games, and Rom Lukaku had no respite because Arouna wasn't available to give him a break. You need the competition, whether you like it or not.

You always want the team to win, no matter who is playing.

I always have done anyway. But you're also in direct competition with that person who is playing in your position. There are many positions for which I can compete. It's been a positive at times but it can also be a negative.

I could play four or five games in centre-mid, do quite well and deserve to stay in the team. But, for example, Jack Rodwell could return to fitness after an injury while Jose Baxter has been on the right wing. The gaffer would rather have a Rodwell back in and a young kid like Baxter dropped to the bench because that will strengthen the side. But Rodwell can't play on the right, so even though I've been playing well in centre-mid for a while and it's all going sweetly, he will come into the middle of the park, which means I have to go and play on the right. If I then don't play so well on the right because I've not been there for a while, I could be out while Rodwell stays in. I could be left thinking, 'what's happened there?'. That can be frustrating.

I've been at the club so long I've competed against many people. There has been Steve Watson, Simon Davies, Andy van der Meyde, Mikel Arteta, Steven Pienaar and Royston Drenthe. And that was when I was playing out wide. There were people like Jack Rodwell trying to come through and Felli in the middle. At different periods I've been competing against them all.

I always want to be in the team but I will never sulk about not being picked. If you sulk, things will only get worse and you'll never achieve. The wife tells me off if she thinks I'm sulking and says she prefers it when I get angry (I can't say the same about her!). When I was dropped against Millwall in the FA Cup in January 2006 and came on and scored, you could see that there was a lot of anger and frustration released in my celebration.

I'd like to say that I channelled my frustration correctly and it ultimately benefitted the team.

I always feel I play better when I'm relaxed but some people tell me I play better when I'm angry, or I've got someone or something to be frustrated or annoyed about. It seems to make me compete more. Maybe that's why I've managed to stay around the team for so long because any frustration I might feel at not being selected is controlled and then released on the pitch. Whether I get five minutes, 20 minutes, an hour or the full match, I will run around like a madman.

I used to laugh with Jimmy Lumsden about this. Teams are obviously always scouting for new players, which they have to – you can't stand still. Jimmy would tell me he was watching a player in my position and he'd say, "oh Ossie, he's brilliant. Quick, strong, two-footed, scores goals" but then he'd add: "Don't worry, though. I like you. I'll keep talking you up in the meetings with the gaffer."

Some players can't hack it if they've not played for a while. They will just sulk and eventually move on.

For instance, that summer we signed Leighton Baines and Phil Jagielka. They were the captains of, respectively, Wigan and Sheffield United when they left. They came to us and neither of them played for three or four months. In fact, it took Bainesy nearly 18 months to properly break into the team. When I was doing this book and looking back at past fixtures, I was shocked to see how often he was on the bench in that time. Jags was played out of position in midfield when he first arrived, then he dropped out of the team and only got in after about four months because Stubbsy was coming to the end.

I think Bainesy may have been close to leaving. If you spend

18 months on the bench, you are going to get frustrated. He may have spoken to the manager and he may have considered leaving – I don't know the ins and outs – but I do know he didn't walk around the training ground sulking. He was never defeatist and he was always very professional. Look at him now – the first name on the Everton teamsheet every week and England's World Cup left-back. You just have to keep your head down and set yourself targets.

When Simon Davies was playing, I said to myself 'I've got to get ahead of him'. Maybe I always tried to be better than him at everything we did in training. The relationship between players competing for a position at one club could be awkward but it's never been like that at Everton. People wouldn't allow it. For instance, at Chelsea in February 2014, I was substituted when it was 0-0. I was properly frustrated because I was playing well but I would always shake hands with the person coming on, in this case Ross Barkley, because it's not their fault. Kev Mirallas was taken off in the same game and he was frustrated to the point where he didn't shake the substitute or manager's hands. He had done it at Crystal Palace earlier in the season and the manager went mad at him. I think that's right. You're a team, a squad, and you need each other. I think Kev got the message and I don't think he'll do it again. And by the way, it was 0-0 when I was hooked at Stamford Bridge…the final score was 1-0 to Chelsea!

It's very much a squad game these days and if we want to win something moving forward, we've got to sign good players to strengthen and everyone has to be welcomed. Everyone wants to play but there are only 11 places. It's part of football. You have to deal with not playing, especially given the size of squads now. Look at Edin Dzeko at Manchester City – he hardly played a league game in the first half of 2013/14, yet by the end of the season he was the most important player. Over the course of a season, more often than not, you will get a chance and you have got to take it. If you're still sulking, you'll not be in the right frame of mind.

Years ago, I would say to my dad: "Wherever I play, Davey Moyes feels the need to strengthen. What is it?" Dad would say: "Well, you're the versatile player and if you go there, it shows where he's probably weak. If he fills that, you can play some-where else. And anyway, whenever it has happened, you've got yourself back in the team. Don't worry about it – just keep going."

My first real bit of competition was Matt McKay in the youth team. I was the first-choice central midfielder and we signed a kid from Chester who was three months older than me and we'd paid money for him. I decided 'I've got to beat him' but he ended up becoming one of my best friends. It happens in football. That's one of the great things about our club. We are a people club, not just the people's club.

Our second game of the season was at White Hart Lane. It was a night game and it poured down with rain. Joleon had developed a habit of scoring and gave us the lead but Anthony Gardner, who ended up joining us that January, equalised be-fore I made it two goals from two games by putting us back in front.

Mikel crossed it to the back stick and you could see Victor's eyes light up. As he was poised to head it in, their right-back got to it but the ball fell for me and I managed to chest and volley it into the top corner. I ran to the corner flag and did a Klinsmann dive – maybe there was something subconscious about that because it was White Hart Lane. Stubbsy scored a free-kick just before half-time to make it 3-1 and we held out comfortably.

We celebrated goals differently then. We go to Spurs or Man United now and expect to score goals and hopefully win. When we score it's a case of 'get in, there it is, let's keep going'. Back then every goal was a bit more unexpected and a cause for a major celebration. We went to Spurs hoping we could win. Now I think we expect to win. That shows how far the club has come. Seamus Coleman tells me I don't celebrate as much because I've scored loads of goals. He says: "When you celebrate, you're so calm. When I celebrate goals, I feel like my heart and lungs are going to burst out of my chest. I feel like I'm going to explode. It's probably just because you've been doing it so long." We had a laugh about that because I was like him when I was younger but I never went as far as booting the advertising boards which is what Seamus did at Swansea in December 2013!

We were into the Lucozade money during '07/08 – we were paid every time we were seen on camera holding a Lucozade bottle or drinking from it. I think each time it happened they put £300 into a fund which you could spend as you wished at the end of the season. One year we gave it to the youth team to buy a new bus.

At the end of the Spurs game, Stubbsy and I were interviewed by Sky and we were making a big effort to get the bottles in shot. Each time the interviewer turned to either one of us we'd suddenly develop a raging thirst and have to guzzle Lucozade.

Sky zoomed in for close ups of our faces as they knew what we were up to but we still managed to get the corner of the bottle in shot. The pair of us were laughing our heads off while the Sky fellas were going mad. The Bolton Wanderers lads were brilliant at it – I think they earned the most money every year. I used to laugh every time I watched the post-match interviews on Sky. One trick was to wipe the sweat from your face as the interviewer was asking his question – using the hand that was holding the bottle.

Cars, Kevin Kilbane and David Weir would also do it. "Quick, get the Lucozade" someone would shout as we spotted the cameras waiting for a post-match interview. It wasn't about the money – it was just a laugh. I was still doing it last year, even though the payments had stopped four years previously.

We started that season in such a positive manner and every time we had a good start to a season under Moyes we pretty much always achieved something.

What probably helped, believe it or not, was the defeat at Reading which followed because it stopped everyone getting carried away. Stephen Hunt snuck in between me and Hibbo and scored the only goal. We were blaming each other and someone else was blaming someone else. It was a frustrating, horrible game, made worse by the fact that it was the only time in my career that the heel support fell off my boot. Had I been a kid again playing with my mates in Skem I'd have been fine because I'd have ran with one leg on the kerb…but this was the Premier League. I carried on as though I had one boot and one flip-flop until Jimmy Martin ran back to the dressing room for a spare.

At the start of that season, we had Cars and Phil Neville

playing centre midfield and after the Reading game, Davie Moyes told them: "You two are the worst centre-midfield pairing I've ever seen in my life." He was really angry. They were both mature and experienced but it was very rare for them to play together in the middle because they weren't ball-playing midfielders. Jags even played in the middle of midfield to begin with and when we played two defensive centre midfielders, we had no real flow. Moyes changed it and, later on, we ended up with myself, Pienaar, Arteta and Tim Cahill in the team. It was a lot more free-flowing with people wanting to get on the ball. That worked out really well.

Our next match was at home to Blackburn Rovers, but in the week leading up to the game the focus of the entire country was on the killing of 11-year-old Evertonian Rhys Jones, who was shot in the Croxteth area of Liverpool on the way back from football practice.

When you see things like that on the news and in the newspapers, you are saddened and appalled, but it's only human to feel slightly removed from it. Even though you know the details, and it's in Liverpool, it is still at arm's length – there is still a distance between you, your family and the awful reality of the situation.

But when all the players went to the scene to lay flowers and pay tribute, it really brought it home. We went on the team bus and walked along the path by the pub car park where it happened. There were a lot of people around but it was eerily quiet. You could only hear footsteps, the odd murmur and the breeze.

There was police tape around the scene and that somehow made it all so real. That was the moment it sunk in with me – 'oh my God, this has happened to a family and a young lad'.

I started to associate it with, and compare it to, my own family. How would I feel? How would I even begin to get over it? It was a very solemn journey back to Bellefield.

We saw Melanie and Steve, Rhys' mum and dad and his brother Owen when they were guests of the club at the Blackburn game. We had recently lost Alan Ball and Brian Labone but, although they were taken sooner than we expected, they had lived a life and achieved something. But this was a young kid of 11 who was in the wrong place at the wrong time and had his life ahead of him. It makes you realise that anything can happen at any point. You come home and hug your kids more. Goodison paid tribute before the game as did Blackburn Rovers – Brad Friedel was great with the Jones family before the kick-off. Things like that will always affect you on a matchday but it was entirely right to honour a boy like that. It united the city, as Everton and Liverpool paid tribute to Rhys. Although we have a big divide when it comes to football support, the city and surrounding areas stick together when it really matters. And at that time it mattered a great deal.

Back to the football and there was great excitement amongst our fans when Yakubu joined us towards the end of August. You are never quite sure when you're signing a striker because they can be hit and miss. You can bring in a striker with a great pedigree but he may not get going. Yak got going within 10 minutes, scoring on his debut at Bolton when he turned in a cross from AJ.

The Yak was such a loveable character with his big wide smile and the way he chuckled. He was a bit like Muttley from Wacky Races. He used to call Joe Yobo 'Chief' because Joe was the big-hitter in the Nigeria squad. Yak called me and Pienaar

'Smalley'. I loved Yak's 'hands' celebration when he scored. It was great that he scored on his debut and, after a Nicolas Anelka equaliser, Joleon got the winner in the last minute. We were all dancing in the dressing room afterwards. I remember Moyes saying: "You know this feeling? You've bloody earned it. Well done. Let's keep going."

That September we had a UEFA Cup qualifying play-off against Metalist Kharkiv from Ukraine. These two games were incredible. In the first leg at Goodison we led 1-0 when we were awarded a penalty. AJ scored but it had to be retaken because Victor had encroached into the box. AJ missed the re-take, Kharkiv equalised and then we were awarded another pen, which AJ again missed. Unbelievable! Oh, and Kharkiv finished the game with nine men. We dominated the match and could easily have won 3-0 but came out at 1-1. AJ was inconsolable after the game but we rallied round him and told him he'd put it right for us. I pulled him to one side in the dressing room and told him not to worry…the balls from his penalties would soon be found and returned to the club! He tried to force a smile but it was probably too early.

We were still confident for the second leg but didn't realise at that stage how different European aways can be. We trained at their stadium the night before and it was like playing at Skelmersdale United, with all due respect to my local team. In fact, having been to Skem United, I'd say it was worse. The lights didn't quite cover the whole pitch and it was dim. The pitch was like something my dad would have played on during his Sunday League days, undulating and uneven with patches of sand. There was a stand missing and you could see a school and a car park over the wall.

We were quite attacking in our approach, which is something Moyes would sometimes get wrong in Europe. We needed to score but we should have kept it tight. In the first 20 minutes we got absolutely battered and were arguing amongst ourselves. We were all over the place and it was no surprise when they scored.

Eventually, I dropped deep, we tightened up and kept it to 1-0 at half-time. Moyes gave quite an emotional speech during the break, basically telling us we had 45 minutes to sort ourselves out if we wanted to stay in Europe.

If things were going okay at half-time, he'd tend to shout at us. In one game we were 2-0 or 3-0 up and he went mad. Instead of going back out happy and a bit lethargic, it would help keep us on our toes. If we were losing, or if things weren't going well, he'd tell us what we should and shouldn't be doing. He would send us out with information, rather than having a rant for the sake of it. There were occasions where it had gone so badly that there would be a kick up the backside and he'd have a right go, but I'd say 85% of the time it would be a calm chat if we were getting beat.

In Kharkiv, Joleon equalised early in the second half. Suddenly we were back in the game and full of confidence, but within just four minutes they were back in front, knocking the stuffing out of us. The crowd was hostile, the pitch was crap and the lights were dull. It could easily have got away from us but we kept believing. With less than 20 minutes left, Faddy picked up the ball just outside the area and I screamed for it because he could have put me in. As he turned his marker, I was yelling: "Faddy give it, Faddy give it, Faddy for fu…yeeeessssssss!"

His goal meant we were ahead on away goals but it got tense

and frantic as they threw people forward. Late in the game we cleared it and Victor took his time on the bobbly pitch, keeping his composure, to make it 3-2.

In Europe, teams did not know how to deal with Victor. We could leave him up front on his own and if the ball was cleared up to him, he could wait for it and knock the defender out the way with his sheer strength. He was great in Europe and I think it was because he knew he could bully the defenders knowing full well that he'd never meet them again. He had all the tools to be a great centre-forward…except aggression. If he had James Vaughan's temperament then Victor would be priceless.

He used to get very nervous, Victor. He would never confess to being nervous, but I could tell by his body language.

Kharkiv was an incredible night. We went up to our fans after the game and they were so noisy. That was one of the top nights I've experienced – it was like a cup final. The support inspires you and you want to do well for them, because the away European trips can be hard for them. If things don't go right, like against Fiorentina where they were effectively penned in a cage on a night of non-stop pouring rain, it is horrible. Ashamed is too strong a word, but you are gutted for the fans. You feel like you've let them down. We had lost two play-offs in Europe two years previously, so it was so vital that we got through to the group stage this time. There was such relief and joy afterwards.

In the international break before the Merseyside derby that October, we moved to our new training complex at Finch Farm. There was excitement, obviously, but there was also massive sadness about saying goodbye to Bellefield.

The history that place had was something else. The entrance was virtually an alleyway between two houses, with just two proper pitches and patches of grass. The facilities were basic to say the least and it was very dated. We needed Finch Farm but Bellefield was brilliant and nobody wanted to leave.

The gym was roughly 15 yards by nine yards. On the side of that was effectively a closet, which served as the medical room. You could get two beds in there and one machine, so only three people could be treated at one time. Anyone else had to stand and wait. When I first started in 1997/98, we had about 15 injuries at one point so there would be a long wait to be treated. Injured players would bring in magazines and books because they knew they'd be spending time in the 'waiting room'. A Portakabin had to be brought in to give us somewhere bigger, and we couldn't all fit in the canteen at the same time when it was time to eat.

There were a lot of limitations but there was a feeling of togetherness from Bellefield. Everyone loved the place. If you wanted to find someone, it didn't take long. There was the canteen, gym, treatment room and dressing room. You could walk along the corridor and put your head in all four of those rooms within 20 seconds.

When we moved to Finch Farm, the biggest change was that you couldn't find anyone. It seemed too big for us, but we soon settled because we took the Bellefield spirit with us. I recall Alan Irvine in particular regularly saying that we needed to do that. Finch Farm is fantastic. There is a pool for rehab and cooling down, a treatment room with six beds, a massage room with two beds, dressing rooms, a big gym, a laundry, loads of offices upstairs for the staff and analysts – and that's not even including the Academy side of the building. We've even got a table tennis table and a pool table in the canteen, which is perfect for the kitmen to help fill their time (before Jimmy, Tony and Shaun start phoning lawyers, I'm only joking!). It's a first-class complex and in fact, as we've progressed as a club in the years since, we could actually do with it being bigger now.

There would be all kinds of fun and games at Bellefield. I recall a head tennis tournament in which Jamie Milligan and Phil Jevons were drawn to play Dave Watson and Walter Smith. The youngsters went two sets up and it was first to three. A crowd gathered while Walter and Waggy were telling Millie and Jevo: "If you want to stay at this club, you won't be beating us." The lads at the side were shouting at them to take no notice and to not be intimidated…even though we'd have all been terrified if it was us. Needless to say, the younger team crumbled and Walter and Waggy won again.

One year we got a table tennis table in the big gym. Duncan Ferguson, who was injured at the time, sent the groundsman to pick up six buckets of KFC so instead of playing for money we were playing for chicken wings and Zinger burgers.

Paul Gascoigne was a great guy, with such a warm heart, but he couldn't keep still. There was a competition one day between himself and Dunc to see who could do the most press-ups. Then he upped the ante and challenged Dunc: "Let's see who can lift this metal skip above their head the most times." There was £50 riding on it.

Gazza gave it absolutely everything he had and was dying on his feet when he reached 50. The sweat was pouring from him and he was physically exhausted when he gasped: "Beat that Dunc."

Duncan didn't flinch, carried on reading his newspaper and replied: "Nah, I can't be bothered. Here's the £50."

Gazza was devastated even though he'd won the bet!

The Bellefield site is a housing estate now and I actually considered buying a property for old time's sake. I've spent a lot of time at Finch Farm now and I'm comfortable there but you do miss the history. I used to drive through the gates of Bellefield and I would honestly think of players that had done the same thing – Alan Ball, Joe Royle and Bob Latchford, amongst many others. You could go on and on. We lost that when we moved to Finch Farm but hopefully, in time, we'll get it back. We have pictures and slogans on the wall to let everyone know what our club is and what it means to us. Our lockers have our names on, and there is a plaque underneath telling you who has previously used each locker. It might not seem much right now but if we're still using Finch Farm in 30 or 40 years time, a young kid will be able to look and see that 'Tim Cahill changed here' or 'I've got Arteta's space'. Or maybe he will think 'Oh no, I've got Ossie's locker'.

12

Nuremberg
And Beyond

Towards the end of October 2007, we faced Liverpool at Goodison in the first derby of the season. It became known as the 'Clattenburg derby' after a series of controversial decisions made by the referee, Mark Clattenburg. It's a match that is still talked about bitterly after all these years.

Sami Hyypia scored an own goal to put us 1-0 up but we deserved to be leading 2-0, maybe even more. We pinned them back at the start of the second half but they broke from a corner, and the course of the game changed.

Hibbo chased Steven Gerrard all the way and Gerrard was clever, doing what a lot of players do now, in getting himself in front of Hibbo and waiting for contact in the penalty area, so a penalty was awarded when they went down. Clattenburg did well in keeping up with play but as he had his hand on the yellow card, Steven saw it and muttered in Clattenburg's ear. I don't know exactly what was said but the ref took his hand off the yellow card and gave Hibbo a red.

Dirk Kuyt put the penalty away to equalise, and we reorganised to keep it tight, which we did until the last minute when Lucas Leiva had a shot which Phil Neville saved on the line. Another penalty, a more straight forward red card and Kuyt scored again. We were losing 2-1 and down to nine men.

However, we went straight down the other end from the kick-off, sent in a long throw and Jamie Carragher dragged Lescott to the ground. I have never seen a more blatant penalty in my life. At the time we all knew it was a pen and so did Carragher. That was the main frustration for me. I went mad at Clattenburg and we all swarmed around him but within 20 seconds he blew the full-time whistle. You aren't supposed to act like that but when a referee makes such a poor decision, it's difficult not to get frustrated.

What made it all the more frustrating was that when it was still 1-1, Dirk Kuyt had made a flying, waist-high, two-footed challenge on Phil Neville which should have been a blatant red card. I don't know what Kuyt was thinking and I'm sure he was expecting to be sent off, so for him to go on and score the second penalty was a total injustice.

We were seething after the game. I just felt that something wasn't right about it. I have absolutely no idea how Clattenburg's performance was perceived by the football authorities but he didn't referee us for over four years after that, and didn't come back to Goodison until December 2013.

I actually like Mark Clattenburg as a referee, I think he's very good. When I was in the ressies, he was in charge for quite a few of our games. We sort of came through the ranks together and when he refereed our game at Palace at the start of the 2004/05 season, we spoke on the pitch, greeting each other like old friends. That derby game must have just been a bad day at the office for him.

At least he talks to you during matches, which I prefer. I hate referees who are really dismissive and tell you to go away. It's their job to calm you down, not make you angrier. Whether they've got it right or wrong, I don't mind if a guy explains and tells you the reasons behind their decisions. Howard Webb is very good at it, as is Clattenburg. I like Phil Dowd and Peter Walton was good. Those referees allow you to have a conversation.

The ones who say "go away" as though you're a naughty schoolboy, frustrate the life out of me. Your Martin Atkinsons, your Mike Deans, Andy D'Urso a few years ago. To be honest, Martin Atkinson talks to me a lot more now, but he used to wind me up by telling me to go away.

Referees won't always have a good game. It's impossible. Players won't, so why should referees? They have one chance to see things on the pitch. Although they should talk to the players during matches, I don't think they should have to talk to the media and explain why they made certain decisions, as that would get ridiculous. But if they speak to players to explain a decision, it deflates the bubble and the anger subsides.

I had a big argument with Howard Webb's linesman at Goodison once. I think it was against Chelsea and it was over an offside decision. I went mad at him and the linesman told

Howard that I called him a cheat. I'd never do that. I might get over-excited but I'd never accuse them of cheating or swear at them. I nearly lost it with that linesman. That's probably the angriest I've ever been at an official. I've never hit anyone in my life but I wanted to then. I still mutter under my breath whenever I see him.

Five days after that controversial derby, we had our first UEFA Cup group game against AE Larissa of Greece. It was a good job that match followed on so quickly because it gave us something else on which to concentrate.

Maybe the manner of the Liverpool result galvanised us because we then went on an incredible run. Davie Moyes had told us: "We're not getting any help from the officials. No one is going to help us; we're going to have to do this ourselves." From that point until the Anfield derby in late March, we only had a handful of bad results.

Against Larissa, Tim Cahill played his first game of the season, which was a big boost for us as he returned from a broken metatarsal. Tim wasn't the typical number 10 who peeled off into space and threaded a pass, like a Gianfranco Zola or a Dennis Bergkamp. He was all action, physical and could do all the jobs – striker, in the middle of midfield, or on the left or right. It was good to have him back and it was good to play alongside him for years because he helped everyone out and scored some very important goals.

In true Tim style, he returned with a goal to put us 1-0 up before I scored what turned out to be our goal of the season. It was a brilliant team move. It went to Leighton Baines, who ran up the left touchline and exchanged passes with Tim; Baines played it inside to Steven Pienaar and he back-heeled it into my path, about 25 yards out. I don't usually hit shots from that far away, I would usually take it on, but for some reason I thought, 'he's set this, I'll hit it'.

I did a hop, skip and a jump to make sure my stride pattern got me to the ball at the right time. I knew I was in line with the post, so I couldn't screw it. I hit across it and the action on the ball was brilliant, it seemed to go round the defender and keeper as it swerved into the net.

Tim Cahill nearly threw me into the stands as we celebrated. I tried to grab the corner flag to stop myself going over the top and he pushed me that hard that I plucked the flag out of the ground. Larissa got one back but Victor settled the nerves with his customary European goal and, with a 3-1 win, we could begin to enjoy the European campaign more.

Our next UEFA Cup tie was in Nuremberg, a trip now legendary amongst Evertonians. My mum and dad went and had the time of their lives. The squad stayed in a hotel close to the centre of the city and on the afternoon of the game, we tried to have a nap in our rooms. It was impossible. The fans were stood outside drinking in the square and then moved towards the hotel as word spread that we were staying there.

My room was on the corner of the hotel, closest to the town, and all I could hear was Evertonians singing and dancing. I was looking out the window, thinking 'shush, I'm trying to sleep here'. Then I started thinking, 'actually, I wouldn't mind being down there, that looks so much fun. I want to get involved in that'. For one mad moment I got caught up in it all and I was considering nipping down to find my mum and dad and buying them a drink, but I soon came to my senses and went back to bed.

When we travelled to the game, there were people shaking the bus, screaming "Ev-er-ton". It was as if we'd won the European Cup, with people on top of bus stops and surrounding the vehicle. It was all good natured and the atmosphere was incredible.

After all that it was a match that we dared not lose. We just couldn't disappoint the thousands of Evertonians who had virtually made it a home game. As well as the big section behind one of the goals, our fans were scattered everywhere. Every side of the ground seemed to be singing for us. There was only going to be one winner that night and we won it with two late goals, through Mikel and yet another one from Victor. When people talk about our European run, Nuremberg is the first thing to be brought up. My mum and dad certainly enjoyed themselves!

It was back down to earth the following Sunday when we played Chelsea at Stamford Bridge and Michael Essien nearly broke my leg with a studs-up straight-leg tackle, right down my shin pad. It was nasty. Not many players have done that to me. John Terry was sent off for a tackle on me at Goodison in December 2008. It hurt me and I struggled on for half an hour before I was subbed but I knew Terry had gone for the ball. I felt that Essien didn't. If anything had happened to me, I don't know whether I'd have forgiven him. I don't like that in football.

I know Kevin Nolan and I like him, but in my opinion his challenge on Victor Anichebe in February 2009, at Newcastle was also nasty. There is no place for that in football. That could have ended Victor's career and he was out for nine months. Kevin Nolan missed three games. If you are responsible for a nasty tackle that puts a player out for nine months, then maybe you shouldn't be able to play for the same length of time. There needs to be a stronger deterrent.

At Chelsea, Tim Cahill scored an incredible overhead kick to get us a point and in our next match at the end of November, we hammered Sunderland 7-1. It's the only time I've ever won by that scoreline. Roy Keane was their manager and he became progressively grumpier as the goals went in. He was livid with his players but afterwards he told the press that his team had been well beaten by a 'proper football club' which I thought was a touch of class. Mum and dad bought the DVD of the game and I think she still gets it out when they have visitors!

Shortly after that, Yakubu scored one of the best hat-tricks I've ever seen. He was unplayable that day against Fulham. The Yak was probably the most natural finisher I've ever played with. Only rarely would he whack anything. He would give you the eyes and roll the ball into the corner. Sometimes the ball would barely reach the net. He would always put just enough power on his shots. It was as if he was playing a game where he was trying to score without the ball touching the net.

That period, culminating in two matches at West Ham, was just great for me, but I broke my toe and missed eight games after that. Although I eventually came back and thankfully stayed in the middle of the park, I lost a little bit of momentum and, I think, so did the team.

Because we were playing twice at Upton Park in four days,we decided to stay down in London. In the first match in the Carling Cup we went behind to a Carlton Cole goal. Shortly afterwards I broke the big toe on my left foot, stubbing it on the floor as I went for a full swing. The tip of my boot didn't stop me; it was all contact with my toe. I was limping but told myself it was just a little sore and I'd get over it. A couple of minutes later we had a nice interchange between Cars and Pienaar and I stroked in the equaliser. The Yak scored the winner in the 88th minute and we were suddenly through to the semi-final of the Carling Cup.

I'd taken two paracetamol at half-time to get through the second half. The next day we had a warm down on exercise bikes in our London hotel and my toe was killing. I put ice on it and took anti-inflammatory pills. I was offered an X-ray but dismissed it, saying I'd be alright. However, on the Friday I couldn't train, and hobbled around the pitch with our physio, Baz Rathbone. He asked if I thought it was broken but again I said no. I asked for a pain-killing jab so Dr Irving gave me an injection at 11am on the day of the Upton Park league match. Five minutes later I jogged along the hotel corridor and there was no pain, although I couldn't feel the toe because it was completely numb.

I put my boots on and it seemed fine but when I returned to my room, I started to feel it again. They had told me it would be numb for two hours, but the pain relief lasted for just 20 minutes. I had more jabs at the ground before the warm up but after that was finished, I could still feel it. More jabs followed but, 20 minutes into the game, I was struggling badly. I had four more jabs at half-time and, I think, 12 overall.

During the match I had a chance which, for all the world, I should have scored but I missed. Moyesy shouted: "Are you blaming that on your foot? Can't feel a bleeding thing, eh?" He was being sarcastic. Somehow I got through the game, which we won 2-0, but I felt sick because I was in so much pain. I could only put my flip-flops on afterwards. We flew back and when we got to the airport, to be fair to him, Moyes said to me: "Well done, you've played really well in the last two games. If you're in pain, let's try and get as much treatment on it as possible so you can make it for the Man United game."

I was taken for an X-ray and it showed I had two fractures right the way down my toe. I ended up missing five weeks, which I was really sad about because I was in the position I wanted to be in and the team was playing attractive football and getting results. I was desperate to be available for the first leg of the Carling Cup semi-final against Chelsea early in January

You do everything through the ball of your foot and your big toe so I had to wait until the pain subsided. It wasn't 100 per cent healed when I resumed playing but it was set and someone would have had to stamp on it for it to go again. I'm terrible when I'm injured, as the physios will confirm. I'm impatient to get back. If I've got a thigh injury, I'll be poking it every 10 minutes to see if it has miraculously healed.

If I'm at the training ground when I'm injured, I have to keep busy by playing practical jokes or generally messing around. If me and Hibbo are injured at the same time, it's absolute mayhem at the club. It's the worst-case scenario for the medical team, the media guys, the kitmen and the caretakers. All sorts can happen. We know we're being nuisances but we can't help ourselves.

One of our favourites is to find someone's mobile phone and send random text messages. We once got Jimmy Martin's phone because we knew he never locked it and we sent Walter Smith a message saying 'I miss you Walter and I think I'm in love with you x'. I can't print what Walter texted back! Another time we got hold of an evertontv cameraman's phone and sent texts to random males on his contacts list saying that 'I'm sorry but I am madly in love with your wife'. We got some very funny replies then too!

When in I'm in work, I can't keep still. When I'm at home, I can't keep still enough. Jenny calls me 'precious'. "Love, can you get this for me? I can't do anything because of my thigh," I'll say. She goes mad at me. "I'll bet you're not like this at work." She also thinks I'm boring at home. We have three kids and the boys have football most nights, one plays Saturday and they both play on a Sunday. There is a lot of running around and it'll be worse when my daughter is old enough to do stuff! When I'm at home, I like to take my shoes off, get my comfy pants on, have a cup of tea and watch TV or read. If I'm not precious, I'm boring. She calls me a boring old man!

If having three children wasn't enough, we've also had a number of pets taking over our household at times. Jenny would tell me that having them in the house is good for the children but I always felt we wouldn't have enough time.

We started off with some fish when Cole, our eldest, was still a baby. We bought eight tropical fish with a tank, rocks, all the accessories – the works. It looked pretty good. They lasted about two or three months before, one by one, they started to die off until we were left with two. I said: "Look, love, see: They're dying and you want to get a proper pet. We can't even keep fish."

Anyway, the two surviving fish clearly enjoyed each other's company and when we woke up one morning we had 58 fish in this little tank! Things went quite well until a nephew of ours dropped a Fairy washing tablet into the tank. In no time it looked like a Jacuzzi and 57 of the 58 fish perished.

One day we passed a pet shop and, before I knew it, we had a rabbit called Daisy. Jenny had convinced me again. Within two weeks, I was doing all the jobs for this rabbit that she wanted.

It was always running under the decking in the garden and I'd have to chase after it, trying to scoop it out. It was a nightmare. In the end, before I strangled the thing, my mother-in-law kindly offered to take it to her house.

We then went another peaceful year or so without a pet until Muggins here gave in to the request for a cat. The kids called it Buzz Lightyear. It was a nice cat, very playful, and the kids loved it. We had Buzz for four years until it got knocked over and killed. I was away on pre-season in Austria when Buzz met his end. I was beginning to doze off at 11.30pm when my phone rang. It was the wife and she was screaming, crying; the works. My heart was racing. "Oh my God, Jen. Stop sobbing. What is it? What is it? Just tell me." I almost had a heart attack because she couldn't get her words out. I thought something had happened to one of the kids and I was relieved when it was poor Buzz.

Of course it was my job to tell the kids when I got back home.

Another 18 months passed before Jenny decided that we needed another pet because it was 'good for the kids'. I was very reluctant because it's always me who ends up doing the donkey work. This time I dug my heels in and the fact that we now have a dog in the house is all Andy Murray's fault!

We were watching Murray's quarter-final against Fernando Verdasco in Wimbledon 2013 and when he went two sets down one of the boys said: "Dad, if Andy Murray wins this match, can we get a dog?" I was thinking to myself, 'he's two sets to love down; I can make myself to be a good guy here.'

I thought I was onto a winner and agreed to the bet. The

smug smile was wiped right off my face as Murray stormed back into it. He won 3-2 and I must have been the only Brit in the country with my head in my hands. I managed to convince the kids that the bet rested on Murray actually winning the tournament. Again, I thought I'd be safe. He still had Djokovic to play and no Brit ever wins Wimbledon! We all know what happened…and that's why I never bet on sporting events, especially with my kids.

We called our new arrival 'Andy Murray' as a tribute and, as ever, it's my job to take him for walks or to the vet. We get some funny looks off people when we're trying to bring him to heel. You don't often hear people calling 'Andy Murray!' in an Ormskirk public park.

By the time the first leg of the 2008 Carling Cup semi-final came around, I'd had three weeks to come to terms with being injured and I was a week away from coming back. It's more difficult when you are injured the week of a big match.

While I was injured, I watched our FA Cup third-round tie against Oldham from the Upper Gwladys. I went with my brother, put my hood up and made myself inconspicuous. Hibbo tried the same thing a few years later when he went, ironically, to a cup tie away to Oldham. He was spotted straight away and the match was a nightmare for him! At Goodison I was right behind Gary McDonald's shot that won the game for Oldham but Stefan Wessels should have saved it. That's one of the pitfalls of the FA Cup though. Results like that happen. I was very disappointed because we had shown what we could do by reaching the semi-final of the Carling Cup.

We have a good cup pedigree now. We know how to win these

games; we know how to get to quarter-finals, semi-finals and finals. For us, it's about making that next step. When it's the big game and there's a lot riding on it, having the know-how to win the games. I think we're getting there but, for a time, we came unstuck when we were expected to win.

I watched the Carling Cup semi-final first leg at home. Injury or no injury, I was out my seat when the Yak equalised, but it really deflated us to concede right at the end, especially as it was a Joleon Lescott own goal, and it made it that much more difficult for the second leg.

I was back in the team for the return at Goodison two weeks later when both sides were without key players who were taking part in the African Cup of Nations. The difference was that Chelsea had players for every position, so they could lose three or four men and bring in internationals that could slot straight in. You wouldn't even realise they had players missing. We could suddenly be without Yak, Joseph Yobo, Victor Anichebe and maybe Steven Pienaar. Us losing players was a bigger hit – Yak was our top scorer.

Although we were missing players, we still felt we could get through, but it wasn't to be. It was a frustrating night because we never had THE chance. It was like we were jabbing them but couldn't find an opening. We never built up a head of steam,but they were a hell of a defensive unit and could hit you on the counter-attack, as Joe Cole did to us with the only goal of the night.

After the disappointment of missing out on getting to Wembley, we gradually began to pick up momentum again and enjoyed a good win over SK Brann as the UEFA Cup resumed. The first leg was in Bergen, Norway, and I didn't play well for the first hour. The ball kept bouncing away off my shin but the poor nature of my play helped contribute to our first goal.

I lost the ball for the umpteenth time and Tim Cahill – good old Tim – won it back. The ball was crossed over and a Brann defender headed it out. It was coming straight towards me, just outside the box on the angle. It went through my head 'if you try to control this, it will come off your shin again. Just hit it'. I caught it on the half-volley and it bent like my Larissa goal round everyone and nestled in the bottom corner. I enjoyed that goal. It was one of my favourites…but as you are slowly but surely discovering, EVERY goal I score is among my favourites!

There was a funny incident at the end, just after Victor had made it 2-0. Bainesy was sub that night and Moyesy introduced him right at the end, replacing Yakubu. Leighton may have made a bit of history that night because he touched the ball in play but didn't actually step on the pitch. You may think that's impossible but you'd be wrong. We had a throw-in on the left corner of the pitch. Yak ambled off and Bainesy trotted down the touchline to pick the ball up and take the throw. As he threw it in, the ref blew the full-time whistle. I've spoken to him it and he told me he didn't see any point in going on the pitch so he walked straight back to the dressing room.

We hammered Brann 6-1 in the second leg a week later to reach the last 16, before outclassing Man City and Portsmouth to stay close to Liverpool as we contested fourth position.

Then it was Fiorentina, in Florence firstly, and we let ourselves down as we conceded two in the last 20 minutes. It was naïvety from us as a team as well as the manager. I felt like we opened the game up when we didn't need to, replacing Tony

Hibbert with AJ when it was only 1-0. We should have kept it tight and not gone chasing the game.

Being 2-0 down made it so much more difficult in the second leg but we so nearly pulled it off. The atmosphere that night was unbelievable. It was electric like the Manchester United game three years earlier but probably even better. AJ got the first goal, Mikel scored in the second half and it was level on aggregate. I swear that Goodison Park was shaking. The noise got to the Italians and we were battering them and genuinely thought we were going to do it, but we just couldn't get the third goal.

The gaffer brought Tommy Gravesen on at the very end of extra-time just for the penalty shoot-out and he scored but, sadly, Yakubu and Jags didn't. Yak always waited for the keeper to make a move but Sebastien Frey, their keeper, just stood his ground and when Yak tried to flick it into the corner, it came back off the post. When Jags missed his, we were out.

That was devastating. We should have been in the final that year. That's one of the best teams I played in. We had the Yak banging goals in, Pienaar and Arteta out wide, me, Tim Cahill and Lee Carsley in the middle, for the most part, and we had a solid back four.

You start to think that 'we didn't quite do it this year, but we'll do it next year' but you don't realise that once your chance is gone, it might not come again. We drew Standard Liege in the qualifying round the following season and ended up going out. You need to take your chances when they come along and that's something we've failed to do.

Maybe there was then a hangover from going out of Europe and as injuries began to mount – we soon lost Mikel and Tim for the remainder of the season – our form tailed off following what was then our customary defeat to Fulham at Craven Cottage.

After we lost to Liverpool at Anfield the gaffer took us to Marbella for one of our training/social trips. While we were there, Jags gave one of the best training performances I've ever seen. We'd been out the night before and had a few beers and for the first 20 minutes of the session he was abysmal. We then changed drills and he suddenly started doing overhead kicks, back-heels and nutmegs. By the time the staff joined in, he was flying and started calling the gaffer 'Davie'. Then it became 'mate' then 'the big cheese' and eventually just 'cheese'. We couldn't play for laughing. If the gaffer was in possession, Jags would scream 'yes, cheese' or 'give it here cheese'.

Moyes didn't know how to react but he seemed to take it in his stride. Whenever the gaffer took us away for a week, I usually had a great game when we came back. I'm sure it was unconnected but it always seemed to have a positive effect on my next game. Or perhaps that was the idea in the first place. We were terrible against Derby when we got back from Marbella but I was on fire. The gaffer said in the dressing room at half-time: "Ossie's the only one who looks normal." I was thinking 'take me away every week and I'll be your Player of the Year!'.

I scored the winner in the second half and was happy to celebrate, even though I'd been on loan at Derby four years previously. Scoring a goal is so difficult to do and such a good thing, you should be able to celebrate it.

I didn't go mad – I'd never be so disrespectful – but I don't understand why so many players make a big deal of not celebrating against former clubs. You're playing for a club that pays your wages in front of supporters who are desperate to see you score…so when you do you should celebrate with them, regardless of the opposition.

We sealed UEFA Cup qualification and a fifth-place finish with a 3-1 win over Newcastle in the final game of the season. It was absolutely scorching in the first half that day and I struggled to breathe and run. I couldn't move. Thankfully, at half-time it clouded over and in the second half there was an electrical storm with thunder and lightning. The temperature dropped 10 degrees and suddenly I had loads of energy.

I don't know why but I am terribly affected by the heat and it happened to me again 12 months later in the biggest football match of my entire life…

13

Wembley

In the summer of 2008, we made another pre-season trip to America and I was delighted that we travelled to Dallas, Texas, as it gave me an opportunity to visit the site of the assassination of President John F Kennedy. I'm fascinated by the Kennedy assassination and will watch anything to do with it. I have read so many books and watched DVDs about Kennedy that to actually go there was an opportunity I couldn't pass on.

It was a 40-minute bus ride from where we stayed and when the question was asked if anyone fancied travelling to Dealey Plaza and the Texas School Book Depository my response was "hell, yeah".

The sixth floor, where Lee Harvey Oswald is supposed to have shot Kennedy, is a museum now and the corner where it apparently happened is encased in glass. It looks like it hasn't been touched since the 1960s. I saw the view down to where Kennedy's motorcade was passing through when he was shot. There were some 'Xs' on the road where each bullet was supposed to have hit him. It was so interesting and I didn't realise how big the Plaza is, or how hilly it is. I stood behind the grassy knoll and it was a really strange experience. To be standing in an area of so much historical importance was all a bit surreal but I was glad I did it.

By the time the season started we were short on players. Lee Carsley had left, Andy Johnson was sold to Fulham and we hadn't signed anyone. I am always of the mindset 'what players have we got available? Right, let's get on with it'. Quite a lot of players take a different view: 'We haven't got any signings? What are we going to do? We're too short, we can't compete'. They can get really affected by not signing players. You should have extra bodies at the start of the season but we had Jack Rodwell and Jose Baxter, 17 and 16, having to play because there was no-one else available.

We lost to Blackburn in a to-and-fro game on the opening day and got a victory at West Brom the following week, which was massive. Rodwell had a goal disallowed from a corner, which was unlucky because it was going to be his first goal, but shortly after I scored to put us in front. Because of the pressure we were under, that goal got quite an emotional response from me. I went mad! Yak scored the second and we went on to win 2-1.

We conceded three at home again against Portsmouth a week later before a busy transfer deadline day when we brought in Louis Saha and, for a club record fee, Marouane Fellaini.

Fellaini arrived from Standard Liege as our holding player

and it didn't take long to realise that wasn't his best position. He wasn't disciplined enough, he didn't get involved in the game enough and he probably wasn't a good enough passer. However, if you got the ball to him in and around the penalty area, he was almost impossible to compete with.

I remember the first derby he played in well – because we almost came to blows! It was after Liverpool beat us 2-0 at Goodison. Something happened late in the game after Tim Cahill had been sent off and back in the dressing room, Felli got in my face, pointing at me. I went mad at him and shouted: "Come on then! You and me outside now!" I was proper angry at him for trying to front me. Hibbo got between us in the end. Temperatures were high. I don't know if he thought he could have a go at the little guy but, having lost a derby, I wasn't in the mood to back down.

When I deal with things, I deal with it myself. On the pitch, if someone is kicking me, I won't immediately react but will keep my cool and try to get them back later in the game. Hibbo is the opposite.

He once had a scrap with Mikel Arteta over me at Finch Farm. It was something and nothing. Mikky is a really nice guy but he spat his dummy out over a few decisions in training. Davie Moyes gave him a couple of free-kicks, partly, I think, to pacify him. Then we both went for the ball and Mikel claimed a free-kick but the gaffer said no. Mikel went mad and tried to whack the ball at me. I was a yard away, saw it coming and stuck my leg up to block the ball with the bottom of my foot. Irritated, I asked: "What are you doing?"

Hibbo wasn't having it because Mikel had been acting like a brat for the whole session. He got straight in his face and they grabbed each other. The next thing they were wrestling. Moyes tried to split them up and there were arms flailing as the three of them rolled around on the floor. Steve Round tried to break it up and so did Sylvain Distin. At one stage there were seven or eight people rolling around and I stood back and thought 'Woh, what's going on here?' It took a good few people to eventually split it all up.

We'd also signed the Ecuadorian midfielder Segundo Castillo in August 2008 on loan and he scored a cracker in the first leg of our UEFA Cup qualifier against Standard Liege. After that goal, everyone thought 'wow, what have we got here? What a player he could be'. But that was just about it. He didn't show much – other than his backside. Before every game he used to get an injection in his bum. I think it was a vitamin boost. I'd be getting a strapping applied before a match and he'd come in, whip his kecks down, bend over and the doc would stick this needle in his backside. Off he then went to get changed. That's my main memory of him, which is a shame because he was a decent lad.

We drew 2-2 against Liege at Goodison. The second leg in Belgium was tight but they edged it 2-1 for a 4-3 aggregate win. They were a good team and I'd say they were simply better than us. It was unfortunate that we drew them in a play-off round. We have beaten teams that were better than us over the years but not that day.

It took us until November before we got going properly. The catalyst for a big improvement was a 1-1 draw with Manchester United and specifically a crunching Phil Neville tackle on Cristiano Ronaldo. Nev wasn't a great tackler. It was shit or bust with him. He was a good full-back in that sense because he got the winger or the ball. Either way, not many got past him.

Goodison was a bit flat until that tackle. Nev thundered into Ronaldo right in front of the Bullens Road fans and they went berserk, on their feet roaring and cheering like mad. Ronaldo was squirming on the ground, Rio Ferdinand was furious and he and Ryan Giggs dashed over to front Nev.

We all rushed to back up our skipper and there was a bit of pushing and shoving. Our crowd loved it! Us v them, a bit of animosity. Goodison was a cauldron but Nev was calmness itself and just walked away, ignoring the threats and abuse from his former team-mates. I think it was the moment our fans realised that Phil Neville was now a 100% Blue. United were rattled, we were determined and Felli scored an equaliser with his first goal for us.

A few days later Felli scored a last-minute winner at Bolton. That can do so much for you as a team. The confidence, the relief, the excitement, the buzz. You take it on into other games and we did that, beating Fulham on the Saturday after I put over what may have been the best cross I've ever supplied for Louis Saha to rise like the proverbial salmon and head another late winner.

It became a habit. Against West Ham a week later we were 1-0 down into the last 10 minutes before going 'bang-bang-bang' with three quick goals. That was one of the times I ended up celebrating in the crowd. I love it when that happens. It's difficult to describe your feelings when you've just scored a goal and made thousands of passionate Evertonians deliriously happy. You just want to jump in and hug every one of them and join the mad celebrations.

It doesn't always go right though. We were very poor in losing to Wigan not long after. We didn't even look like a team that night and the fans understandably went mad. They were waiting for us by the bus after the game to boo us and shout at us. It was a bit scary actually and it gave me a taste of how intimidating our fans can be.

We reacted with our third win on the trot at White Hart Lane but it was soured as Yakubu ruptured his Achilles tendon. No one really knew what had gone on. He walked off the pitch so it was a shock to hear afterwards that it was such a serious injury. Louis Saha hurt his hamstring in the same game and we later discovered that James Vaughan needed an operation. We had no recognised strikers available so Cahill and Felli had to play up front for us. We used to joke about winning games with a 4-6-0 formation. The bizarre thing is it actually worked for us. We lost a crazy game to Villa at the start of December but, apart from a single defeat at Manchester United, we didn't lose again until March.

What a match Villa was. 1-0 down after a minute, Joleon Lescott scored, then we went 2-1 down. I played right-back for the only time in my career in the last five or 10 minutes as we went after an equaliser. Into stoppage time I put a diagonal ball in, which I thought I'd overhit, but Jags headed it back and Joleon volleyed an absolute belter for 2-2. We were celebrating a dramatic point and Moyes chucked his coat into the crowd because he'd had some stick from them but we were devastated when Ashley Young went straight up the other end to make it 3-2. It was a sickener.

As players, we argued about who was to blame, but a couple of days later the manager accepted it was his fault. Moyesy would always analyse himself first and he was always man enough to concede it had been his fault if he thought it had been, rather than point fingers. Jags had been pushed forward for the last 10 minutes and he asked if he should come back once we'd made it 2-2. The gaffer said: "No, stay up front. We might get another one." I was still right-back and after Mikel lost the ball with a loose pass, they broke at us and we were all disjointed.

We should have tightened up and accepted 2-2 but you can get caught up in the emotion of Goodison and go for the win. It needed someone to step back and say: "No, that's it. Never mind what the manager is saying, we are shoring this up." We could have argued about that afterwards with us sitting on a point. That was a big learning experience for me that day. Captains can make decisions on the pitch, overruling the manager if he thinks it's necessary, and we'll argue about it later.

Our FA Cup run began at Moss Rose, Macclesfield, where I had scored my first ever professional goal just over six years earlier. When we played at the lower league clubs in the cup, Moyesy liked to take us to the ground the day before, so the newer lads could get used to it.

At Macclesfield, the dressing rooms were like a shoe box so we decided to change at our hotel. So the players of Everton Football Club left the Wrightington Hotel just outside Parbold at 1.45pm in full kit, carrying our boots.

Macc played really well that day but we always had enough and I scored a late goal, a half-volley from the edge of the box into the top corner.

It was well struck and I was very pleased with it. What I didn't realise at the time was that it was a goal that started a journey that would take us all the way to Wembley.

Because I'd scored the winning goal, I had to speak to the

media after the game. The interviews were pitchside and as the stands were low, I could see the houses behind the stadium, with the team bus parked on the main road. I was going from press to radio to TV and it was taking ages. I was panicking about them leaving without me but our press officers reassured me during my Everton TV interview.

Then I saw a team bus pull away.

"Is that our bus?"

I grabbed my stuff, ran out of the stadium into the main road and set off after it, shouting for it to stop.

I caught up to it in traffic and banged on the back but the driver thought I was a fan and kept on going. As I continued to run, I felt something fall out of my pocket, heard a crack and a bang, but kept on running. I eventually caught up to the front and made my presence known. They stopped the bus and opened the doors.

As I was getting on, a kid ran up to me and said: "Osman, you've dropped your phone." As I thanked him, he added: "The bus ran over it."

As we had drawn Macclesfield in the third round and I scored the winner, I decided to avoid the fourth-round draw so it could provide us with more luck. I took the kids to the cinema and when we walked out afterwards, I saw I had a load of voicemails and missed calls on my battered phone. When I first read a text that we had been given Liverpool away, I thought it was a joke. But as I read and listened to all the messages, it became obvious it was true. The initial reaction was disappointment at such a difficult draw – they were challenging for the Premier League title that season – but it wasn't long before you're feeling excited about going to Anfield.

Coincidentally, we played them in the league at Anfield on the Monday night before the cup tie and we equalised late on through a Tim Cahill header. That goal made such a difference to us, mentally. If we had lost that game, we would have gone into the cup tie feeling down and it would have been a lot tougher. The fact that we got something out of that game gave us a lift and extra belief that they wouldn't beat us if we all did our jobs.

The cup match was tough. Marouane Fellaini was suspended, Mikel Arteta injured and Liverpool dominated possession and territory. Despite that, we managed to take the lead through Joleon Lescott before Steven Gerrard equalised early in the second half. We were under a lot of pressure in the last 15 minutes. We had tired legs and tired minds and just wanted to see the game out.

I don't know why we haven't won at Anfield in so long – 15 years and counting as I write this. Maybe it's a mental thing as much as anything else. A lot of the time we've gone there to be tough to break down, trying to sneak something, rather than going there all-out to win.

It was all summed up when we were in great form in 2011-12, they were struggling, but we lost 3-0 as Steven Gerrard scored a hat-trick. We had an FA Cup quarter-final against Sunderland four days later and made six or seven changes but we hadn't won at Anfield for 13 years. As shown in the league game in 2009, that first 1-1 draw set us up to get the second one. Mentally, if we'd got something from that league game in March 2012, it would have set us up in the cup semi-final a month later. It's important that we win a derby at Anfield and I'm not sure we have always given ourselves the best chance.

On the flip side of that, Roberto Martinez's first attempt to win an Anfield derby in January 2014, showed that you can't go the other way either. We went all-out to win and got thrashed 4-0. There has to be a happy medium between the two. Hopefully, we'll learn that because I'm desperate to win at Anfield before I finish playing.

Thankfully, we did defeat in them in the fourth-round replay in 2009 – the Dan Gosling derby when ITV went to an advert break in the build-up to our goal. Gerrard had to go off injured early that night and mentally that was a big boost for us, players and fans alike, because he's their talisman.

It was a tight, tense occasion and in the second half I had a great chance to win the game, slicing my shot and hitting the post. That's one of the moments in my career I'd love to go back and change. I should have scored.

We went on to win through Gosling's late goal in extra-time. It looked like it was going to penalties. Both sets of fans were probably wondering who was going to step up. I was worried that I would have to take one, although I'm not sure Moyesy would have let me. The scars from Middlesbrough and 2003 still had not completely healed. I asked a couple of times after that, when I started to feel a little braver, but he seemed to have completely lost confidence in my penalty-taking ability. I've always practised to improve my technique in case I've ever had to take one but I wouldn't put your money on me.

We had Aston Villa at Goodison in the fifth round – tough opposition who we often competed against for European qualification at that time, but you can't complain at a home draw. I was injured so sat in the stands and watched Victor Anichebe destroy Curtis Davies as we won 3-1.

We'd not had an FA Cup run under Moyes. Getting to the semi-final of the Carling Cup the year before helped us and showed us how to win these games. We were now one game away from Wembley.

It was another home draw in the quarter-finals, against Middlesbrough. It was so tense that day. We went 1-0 down just before half-time and Moyes gave us a right rollicking at the interval.

He said: "This is your one chance. You've got 45 minutes to get to Wembley. If you want to get there, you've got to go out and do it in the second half. The fans will be right behind you. They want it as much as you. There is not much tactically I can do. You look like you're all too uptight. If you want it, go and show it."

We did. Within 15 minutes we'd scored two goals and we held on to get through. We were all dead excited in the dressing room afterwards and a few of us were saying: "Come on, we've got to have a night out. All of us, we're going into town."

We went to a few bars but because it was a Sunday night, it wasn't too crazy. A few people went home after a while but myself, Hibbo, Dan Gosling, our Danish right-back Lars Jacobsen and a couple of the staff stayed out.

Someone suggested The Grapes on Mathew Street because it would be livelier. I knew what The Grapes was all about and it was chocker when we went in.

We were greeted by massive cheers as most people in there were Evertonians who had been the game. Lars freaked out, left and went home immediately! The rest of us stayed with the fans for hours, singing Everton songs, doing karaoke and dancing on the tables.

Dan was quite uptight and taken aback by fans singing in his face so I told him: "This is a good thing, mate. They love you. You scored the winning goal in a derby. Enjoy it." Everyone was delighted we were going to Wembley.

The atmosphere at the semi-final against Manchester United was incredible. It sent shivers down your spine. The noise, the sea of blue and white – it really was brilliant. The whole occasion was great.

United were going for all five competitions at that point, having already won the Community Shield and League Cup and reached the Champions League semi-final, but we went there to win. When we saw they were playing a weakened team – Wayne Rooney, Cristiano Ronaldo and Edwin van der Sar weren't even on the bench – we got a mental boost and grew an inch before we'd even got out on the pitch. We felt the United team was beatable, although Rio Ferdinand, Nemanja Vidic and Carlos Tevez were still starting.

Like the cup replay against Liverpool, it was a very tense affair with not much in it. Again, it was 0-0 into extra-time and penalties loomed. Again, I was worried that I would have to take one. I did put my hand up and Moyesy told me I could go sixth. That was nerve-wracking enough, to possibly have to take one in sudden death.

Thankfully, it never came to that. Everton's historically poor record in shoot-outs was not on the players' minds. A lot of them were fairly new and wouldn't have known anyway. We had practised pens for months, all the way through the cup run, and we all knew what we were doing.

I knew Tim Cahill was going to go down the middle with

that first penalty, but, unfortunately, so did Ben Foster, who stood still, and that's why Tim put a bit extra on it. Too much, as it turns out, as he blasted it over the bar. Until that point Tim Howard had not made a significant penalty save for the club, but he was big for us that day, keeping out United's first two pens from Dimitar Berbatov and Ferdinand. As Leighton Baines scored with our second effort, we had the advantage.

It is tense when you watch your team-mate go up but because we'd been practising a lot, I knew where every Everton player was going to put their pen. I watched Foster to see what he was doing and if he didn't dive the right way, like with Phil Neville's pen, the relief would hit me straight away. I thought Nev was really brave to take a pen against his former club. He played a true captain's role that day.

When James Vaughan stepped forward with us 2-1 up, I was nervous. He's such an emotional guy and he always wanted to take responsibility. He was a young lad and hats off to him. I think he tried to take a similar pen in the pre-season straight afterwards and it went over the stand. At Wembley, Foster went the right way but Vaughany hit it out of his reach. It was a great pen.

Phil Jagielka had the penalty to take us to the final. I knew Jags was going to score. He'd had his pen saved against Fiorentina the year before but he practised a lot in the following 12 months. He had a quick run-up and it looked like he was going to smash it, before stroking it in the bottom corner. I was sure that Foster wouldn't know what he was doing – Jags is a centre-half and a keeper is not going to expect him to pass it in the corner. As soon as he hit it, the keeper hadn't moved and I knew it was going in.

We were all stood watching in a line. When Jags' pen hit the net, the lads set off in different directions – some went to Jags, some went to Tim Howard. The pens were taken at the Man United end, so I ran to the Everton supporters on my own. It wasn't planned – they were our fans, that's where all the noise and cheering was coming from and I wanted to go down there. The feeling was incredible.

It was a great day but I don't believe semi-finals should be played at Wembley. It felt like we had won the final afterwards,mand we hadn't. I'm pretty sure we celebrated on the pitch like it was the final. Then you have to go back there and try to do it all again. It takes something away from the final. We have enough quality stadiums around the country to accommodate two semi-finals.

We were playing Chelsea in the league three days later so the gaffer decided we would stay in London. It was a terrible idea because we won the semi-final, went back to the hotel, had one glass of champagne each before being told it was bed-time because we had a big game on the Wednesday. It was such an anti-climax and in stark contrast to the night out after Middles-brough. We wanted to go crazy because we were in the FA Cup final – it was such a big thing and so exciting but Moyesy put us to bed. I held a grudge for a while over that. Those really good days in football don't come around that often in a career. I've not had enough of them and I felt like we should have cel-ebrated getting to the final, but we didn't. Not properly anyway. You can say you'll celebrate it later but it's not the same as the moment you've done it.

Chelsea beat Arsenal in the other semi-final so the league game three days later at Stamford Bridge was a dress rehearsal.

We played really well and should have won. Brazilian Jo was put through on goal and should have squared it to me for a tap-in. Instead he had a shot and pulled it wide. If we'd won at Chelsea, that would have been massive for us going into the final. We would have known we could beat them, and so would they.

Everything in that week following the semi-final was about Jags, and rightly so. Sadly, his world came crashing down the following Saturday when he suffered a serious knee injury when we played Man City at Goodison. He was going to be leading the defence in the FA Cup final but instead he faced 10 months out of the game. It was devastating, for us a team as well as him.

He's a rollercoaster of emotions, Jags. He's up or he's down and that can change from one minute to the next. When he's high, he's giddy and excited. When he's low, sometimes there is no talking to him. That was a major low point. It was another injury which we didn't need, with Yakubu, Arteta and Anichebe already out long-term.

We did go into the final on the back of a 2-0 win at Fulham on the last day of the league season. I scored both goals. We had won at Craven Cottage for the first time since 1966 and had finished fifth again. It was a great turnaround after such a ropey start to the season. Fulham was one of the good days for me. The last guy to score a winning goal there for Everton was Alan Ball and I was made up. I went into the cup final full of confidence. It was to be another week that sums up football and how things can change so quickly.

The cup final was undoubtedly the worst day of my career. It's difficult to stay relaxed for such big games. You can't help but feel nervous. The best players are the ones who stay the most relaxed and see it as a normal game. I was proper nervous that day!

We stayed in the Grosvenor Park Hotel in London. On the morning of the game, I went for a couple of walks around the grounds, listening to Motown, while taking deep breaths and trying to stay relaxed. It was a scorching day. The sun was burning my head. I felt it was too hot then and knew it was only going to get hotter. I was hoping that clouds would come out in the afternoon.

I saw some of the build-up on TV and it showed our coach, parked up outside the hotel. I remember getting on it later, thinking 'I'll be on TV now', just like all players in the cup finals I watched growing up. I was in the habit of having hot chocolate on the coach on the way to the ground and despite the heat I had one that day. We got to Wembley and there were no signs of any clouds. The Everton fans were in the opposite end to the semi-final and we were in a different dressing room, which wasn't a good omen. Everything was just different.

We went out to warm up and it was so hot. There was a shadow across the middle of the pitch and the difference was night and day. I could operate in the shade, but as soon as I went over in the sun it absolutely killed me. As we lined up to come out, they had these massive flames shooting up at the side of the pitch. The temperature was already 30-odd degrees and that seemed to take it to 50 right by me. The shade went from goal to goal down half the pitch and, of course, I played on the right which was in the sun in the first half.

Because of our injuries we went into the cup final with very few options on the bench. We had little back-up and in the heat and with the nervous energy you would burn in that game, you needed subs. That was an area where Chelsea had a significant advantage over us.

The heat affects most players but I don't know if it affects me more. I would always choose minus 20 before 18 degrees. In the cold and the rain, I can run around all day but as soon as my body gets hot, I can really struggle. Pre-season kills me. I feel like I can barely move. I don't operate well in extreme temperatures.

Ashley Cole ran me ragged in the final. Because he's quicker than me, he could stand as high as he wanted because I would have to go back and mark him. Any ball that came out, he would always beat me to it. I couldn't compete with him that day. What we needed to do was be brave and for me to do what we call in football 'cheat'. That would have meant me staying forward and not going back to mark him, in the hope that it would force him to stay back because he's thinking 'I can't leave him in that position'.

That was another good thing about Moyes, there were never any cheats. You had to do your job and mark your man. That day I basically played right-back because Ashley Cole had me so far up the pitch. Florent Malouda and Hibbo were inside a little and Hibbo was booked early in the game, which only made it more difficult for him.

We went 1-0 up after 30 seconds through Louis Saha. What a start. I hadn't even touched the ball. After the initial celebrations, I couldn't help but think 'I hope we haven't scored too early'. Then I thought 'come on, we're Everton. We're good at seeing results out'. We held the lead for just over 20 minutes before Didier Drogba scored a header, which was devastating.

It was still only 1-1 but we were up against it. Chelsea were doing most of the pressing. Inside the last 20 minutes Frank Lampard had a shot from a long way out that ultimately won them the game.

We were 2-1 down and Chelsea were so good defensively. Chasing the game in such heat was just impossible and we weren't able to create a chance to equalise. It was massively disappointing, walking around the pitch afterwards, having gone from the high at the semi-final to the low of the final. It just wasn't to be.

Our fans were amazing. Hardly any of them left the ground. Almost all of them stayed to clap us and show their appreciation for how well we'd done in the cup and league that season. It showed their character because it was such a big disappointment for all of us, yet nobody left in a huff.

I almost didn't watch Chelsea receive the cup. I was on the pitch but didn't want to look up, but I had a little glance just as John Terry lifted it to the skies and pictured what could have been.

Then we had the party at the Grosvenor afterwards. You've got to plan them in case you win but we ended up celebrating without the trophy we all wanted. Jim Davidson was booked to do a short turn and his act was, shall we say, politically incorrect. Joleon Lescott wasn't happy at all at some of his material.

After the meal quite a lot of the players disappeared to a nightclub, while a few of us had a party around our table – me, Hibbo and our families. We cranked the music up and were still going at stupid o'clock in an effort to console ourselves. The next morning it was back on the plane and that was it. There was no celebratory bus journey around town.

The wait for a trophy went on.

14

Wearing
The Armband

After reaching the FA Cup final and ending the season strongly to finish fifth in the Premier League, we should have been in a position to push on and achieve even more in 2009/10. Instead, we began the new campaign with turmoil surrounding the club as Joleon Lescott sought a move to Manchester City.

Despite handing in a transfer request, David Moyes selected him for our opening-day match at home to Arsenal. When we lost the game 6-1, Joleon was singled out for criticism from both the manager and the media, which I felt was unfair. City suddenly had a lot of money and were potentially going to start winning league titles. They were paying big money to buy players and paying ridiculous wages when they got them. Their then manager, Mark Hughes, wanted him, and Joleon wanted to go. It was nothing against Everton.

Loyalty is a big thing. I am all for it but footballers' careers are such brief periods of time. People try to earn as much money as they can as quickly as they can in their working lives. I know it's different in football, because you can earn a lot anyway, but you still want to set yourself up as best you can for the rest of your life. I don't begrudge any player if they are offered silly money. I don't know exactly but I think Joleon's wages may have trebled. You are also thinking about your family at this point. He had kids and he could secure their future, whether it went well or not.

It was common knowledge that he wanted to go but I don't remember him forcing it. When a player is seeking a transfer to another club, it doesn't make it awkward between players and I spoke to Joleon about what was happening. You might encourage them to do what you want – stay – but you're not scared about asking them about what's happening. Things didn't work out well against Arsenal and Joleon was blamed. Once you go out on that pitch, that's it – the game's ahead of you and you're not thinking about anything else. We lost as a team that day. It was very harsh and wrong to blame Joleon for that result. Whether it was tactical, physical or mental, it wasn't Joleon's fault, but it was certainly a tough way to start the season.

Fortunately, after our hammering by Arsenal, we played Sigma Olomouc in the Europa League the following Thursday and won 4-0, with Joleon dropped by Moyes for what he considered to be his "poor attitude". Then we went to Burnley and lost 1-0. They had just beaten Man United and were on a high.

Mixed emotions, 2005/06: (Above) Letting my frustrations out after levelling at Millwall in the FA Cup; (left) celebrating after David Thompson's own goal at Wigan which I felt I should have been given – what Bainesy is appealing for is anybody's guess!
Below: Another goal at Upton Park...

Goodison goal: On target again against Aston Villa during the latter months of 2005/06

Derby delight: (Above) Celebrating with Andy Johnson and Gary Naysmith after 'AJ' had scored his first against Liverpool in the memorable 3-0 derby victory in September 2006. Right: We were stunned to meet Rocky – Sylvester Stallone – at the Reading home game in January 2007

Training buddies: With Mikel Arteta and Tim Cahill, influential figures at the club in the 2000s during David Moyes' tenure

Flying start: Celebrating the opener against Wigan Athletic on the opening day of the 2007/08 season (above left), and my Goal of the Season strike v AE Larissa in the UEFA Cup (above right)

Final day: (Far left in shot) Receiving instructions from David Moyes during our final training session at Bellefield, October 2007, Jimmy Comer gegging in (far right)!

Memorable moments: (Left) Celebrating our Nurnberg victory in Germany – for the fans; (above) slaloming through to score against Sunderland in our 7-1 victory

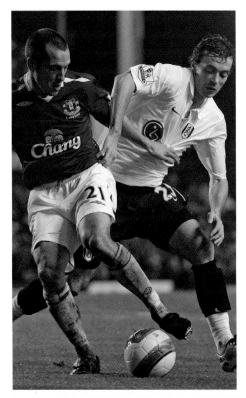

Familiar faces: (Left) Holding off former team-mate Simon Davies, who seemed to have been brought in to replace me; (above) kit man Jimmy Martin and first-team coach Jimmy Lumsden, big influences behind the scenes

Action man: Tim congratulates me after a goal at Hull City in 2008/09 – he really knew how to promote himself as a person and market his potential

Career firsts: (Above) Letting myself go after our 2009 FA Cup semi-final victory over Manchester United, and (above right) part of the mob congratulating Phil Jagielka following his winning penalty in the Wembley shootout

Highs and lows: (Left) The 2009 FA Cup final misery v Chelsea in the heat of Wembley; (below) achieving 'goals' as captain in 2009/10, including a strike at Hull (below left) and against Stoke City

Winter warmers: (Above) Hopefully Andy Reid never caught anything from me after I'd risen from my sick bed at Sunderland; (right) rising highest to head home against Arsenal at the Emirates in January 2010

Manchester magic: (Above) Dan Gosling receives my congratulations following his goal against United at Goodison in our 3-1 victory; (left) beating a familiar face to the ball as we come away from the Etihad with another victory over Roberto Mancini, to the delight of David Moyes, in March 2010

Liverpool goal: A derby first – celebrating my Goodison strike in 2012

Leon Osman: (Left) At my first England press conference, November 2012, which meant a lifetime's memory of Movember…and making my debut – in long sleeves – an occasion slightly overshadowed by Zlatan Ibrahimovic

Football life: 'Blue Crimbo' celebrations with the skipper in 2013 and coming off following my 'collision' with the Goodison turf v Arsenal, April 2014

Family shots: (Left, from top) With the family for Kendall christening; Deacon, Cole and Kendall with their mum, serious as ever; my kids enjoying their summer holiday..

Testimonial memories: (Above) Saluting the fans ahead of the game with Porto, with Kendall and Cole joining me on the pitch; (top right) holding hands with Deacon, who showed great bravery to make my day extra special

It wasn't a good day for us and, to cap it off, I dislocated my thumb and it kept popping out during the match.

By now Joleon had gone and when you see his CV since joining City, it's difficult to suggest he made the wrong decision. He's won two Premier League titles, an FA Cup, a Carling Cup and played in the Champions League.

Without him, we got our first Premier League points of the season through an injury-time penalty from Leighton Baines as we beat Wigan 2-1. It was the first time I played against a team managed by Roberto Martinez. His teams tended to frustrate us. They were always so unusual. You would get used to each club's systems and I'd know where to go to find space, but Martinez was something completely different to play against in terms of his systems and tactics. He would play wing-backs with wingers outside them. I always found it difficult to find space against his teams.

On the same day that Joleon finally left us for Man City, we signed the Russian left-sided midfielder Diniyar Bilyaletdinov from Lokomotiv Moscow. As much as you want the team to improve, you are fighting for your 'spec'. When Moyes brought Bilyaletdinov in and paid £9m for him, I was thinking 'this is a lot of money and I've heard good things about him'. In our first Europa League group match against AEK Athens he played really well, having a hand in three of our four goals. I thought I was up against it and would face a tough battle to be in the team. But his Everton career didn't carry on in that manner.

When you're younger, you see every player as competition and take it as an insult every time you don't play. As you get older, you realise that you can't be fresh for every game because the demands are too much.

In September, I was given the honour of captaining the club for the first time in a League Cup tie at Hull City. I had been passed over almost a year earlier, when Phil Neville missed a league game against Newcastle in October 2008.

Moyes made Mikel Arteta captain for that match. Before the game he called me to one side and said: "Look, you should be captain. I know it, you know it. I've made Mikel captain because I'm hoping it will bring him back to form, but I still want you to act as a captain." What can you say? My response was "Okay, no problem. I'm disappointed, though."

I really liked Mikel but it was another example of 'Ossie will be alright with that'. It makes sense in a way because it stops arguments between players or a player and the manager. You could make the 'right' decision but another player gets upset which dislodges the team's momentum. Once again, I took one for the team.

Finally getting to wear the armband didn't half inspire me. I love cup games anyway. They get me excited; there is something different about them. The fans feel that and so do I. I literally charged around the pitch against Hull. I was trying to lead by example. We were 3-0 up at half-time and I was so proud of my lads as we came back in the dressing room! The night was capped off by me scoring in the second half. The manager said at the end how well I had played and that I had shown how to lead the team. He didn't say stuff like that very often. He never wanted anyone to get carried away.

I was captain for our next league game against Stoke. Again, I was so proud. It was my first game as skipper at Goodison and that was big. Leading the players out of the tunnel to the Z-Cars drum-roll and hearing the crowd roar start was special.

We were 1-0 down and struggling when I had a shot that nearly hit the corner flag. Five minutes later, one of our August signings, Johnny Heitinga, played a one-two with me and I was in almost exactly the same spot. I tried it again and it went in off the underside of the crossbar, into the roof of the net. It was one of my best goals. Andy Holden was pleased I didn't shirk trying that shot again and told me I had "great bollocks to try again" afterwards. Cheers, Taff. I was taken off 20 minutes later, but that's management for you. We didn't play well but got something out of the game. I would have been devastated if my first Goodison captaincy had been a defeat.

A trip to Belarus was on the cards when we resumed in Europe against BATE Borisov. Our hotel was right across from the stadium. Yakubu missed the bus, but because of the crowds and the way we had to enter the stadium, he walked across the road and got there before us. It absolutely poured down. Hibbo, who was centre-half, suffers from terribly bad blisters and has to get his feet padded and play in moulded studs, no matter what the conditions. It was a bog, but we won 2-1 and coming off the pitch, that was a satisfying result. We got so soaked it was fun, like playing with your mates in the park in the pouring rain.

Soon after, I broke my foot. It was a tackle with Wolves' Karl Henry and he stood on the outside of my foot. I had a sharp pain but carried on. I was in real pain afterwards but it took a minimum of 10 days to figure out what I'd done. Scans or X-rays initially showed nothing, even though I was in agony. Eventually, I had a CT scan and it showed a tiny flake off my bone had separated where the ligament joins. The ligament was pulling at this piece of floaty bone.

The broken foot meant I missed the opportunity to play Benfica at the Stadium of Light. We had such a depleted team in Portugal as injuries caught up with us. We had Dan Gosling right-back, while Seamus Coleman made his debut at left-back and Hibbo was one of our centre-halves. I watched it on TV and it was tough viewing as we lost 5-0. Benfica had David Luiz, Ramires, Oscar Cardozo and Angel Di Maria in their team, so we didn't lose to a bad side!

I was finally able to come back for the home game against BATE Borisov a week before Christmas, exactly two months after I suffered the original injury. While I was out we won only two of 12 matches, losing seven. I'd like to say it was all down to me not being in the team but we were hit so badly by injuries at that point.

BATE Borisov was Hibbo's record-breaking European appearance for Everton but we had a very weakened team because we'd already qualified for the knockout stage. Moyes even named his team in the press the day before the game because he wanted the supporters to know that he was playing a very different line-up. Typical, that. Moyes didn't want to hoodwink the fans and I thought that was a class thing to do.

We had Shane Duffy, Jake Bidwell, Adam Forshaw, Kieran Agard and Jose Baxter in the starting eleven and Carlo Nash made his first and only appearance for the first team. Nathan Craig and Hope Akpan came on as subs.

It was literally a kids team with me, Hibbo, Yak and Nashy. Jack Rodwell had some experience but he pulled his hamstring after eight minutes. I played 81 minutes and the manager told me I would be needed at the weekend because our squad was so thin.

After just coming back from injury, the last thing I needed was to get hit by an illness. But that's what happened for our Boxing Day match at Sunderland.

As usual, I had an hour with the kids on Christmas Day morning before we had training. The Christmas Day tradition at the training ground is for the club's chaplain, Reverend Henry Corbett, to tell us a Christmas story, invite anyone present to add anything before leading a prayer. We say "amen" and head out. Halfway through training I started to feel unwell with serious pains in my stomach. Afterwards I went round to my mum's to meet the whole family and I was as white as a ghost... which for me takes some doing! We went home for Christmas dinner with Jenny's family but after half an hour I had to go to bed. I spent the next 16 hours vomiting and also had diarrhoea. I had never felt so ill in all my life.

Jenny was telling me I had no chance of playing the following day but I was insistent I would. I asked her to bring me some food. I couldn't face a proper dinner so she brought me a bowl of Christmas soup. After three mouthfuls I got the sweats and was back in the bathroom.

I spoke to our physio, Mick Rathbone, and told him to give me until the morning. The rest of the squad headed up to Sunderland that evening. They called me at 7am on Boxing Day and I told them I'd been okay since 4am. A fella called Bob, who worked for the club at the time, came to our house at 8am. He drove me to Sunderland, while I took a banana and a bottle of water...and two emergency rolls of Andrex!

By the time I got up there, I was feeling a lot better but still hadn't eaten, other than half of the banana. I played about 70 minutes, as we drew 1-1. I was fuming when I was taken off but when I got back to the dressing room, I had the sweats again. I travelled back with Bob and when we were halfway home, I was hungry so we pulled in at a service station. Bob got me a KFC, I had three bites and it all came back up again. If I'm able to play, I will make myself available. Unless I can't get out my bed, I'll turn up. I might not do well but I'll drag myself there and try. I hate missing matches.

In January we faced Carlisle in the third round of the FA Cup, but I was injured. Because I'd enjoyed my time there on loan so much, I wish I could have played, but it was good to speak to Peter Murphy, who was one of my friends up there, and catch up with the kit man, Buzz-Head!

After a 3-1 win at Brunton Park, disappointingly, we couldn't repeat our FA Cup run of the previous year as we lost at home to Birmingham in round four. We went 2-0 down, I came on at half-time and scored, but luck wasn't on our side that day.

In the same month, we also drew 2-2 at Arsenal in one of my favourite games. We were so much better than them that day.

We battered them, and it was very different from the opening-day hammering at Goodison. I headed us in front from a Landon Donovan corner. It was Landon's debut. He trained with us over Christmas and I wasn't sure what we were getting. He didn't start too well and I needed to be convinced, but then the Major League Soccer season had finished a couple of months earlier. He was soon up to speed and was really influential in the time he was with us on loan.

Arsenal equalised with a deflected shot from Denilson, which I didn't even realise until recently has gone down as my own goal, but we continued to dominate them. Stevie Pienaar scored a great chip to make it 2-1 with 10 minutes left and a minute later James Vaughan had a one-on-one to make it 3-1. He couldn't take the chance and Tomas Rosicky equalised with another deflected shot in added time.

That was as close as we ever came to winning at one of the so-called big four – Arsenal, Chelsea, Liverpool and Manchester United – under David Moyes. We should have seen that game out. It was a real missed opportunity. That could have changed our run of form against those four clubs. After we won at Spurs for the first time in 2006, we then went and won there for the following two seasons. We suddenly had good memories of White Hart Lane. I'm not saying it's a mental thing where we know we are going to get beat. We know we're good enough to win but, with the teams we've taken to Arsenal since, we could have won two or three of them. Maybe a touch of extra belief based on experience would have made the difference.

For that whole period when Landon was with us, we were still short on players but produced some excellent results and per-formances. We lost the derby at Anfield but rebounded strongly in beating Chelsea. I tackled everything, while Louis Saha had John Terry on toast and scored the winner with a fantastic volley. We battled our socks off that night.

We played well again in the last 32 of the Europa League against Sporting Lisbon and led 2-0, but in the 85th minute, Jack Rodwell got a pass back wrong, Sylvain Distin brought their man down and they scored from the penalty. That was crucial. There was such a big difference from us leading 2-0 to 2-1, which, with the away goal, is not even a one-goal advan-tage. With a two-goal advantage they would have had to go at us in the second leg, giving us an opportunity to counter-attack.

At that point, we had signed Philippe Senderos on loan from Arsenal. Phil Jagielka's comeback game was the second leg but he wasn't ready to start. Senderos was a big player, an international who had played for Arsenal and AC Milan, but you wouldn't have known it that night. Walking out the tunnel before that game, Senderos said: "Lads, you're really going to have to help me tonight. You're going to have to encourage me, I'm too nervous." We were looking at each other, thinking, 'is he being serious here? Is this a joke?'.

He made a mistake in the first 10 minutes and was very shaky. Early in the second half he put his hand up and said he needed to come off injured. That was a real eye-opener. Some people can't handle certain situations. Whether people feel it or not, you try to keep it to yourself and tough it out. Jags replaced him and one of his first contributions was to do the Jags' boom – a massive clearance kick. While it was in the air, I shouted: "Welcome back, Jags."

Once Sporting got their first goal, they were already winning. We had to come out and score ourselves and once you do that away from home, the home team generally pick you off. The goal we conceded in the first game, which was something out of nothing, cost us and we lost 3-0 in Lisbon. In Europe, playing a team home and away is a completely different kettle of fish.

In between each leg, we beat Man United 3-1 at Goodison, our first win against them for five years. Dimitar Berbatov scored first but Bily equalised with an absolute whopper three minutes later. He didn't move very well – he was unnatural in the way he ran – but once he got that left foot swinging, wow. Gosling scored to make it 2-1 and Rodwell put the icing on the cake. We thoroughly deserved the win that day.

Later that season we completed a league double over Manchester City by beating them 2-0 at their place, having done them by the same scoreline at Goodison in January. That night at City was a really good victory. With five minutes to go, we led 1-0 when I picked up the ball and wanted someone to pass to. I looked left and right, saw someone running and played it into the space. It was Rodwell, who'd not long come on, and that boy can run. He is an absolute athlete. He set off and squared it, Tim Cahill stepped over it and Arteta stroked it in. We'd won there again.

It's great to play well and dominate matches. With Everton now, we've reached the point where we expect to outplay teams. It's still good to win but we're so much in control of games that we should win. Quite often in the past we might be good enough to win but we haven't dominated possession – we've worked hard, defended like men and dug it out. Those results feel so much better than the ones you should win.

Another change between then and now is the length of the grass at Goodison. It was always really long, partly because the groundstaff would advise the manager at what height it should stay. On the last game of every season they would cut it down so it was like a bowling green and it was always the best game to play. I constantly give our head groundsman, Bob Lennon, stick that we should have our pitch like that all the time, but he says you can't or the grass will be ruined. Anyway Martinez has the grass cut shorter than we did under Moyes. It's only two millimetres but that can make a big difference.

We finished 2009/10 with 61 points, the same total as 2004/05 when we finished fourth but this time that was only good enough for eighth place. What we accomplished in '04/05 was incredible but in the nine seasons since, we have beaten that points total four times, while having European football in some of those years. From 2007/08 up until now, we've had some really good teams. If we hadn't had so many injuries in '09/10, we could have accomplished more that season.

Sadly, we would go backwards the following year. Finishing eighth was not good enough to get us into Europe. Once you get there, you need to stay there. That set us back, though we didn't realise it at the time, because it makes the club less attractive to new signings.

The club concentrated on keeping our star names that summer – Tim Cahill and Mikel Arteta – and both players signed new and improved contracts. Our big signing was Jermaine Beckford on a free transfer. By giving those big contracts out, we had no kitty to sign anyone else. Although we had fewer games with not being in Europe, we still needed to strengthen the squad. Competition for places is important. We only brought one significant player in and that set the tone for the season because we needed to reinforce more than we did. We had a running joke as players – "Come on, Moyesy, where's the signings?"

As usual, we began poorly, losing 1-0 at Blackburn on the opening day after a Tim Howard mistake. I started right midfield, having primarily played centre midfield for the previous few seasons. I didn't play well and neither did the team. Before the next game against Wolves, Moyes told me: "You're not playing. I don't think you're a right midfielder, it's not fair on you and I won't be playing you there again." I was very disappointed to miss out but, fair enough, he was probably right. I'm not really a wide midfielder. I've obviously played there loads of times and must have done well because I kept getting picked, but I do prefer a central role.

I played in centre-mid and captained against Huddersfield in the League Cup and we won 5-1. I wasn't selected in a 1-0 defeat by Villa but I was back for Man United – and guess where? Yep, on the right of midfield…

We were actually losing 3-1 until injury time when Cahill and Arteta scored within a minute to somehow drag us back to 3-3. It seemed to be the beginning of the end of Gary Neville's career because of how easily we got down his side of the field for those two goals.

We could even have won the game. Moyes came on the pitch at the end after Martin Atkinson blew for full-time when Jags was charging forward. The gaffer and Steve Round were both fined but Moyesy's was about one per cent of his weekly wage and Roundy's was something like 60 per cent, because of their earnings differential. It was hilarious. He was so wound up about it – "it's not fair, it's just not relative." Obviously, I took every opportunity to rub it in.

It was a very slow start and we didn't get our first win until we went to Birmingham in October. It was a horrible game but the result was all that mattered. I was on the left that day and we had to beat them. Our next match was against Liverpool and we couldn't go into the derby – eight league games into the season – without having a win. For our first goal, the ball was played into me with my back to goal and I did a little turn and put a stretching cross into that space between the keeper and centre-halves, and Roger Johnson kicked it into his own net.

I've got a picture somewhere of me celebrating in front of the Everton fans and the veins were popping out of my neck, yelling with my mouth wide open, gums and teeth showing. It's a good picture but all I could see was my crooked teeth.

From growing up, I felt uncomfortable about them so I wouldn't smile properly in television interviews. Jenny would ask why I pulled a funny face and when I explained it was because I was self-conscious about my teeth, she said she'd never even noticed. Bless her! Anyway, I was embarrassed by the Birmingham picture so I started to get my top teeth done. I still wear a plastic brace on and off, although I do forget at times.

Tim scored at the end to make it 2-0 and that was the biggest result of our season. It set us up for the derby, although it wasn't exactly like the titanic clashes I grew up watching, with us 17th and Liverpool 18th.

Evertonians would have been thrilled with a straightforward 2-0 win but it was a bad afternoon on a personal level as I injured my right ankle. You have three ligaments in that part of your body and I snapped two of them in my youth-team days so I have to strap the ankle for every training session and match. I'm fine now as long as I do that, but I hurt it badly in the derby. We were 1-0 up and I was charging round the pitch, going for a one-two by the corner of the Bullens Road and Gwladys Street, when Martin Skrtel made contact with me and I rolled the ankle. With no supporting ligaments, my shinbone may have touched the ground. I ended up in the gravel at the side of the pitch, in agony. The fans were patting me on the head but I thought I was going to vomit, such was the pain. I hobbled back on and couldn't move properly until half-time and there was no chance of going out for the second half.

A few days later I tried to do something in the gym and felt a pop in the ankle. I had a scan and X-ray and I'd taken a big chunk out of my cartilage, which was lodged in my ankle. I had the scan mid-afternoon and received a phone call about 6pm off Danny Donachie, our physio, who told me it wasn't good news. Your heart sinks in those situations. He asked if I could be at Runcorn train station in an hour so I could travel to Basingstoke for an operation. Hobbling around, I quickly packed my bag; Dad picked me up and dropped me at Runcorn where I met another one of our physios, Matt Connery, and we caught the train to London, arriving in the capital about 11pm before a driver took us on to Basingstoke for about 1am. At the crack of dawn we were up and out to go to the hospital; I met my surgeon, had the pre-op and before long was in theatre.

I woke up at 1pm and was taken back to my room. We had a choice of staying another night at the hotel or getting the train home. I wanted to go home but I had to show them I could hobble along a corridor and use the toilet. I did all that but it exhausted me. Matt rang a taxi; I hobbled down and slept for the whole ride. When we got to the station, Matt collected our tickets while I sat down and immediately fell asleep again. I must have looked a picture – a Premier League footballer fast asleep on a bench at Basingstoke station! I then got on the train and dozed off once more. Everything was such an exertion.

I was back for our game at Man City on December 20. We were down in 15th while they were third, but we managed to beat them again on an absolutely freezing night. Carlos Tevez, David Silva and Yaya Toure were wearing snoods. It was Baltic, something like minus 12.

As much as we seemed to have issues playing away against Arsenal or Liverpool, we were so comfortable and confident going to Man City.

The gaffer was buzzing after that game. He developed a thing with City. It started with Mark Hughes signing Joleon and then he had that hilarious scuffle with Roberto Mancini on the touchline when we won 2-0 in March 2010. At this point I really think they disliked each other. I think Moyes felt Mancini was arrogant and it was so important for him to beat the Italian. He would say to us in his team-talk: "We're beating these." There was extra fire in his eyes for those games. As players, you can't help but feel that. Everyone would have the feel-good factor after we beat City, high-fiving in the dressing room.

I don't think there was a different approach when we played City compared to, say, Arsenal, Chelsea, Liverpool or United. Moyes liked to tell us how to stop teams playing, give us a base and then go from there. Everyone had to do a job honestly.

There was no, what we call in football, 'cheating'. I don't mean literally cheating – it's just a phrase players use when a man is left up field with no remit to chase back.

Moyes didn't believe in this. For example, some teams would have a David Silva or a Cristiano Ronaldo who weren't required to run back and help regain possession. I stress they weren't cheating anyone, it was merely what we called it. We never had any of those under Moyes and everyone would have to charge round. But sometimes these players can be your match-winners.

Under Moyes, we all did an honest job, worked hard and won and lost as a team. When we played the likes of Man United, because they were so good at attacking, we found it difficult to get forward because we were back as an entire team. We would work so hard defensively, even our skilful wingers or strikers didn't have a burst of energy to get forward. We could move up the field slowly, via throw-ins, and then go from there but because we didn't have a 'cheat', we didn't have anyone we could kick a ball out to for relief. All our players were working hard to stop the opposition scoring…and the Everton crowd would never have it any other way. The better teams could have up to three 'cheats' in the team. As hard as we were working, they were saving up their energy to hurt us. We didn't have the same freshness to hurt them and I feel that's why we would tend to lose against the top teams, especially away from home.

As usually happens when I've had a long period out and come back for a big game like City, my body rebelled. I hurt my groin in training on Christmas Day and although the Boxing Day match against Birmingham was called off because the freezing weather burst a few pipes at Goodison, I missed our 1-1 draw with West Ham on December 28, and was a late sub in a New Year's Day defeat at Stoke. After a fantastic win against Spurs, in which Seamus Coleman got our winner, I was captain against Scunthorpe and I really enjoyed leading the lads in the FA Cup as we battered them, 5-1.

The following weekend we drew 2-2 with Liverpool in Kenny Dalglish's first game back at Anfield as their manager. We went a goal down but Sylvain scored just after half-time and I then set up Beckford to put us 2-1 in front. We should have been cruising, they weren't showing anything but we gave them a cheap penalty and Dirk Kuyt put it away. He loved scoring pens against us. It was so frustrating. Another opportunity missed.

After a 2-2 draw against bottom club West Ham, I picked up another niggle and was out for another month. Thankfully once we got to late February, I was fit for the rest of the season.

Sadly, at this point we lost Steven Pienaar, who joined Tottenham. We missed his creativity badly, and I'm sure Leighton

Baines felt his absence particularly as they had established such a fantastic understanding on our left side. As I've mentioned, in the previous summer the big-hitters were Mikel Arteta and Tim Cahill. The manager and chairman wanted to keep them so they were both given new, improved deals. Meanwhile, Stevie's deal was slowly ticking away and was up at the end of 2010/11. He'd seen Arteta and Cahill be given better deals and it may have been a case of 'what about me?'.

I don't know if the club was playing hardball but I think the message was 'we can't afford more because we've given them the budget'. Stevie may have felt it was unfair, so he held out. The club were hoping he'd come around but Stevie's very stubborn and decided to leave. He came back soon after and I think he ended up getting what he wanted anyway!

That January, Cahill was away with Australia, taking part in the Asian Cup, where he hurt his foot. He returned injured, missed a lot of matches and completely lost the form he had before Christmas. He didn't score a single goal for us in 2011. We didn't know it then but we had seen the best of Tim Cahill in an Everton shirt. On top of Tim's struggles, Arteta pulled his hamstring against Birmingham in early March and didn't play until the final few matches of the season. With Pienaar having left, the lack of depth in the squad was exposed.

One player who was in superb form early that year was Louis Saha, who scored eight goals in seven matches, including four in one game against Blackpool. Some strikers can blow hot and cold and Louis definitely fitted in that category.

I wanted to play every game. Louis wanted three or four strikers around the squad so that he only had to play once every three weeks. That way when he played, he was sharp and fresh.

We never had much to choose from up front so he didn't have the sharpness to play a whole season. Louis would have bouts where he'd come in and be unplayable – John Terry must have hated him because he was so often amazing against Chelsea – but he regularly broke down.

Louis scored our goal against Chelsea at Goodison in the fourth round of the FA Cup but by the time the replay was played three weeks later, he was injured. I came back for that game and what an afternoon it was.

We were after payback for the cup final defeat two years earlier. We took the game to them and should have won in 90 minutes. It went to extra-time and the gaffer took me off after 95 so I was watching from the bench when Frank Lampard scored. My heart sank. Step forward Leighton Baines. We had half a chance with a free-kick on the edge of the box in the very last minute. I fancied Bainesy to score and he didn't disappoint. Petr Cech didn't move.

There's nobody better in those situations than Bainesy because he is so accurate and so dependable. He then took our first pen in the shoot-out…and missed!

I've been involved in a few shoot-outs where we've missed with our first attempt and gone on to win. Tim Howard was making the goal tiny and he saved Nicolas Anelka's effort while Ashley Cole missed. Chris Woods was our goalkeeper coach and one of the IT guys gave him so much information on where the Chelsea players had placed their previous pens. Ultimately, even with all this data, a keeper still has to pick a side of the goal. Tim was picking the right side nine times out of 10 at this point.

Cole missed his pen after Johnny Heitinga decided to stick his chest out and barge into him as they passed each other after our Dutchman had scored. It didn't surprise any of us. That was Johnny's game, even in training. You'd be talking to him one minute, the game would start and he'd stand on the back of your Achilles. It was his way of beating you.

I was confident when Nev stepped up. I knew where he was going to put it. Again, that was one of those moments. You charge down to celebrate in front of our fans. Nev got there first, of course, and just spread his arms out in front of them. He got some stick for that later! We need to beat them properly at Stamford Bridge but that was the next best thing. We had knocked them out of the FA Cup.

To go from such a high to losing at home to Reading in the next round was such an anti-climax. Jermaine Beckford was meant to start that match but arrived late after getting stuck in traffic on the M62. He came in as we were going out to warm up and received loads of grief off the players before he even met the manager in the dressing room. I can't imagine what was said in there. I'm sure he set off at the usual time...or at least I hope he did. An accident on the motorway – what can you do? He ended up on the bench and was brought on for Bily at half-time when we were 1-0 down.

Becks was a really good goalscorer. He wasn't the greatest player technically but he was a threat. I've played that number 10 position quite often and he was one of my favourite people to play alongside up front, and we were paired together in the latter part of that season as Saha was ruled out for the rest of the campaign.

He complemented me better than most. All he wanted to do

was run in behind. He wanted the ball over the top every single time. He didn't want the ball to feet – that was more difficult for him.

With him running ahead, that gave me loads of space in the hole to collect the ball and turn because the centre-halves would have to run after him. Becks would scare people with his pace. Also, he wasn't keen on going for headers, while I don't mind doing that, despite my size. Any high ball, I would go for the header and he would go for the flick-on. It worked perfectly. I've played up front with other players who want to go for the header but I'm not the best at getting in behind people. I want to drop in the holes, turn and get on the ball. I've played up front with better players than Becks but I don't know if I've played with one more suited to me. We were opposites. I'm not that quick, he was rapid. I like to get on the ball, he likes to run in behind. It was one of my favourite periods playing-wise. We worked together so well.

When Becks scored two against Sunderland the weekend before we lost to Reading, I wasn't sure I was fit to play. I went out and tried and had a great game, set the first up after eight minutes and was involved in the second as well. That's often happened with me. Concentrating on getting out there takes all the pressure of the game away. You can overthink a game, have too many thoughts in your head and get too wound up.

We completed the double over Man City in early May and I was seeing double as Vincent Kompany all but knocked me out when I scored the winner. I had to twist my head to get power on a header from a corner and in the split-second before I was hit, I knew it was in. In a blink of an eye, I was whacked. I heard the cheer as I landed on the floor. People were jumping on me but I was dizzy and groggy and wanted them off me. It was like 10 headaches all on top of each other. I looked like the Elephant Man – my jaw to the top of my head was badly swollen. I was a bit dizzy for a while after that but it was worth the pain as it was another defeat of Man City and Mancini. Moyesy was absolutely buzzing.

In the final game of the season against Chelsea, Becks scored an absolute worldy. He got the ball on the edge of our box and just kept on going. I'd like to say he was in control of it all the way but I don't think he was. However, that doesn't matter. It was the only goal of the game.

He left at the start of the following season. At the time we didn't really have any strikers. Yak had gone, which left us with just Louis and Victor Anichebe, who would blow hot and cold. It was a massive surprise that we let him go considering we were short on forwards, but Moyesy presumably thought £4m was a good fee for a player he brought in on a free.

We ended up finishing seventh, a place higher than the year before, but with 54 points, seven fewer than 12 months earlier. We had our usual poor start, Pienaar and the Yak left, while Arteta, Saha, Cahill and myself missed a lot of games. We actually did well to get ourselves back up the table and finish the season strongly, but it wasn't the most memorable season.

One of the undoubted positives was the performances of Seamus Coleman, who was playing right midfield at this point and, at times, competing against me. What a deal, £60,000 from Sligo Rovers in the Irish League. Unbelievable scouting. After he first broke into our team in late 2009, he went on loan to Blackpool and had his first full season for us in 2010/11. His attacking prowess, running with the ball and taking people on, was unquestionable but the gaffer didn't trust him enough defensively at this point. Seamus would probably admit he wasn't quite there.

He wasn't comfortable as a right midfielder, even though he could dribble, cross and score. He was always a right-back. He worked and worked and over the next 12 months he improved so much. Now he's one of the best right-backs in Europe. The improvements he's made defensively have been so impressive. It was a big step from the Irish League to the Premier League. He had to learn and he did so in style.

Under Moyes, he would charge forward but he always knew that chasing back was the most important thing. Because of what he already had in his game, Moyes was the perfect teacher for Seamus. He taught him the defensive skills and importance of responsibility. Now Roberto Martinez has got the finished product.

Another positive from 2010/11 was the arrival of Sylvain Distin. Moyes had to move quickly because Joleon had left us just before the end of the transfer window but he couldn't have brought in a better replacement. Big Sylv is a consummate professional who everyone looks up to. He's the foreign outfield player with the most Premier League appearances, and you can see why. He works so hard in training that you can't help but be inspired. He is a very big figure in the Everton dressing room and he's like the 'daddy' for any new foreign player.

While Seamus and Sylvain were on upward curves in 2011, Everton, as a team, were not. It was a period of transition and as the year wore on, David Moyes lost his mojo for a period as our best player left and wasn't adequately replaced. We were approaching the end of an era.

15

Leon The Lion

For nearly 10 years, David Moyes had been the boss at our club and his drive had lifted the club out of the mediocrity that had been the norm for so long before him. He emanated fire but, in my opinion, for a few months in 2011, that fire wasn't raging as strongly as it had done before.

Moyes spent a number of years building the team up but we hadn't really strengthened in the summer of 2010 as Jermaine Beckford came in with reserve keeper Jan Mucha, Joao Silva and Magaye Gueye. Beckford only stayed for a year while the others were peripheral players.

Twelve months on and we were actually weakened as Beckford and Yakubu left plus, more significantly, Mikel Arteta, a real fans' favourite. After 2010, Moyesy must have been thinking he'd be able to strengthen the following year. It came and what happened, Arteta went to Arsenal on deadline day and we brought in Royston Drenthe and Denis Stracqualursi.

I wouldn't say Moyes lost his drive, but that special energy he had about him, the determination that he portrayed, went missing for a few months. His shoulders seemed to drop. On the training ground he'd still be as angry as ever but I could see it in his interviews. He seemed deflated.

His downbeat mood was demonstrated most clearly when he talked about "taking a knife to a gunfight" before a league game at Manchester City. That wasn't the attitude we had come to expect before City matches. I suppose he felt like he had built a reputation for himself and the club, but his best player (Arteta) had left and he was still expected to get the same results. I could understand his frustration.

When Moyes was fired up, you couldn't help notice it, pick up on it and be influenced by it. At this point he probably lost the attitude of, 'I don't care who these are. We're going to win today'. It was more, 'I hope we win today, we're going to try our best'. Deep down, he wasn't his usual self at that point, although that would change after Christmas.

You could tell by his body language how he was feeling, whether he was uptight, relaxed or determined. The manager's mood might have affected the players. Players are clever and we pick up on everything. You shouldn't need the manager to motivate you but players can't help but pick up on it. We tried to make light of it but Moyesy did find it tough until January when he felt he was supported in the transfer market.

In the past, especially at home, we'd always give the so-called top four teams a game and win one or two of them. Until

Christmas that season we lost every time we played a top team, home and away. That was unlike us under Moyes' tenure.

The start to our season was delayed by riots in Tottenham, which forced the postponement of our opening-day game at White Hart Lane. As a result, we went two weeks from our last pre-season game to our first Premier League match and QPR benefitted from it as they sneaked a 1-0 win at Goodison. We still should have won. Tim Cahill missed two absolute sitters and they scored with their one shot. If we'd played the weekend before, I'm sure we would have beaten them comfortably.

After signing off with a last-minute penalty at Blackburn to win us the game, Arteta said goodbye. It was hard to take in. I was pleased for him but I was disappointed that a player of that quality was leaving us. I was hoping that we had a trick up our sleeves but it was so late on deadline day.

The club wasn't strengthening at the time. We were shipping players and not bringing enough quality in. The striker Denis Stracqualursi, who was such a nice guy, was signed. Honest as the day is long. He would chase a crisp packet for you. But he couldn't get you a goal on his own. He waited for a cross and even then he didn't attack them with much conviction.

As for Royston Drenthe, he was an enigma, a bit like Andy van der Meyde. One day he'd be in a Ferrari, the next day a Maserati. It was one flash car after another. He must have spent his money as soon as he got it. Roy wanted to play poker all the time on the bus and he tried to raise it for stupid amounts. He'd have nothing in his hand – a total bluffer. But he was a nice guy and always had a smile on his face.

One day he turned up with two Rolls-Royce Phantoms. About 16 people emerged from the two vehicles. It was his family who he'd decided to chauffeur around and bring into training. They stood on the side of the pitch and he took them to the canteen to eat their dinner. It was like a day out for them. This was training – it wasn't a family day out for us.

After one incident too many before the FA Cup semi-final later that season Moyes lost patience and told him he wasn't travelling. That was the end of Roy at Everton.

Another player new to our first team was the Greek striker Apostolos Vellios, who we'd signed in January. He scored in a 3-1 win over Wigan in September and barely did a thing after that. He was a massive believer in his own ability but he never cut it for me. Tolis thought he was Zlatan Ibrahimovic. He wore the same clothes, tried to walk like him and tried to do the same things in training. That was where the comparison ended.

James McFadden returned to us as a free agent in the autumn. Things didn't work as well for him this time but it was great to have my mate back. There wasn't much to be excited about on the pitch in this period.

We lost the Goodison derby after Martin Atkinson had sent off Jack Rodwell for a perfectly legitimate challenge on Luis Suarez. What a bad decision that was. It was the first time he'd 'reffed' us since the Man United 3-3 – there was worry from Moyes before the game, and he was proved right. Suarez screamed before Rodwell, who won the ball, even made contact with him. It's always going to be tough playing with 10 men in a derby for so long, and they picked us off with two late goals.

We were in the early stages of a bad run, losing eight of 11 league matches. It was important to stop the rot and I scored in consecutive games leading up to Christmas, a 1-1 draw with Norwich before getting the winner against Swansea – I was the big man arriving to meet Royston's corner. I had to go and celebrate with him. Usually everyone runs to celebrate with the goalscorer but he would celebrate all on his own. If he was involved in a goal, it was his!

I played in our first home match of 2012, against Bolton, despite my wife Jenny already being in a slow labour with our third child. I told her: "Hang fire, don't be having the baby yet. I've got a game tonight and I want to play." She was told to go home and advised that if we wanted to hurry the labour along, she should go for a long walk. I told her to get in bed and arranged for her mum to come round so she wouldn't have to move very much.

As it turns out, I would have been better off missing the match because I injured the cartilage in my knee and needed an operation. Jenny and I left hospital on the Saturday with our new daughter, Kendall; Jenny was recovering from a caesarean section and I was on crutches. I had an op in London two days later and that meant an unplanned period of paternity leave for me as I was out for nine weeks.

During my absence, Moyesy was busy in the transfer market, signing Nikica Jelavic from Rangers and Darron Gibson from Man United, while Steven Pienaar came back on loan from Spurs and Landon Donovan returned. It lifted the mood of the whole club, including the manager, and results immediately improved. We were suddenly revitalised.

Moyesy started clicking again, literally. If he was unhappy, he might say a gruff "morning" but he wouldn't really look at you as he scowled. If he was happy, he'd say: "Morning, ladies. How are we?" Then he'd start clicking his fingers. It was hilarious. Bainesy still does it now and again.

Moyesy had his mojo back and a win over league leaders Man City on January 31 only made him happier. We were 14th going into that game but started climbing the table from that point.

A key factor in our improvement, particularly from March, was the form of Jelavic. He picked up an injury straight away and didn't start his first game until Spurs in March, when I was just returning. I set him up for the winner with a cut-back and he finished it brilliantly.

That became Jela's trademark. A first-time finish from a cut-back. Lots of strikers score their goals in the six-yard box so most defenders look after that area. Jela came from Scotland and hadn't been watched every week so, when he first came, most defenders protected that six-yard line. Jela always pulled back so he was available for the cut-back. His one-touch finishing was really good. But he started struggling from the middle of the following season because defenders had watched him and realised they didn't have to defend the six-yard line. They man-marked him in the box and they made it a lot more difficult for him.

As we found form, we reached the quarter-finals of the FA Cup and a home draw against Sunderland. Four days before the tie, we had the Anfield derby and Moyes made six changes from the Spurs game with the cup tie in mind. We all wanted to beat Sunderland but this wasn't Fulham at home or West Brom away. This was Liverpool in the derby. There were not many times I disagreed with Moyes' decisions because he was a fantastic manager for us. But to make that many changes for a derby at Anfield was wrong in my opinion.

That was unlike him because, under Moyes, there was no

proper squad rotation. You were either in the team or out of it. Roberto Martinez rotates the squad and will pick horses for courses. If he's got a game that is suited for a particular player, he will make a change, even if the other player scored a hat-trick the previous week. With Moyes, if you were in form, you were in the team. Steven Gerrard scored a hat-trick, we lost 3-0 and another Anfield derby had passed us by.

We didn't even manage to beat Sunderland and had to go to their place for a replay. At Goodison, Phil Bardsley scored after 12 minutes and it was a bit like the Wigan quarter-final 12 months later. The tension round the place was incredible and that seeped onto the pitch. You try not to get influenced by it, but you feel it. We felt the panic from the crowd when they scored first but did well to equalise through Tim Cahill.

We made it difficult for ourselves by needing a replay but, at Sunderland, all the tension was on them. Their crowd were panicky and nervous. Now Moyes was emanating the fire on that occasion. He wanted it that night…and the local police force making us very late for the game served only to make him even more determined. Our coach driver had warned Moyes that we were leaving the team hotel for the game far too late but the police wouldn't hear of it. The coach driver's fears were correct. We left too late, the traffic was horrendous and we arrived half an hour before the kick-off. Tony Sage, kitman, and Darren Griffiths, Press Officer, had to hand the teamsheet in to the referee along with Lee Cattermole and Steve Walford as they were our only people at the stadium! This was an FA Cup quarter-final. Moyes was absolutely livid. He stormed off the coach, straight to the policeman who was outside the dressing room and shouted: "Get me your boss NOW."

He kept us all focussed though and, again, was on top form as he used what little time we had to prepare for the kick-off. He certainly let the police have it after the game. Somebody mentioned later that we were far from the first club to have it happen to them in that neck of the woods.

We kept hold of the ball, went in front through Jela and played really, really well. I hit a half-volley that skimmed the top of the bar. Now THAT would have been my best goal had that gone in! I wonder if people remember that. It would have been some strike. It didn't matter as a David Vaughan own goal ensured we were through to the semi-finals where Liverpool awaited.

Five days before the semi, we hammered Sunderland 4-0 at Goodison, with nearly identical curlers from Steven Pienaar and myself. We were all set up for Wembley.

Sadly, the semi-final would be another crushing disappointment. We were in control in the first half and took advantage of a mistake from Jamie Carragher to go 1-0 up through Jela. We were the best team in the first half and at half-time the manager said: "Keep doing what you're doing." They came at us early in the second half, Andy Carroll missed a chance but we had weathered the storm. Then Sylvain made a bad back-pass that allowed Luis Suarez to equalise and from that moment we were under so much pressure. We didn't keep the ball well enough. Seamus came on and made a rash decision, getting too close to Gerrard and giving a free-kick away. Gerrard put it in the right area and Carroll wasn't going to miss.

As a team, we were poor in the second half. Tim Cahill was one of those who didn't play well and he was very much a big-game player. Every time the ball came to him, he was trying special passes when we were desperate to keep it. Bainesy had played 99 games on the run and the gaffer had left him out of the Sunderland league game. He then pulled his hamstring against Liverpool. Some people just need to keep playing.

It was tough for us that Steven Pienaar was cup-tied. I think we'd have won if he was available. Magaye Gueye started and that was great for him but it showed the limitations in our squad at that time. The whole day was massive a disappointment. Our families had come down on the train and it was a sad ride home, although my Liverpool-supporting brother-in-law was grinning from ear to ear. The Osmans and Hibberts commandeered a carriage and had a bit of a sing-song to try and cheer us up, but it was tough.

A week later – forget Sergio Aguero's goal – we basically won Man City the league, scoring two late goals to draw 4-4 at Old Trafford. Patrice Evra headed my temple early in the second half and I had to go off and lie down in a darkened dressing room while it was all happening.

The goals were flying in for us in our final two home games. We destroyed Fulham 4-0 as Cahill scored his last goal for us, before we did a job on Newcastle. This was the season Alan Pardew turned up, telling everyone that Newcastle were a class above us. That really riled Moyes and got his back up. It was up there with Man City and Mancini. "We've been consistent over so many years. They've had one good season. You get out there and batter them today and show them."

They had Demba Ba, Papa Cisse, Hatem Ben Arfa and Yohan Cabaye, and we absolutely steamrollered them. We are a better team than Newcastle and they have struggled since. They've had such turnaround of players in that time.

Stability has been the key word for Everton, of managers,

staff and players. If you are constantly changing players, there is always a bedding-in period.

Look at the team that played against Newcastle: Tim Howard was finishing his sixth year, Hibbo his 12th, Heitinga his third, Distin his third, Jags his fifth, Baines his fifth, Phil Neville his seventh and Felli his fourth. Myself and Cahill had done eight years; Pienaar had managed four years with a year at Spurs while Gibson and Jela were new. Within 11 players, we had a great deal of experience.

Two-and-a-half years later, Howard, Hibbert, Distin, Jags, Baines, Gibson, Osman and Pienaar are all still here. That's the difference. That's the foundation.

Against Newcastle, Cahill was sent off after the final whistle following an altercation with Cabaye. It was a neat way to finish his Everton career – sent off for his first goal and sent off for his last appearance.

Tim was complaining about his body at the time and saying it was getting tougher for him. He was all action and he was getting older. The New York Red Bulls made him an offer to go out there and promote Tim Cahill the brand, and he couldn't really turn it down.

It was sad to see him go. Tim Cahill, Mr Everton, a fans' favourite. He was a big part of my time at the club but the club moves on. At the time he wasn't starting because Felli had taken over that role off the striker and Tim wasn't a back-up player, that's for sure.

It made me realise the shortness of careers. That's why when it came to my testimonial, it made me appreciate that I've done so many years in the first team. People like Arteta and Cahill, who stayed for a long time and became crowd favourites, didn't manage one. Neither did Duncan Ferguson. It made me see my testimonial as an achievement.

Jack Rodwell also left, joining Man City for £12m. Jack had shown early promise and hadn't got anywhere near fulfilling it. He hasn't really done much since. He's gone to Sunderland now and I wish him so much luck. He's got potential but some players are all potential. I hope he's not one of those because he's a great lad.

We had finished seventh again in 2011/12, finishing above Liverpool for only the second time since 1987. The new season, like the previous one, began with a riot. This one was on the pitch rather than the streets of Tottenham, as our fans poured on to celebrate Hibbo's goal in his testimonial. It was a great occasion with his daughter coming on the pitch with him before the kick-off and Hibbo receiving a presentation from our chairman, Bill Kenwright. It meant a lot to be part of his big night.

When the 2012-2013 season began, we finally broke our habit of slow starts. Starting off with a home game against Manchester United did us no harm. We thought it might be a good thing to play such strong opponents. As it was a Monday night match, we had to wait the whole weekend before we got our chance. When it arrived, we battered them. Felli scored and we ran all over them in all departments. It confirmed that the mojo was back, for us and Moyes.

The manager would go through periods of trusting me in certain positions. Against United, I played wide right with Nev and Gibbo in the middle. Hibbo was injured before our next match at Aston Villa game so Nev went to right-back and I came into the middle with Gibbo. Steven Naismith, who had just joined us, went out on the right with Pienaar on the left.

With no disrespect to Nev, it was positive to have four footballers across the park. That's what the top teams do. Look at Real Madrid, they have Luka Modric in the holding role. Footballers will keep the ball.

We certainly did that at Villa. In the first half, we were hardly out of possession. Steven scored early and we could have managed six in the first half alone. It was one of the many times I've enjoyed going to Villa Park. There was only one team flattered by a 3-1 scoreline and it wasn't us.

After losing at West Brom, where we were thrown off course by an injury to Gibbo, we somehow failed to beat Newcastle in another Monday night match and then went to Swansea and won 3-0 before blowing the League Cup again, losing at Leeds. It happened to us too many times under Moyes. Everyone was bubbly when we got to Elland Road; me and Bainesy walked into the dressing room and Moyesy said: "Ossie, Bainesy, eff off. You're not needed tonight." We couldn't understand why he brought us. A few fringe players came in, like Bryan Oviedo and Francisco Junior (who no-one had heard of before and no-one has heard of since). Cisco needed to be alongside an experienced lad and talker in central midfielder. But Felli is not a talker. He'd always say: "Ossie, talk to me." I'm a talker on the pitch and will give out information and instructions. Felli doesn't open his mouth, he's not a leader. To have him and Cisco in the middle of the park was not a good combination, and it was proved on the night.

I was frustrated because I was fit and couldn't influence it. We gave them the opportunity to win. The managers who are in European competition regularly will rotate their squad in games like that. But we only had that competition and the league on our agenda until Christmas. We had no Europe. Win the game. Players can handle a midweek game and a Saturday game. It gets tougher when it's midweek-Saturday-midweek-Saturday. In a one-off game, it's fine.

We responded with a 3-1 defeat of Southampton, in which I equalised but nearly missed it. A cross came in and stopped between the six-yard line and the penalty spot. I followed it in, saw the keeper diving and put it so far in the corner that it went in off the bar. It was a big relief as it would have been a dreadful miss. After a 2-2 draw against Wigan in which our future striker Arouna Kone destroyed Johnny Heitinga, it was derby time again.

In August, we had signed Kevin Mirallas. It took him a while to realise how physical our league is. He has so much skill but he was a bit flaky when he came in, easy to push off the ball. Against Leeds at the end of September, he was still a bit of a soft touch. Since then, he's toughened up, and Kev is one of the better players I've played with in my career. He has been a great signing for us.

By the time of the derby in late October, he was still learning but still really stood out for us. Like we had done all season, we dominated against Liverpool but they scored twice against the run of play. I thought Moyesy showed great resistance not to kick Luis Suarez when he dived in front of him to celebrate their first goal. I was worked up that day and gave it a big "come on" after my goal. It was a great feeling to score in the derby but we were still 2-1 down and had work to do. Naisy equalised and we could have scored two or three more before half-time.

Kev had destroyed Andre Wisdom in the first half but I felt he was a bit soft not to come back on for the second half that day. He did take a knock but no-one could believe he came off at half-time, given the way he had been playing. I'm pretty sure he trained a day or two later. I was disappointed in that.

Suarez should have been sent off for standing on Sylvain's ankle and the second half was more cat and mouse. They changed their system to three at the back. We still should have won but, thankfully, they had a Suarez goal disallowed at the end. I was right in the middle and my initial reaction was to just try to claim offside in desperate hope. I was amazed when the assistant raised his flag. That one worked out for us because Suarez was comfortably onside but then we had a Distin goal disallowed at Anfield later that season and there was nothing wrong with it.

The way we were playing was enjoyable; we were keeping the ball and creating chances. But we weren't killing games off and there's nothing more annoying than playing well but dropping points at the same time. At Fulham after the derby, Seamus made a bad pass late in the game and the next thing Steve Sidwell scored at the back post. It was like a defeat. At least after the game, Sascha Riether, their right-back, told me that we were by far the best side they had played up to that point.

A couple of days after that Fulham game, I got the biggest shock of my footballing life.

During the warm-up for training at Finch Farm, we were stretching when Jags asked me what I was going to do during the international break. I said that I was hoping that the lads left behind would get a few days off.

We trained as normal and when we'd finished, Moyesy called us all over into a big circle. Nobody had a clue what was going on – I actually thought to myself 'this is it, this is the message that we're getting some time off'. What he actually did say left me in a daze.

"I've got some good news boys," he said. "It's taken a long time but no-one deserves this more." Then he paused for effect and I still didn't twig was what coming. Moyesy broke into a huge grin, looked right at me and said: "Ossie's been called into the England squad!"

I was stunned. "What?" I blustered. "Is this a wind-up? Has Jags put him up to this?" But I knew that neither Jags nor Moyesy would do such a thing.

The lads all jumped on me and started cheering. Moyes then said we would finish the session with a bit of shooting, starting on the halfway line and running to the edge of the box. You had to score to go inside and he told me to go first. My head was all over the place. I wasn't thinking straight but I took the ball forward, whacked it and it went right in the top corner. What we call a 'postage stamp goal'. I walked off and all the staff were waiting for me. "Well in, lad. Made up for you. Don't be getting all big-time!" That sort of thing.

I went into the Finch Farm dressing room, checked my phone and sure enough I had an official message saying I had been called into the squad for the international matches against Sweden. It began to dawn on me that this was real. I told my wife first and she was made up. It had already been officially announced at this point so I had a few messages on my phone to say congratulations, although strangely enough my mum and dad still didn't know.

I can't really recall the phone conversation when I told them but Dad would have kept his composure and poured himself a celebratory beer. Mum would have just screamed the house down!

At our next game against Sunderland, it was mentioned as they read the teams out and the fans gave me a massive cheer. I was 31 at the time and these things don't tend to happen so late in your career. I admit that I did feel enormously proud. I've already spoken about the schoolboy internationals I had played in but this was the real deal. I just hoped with all my heart that I'd actually get to play.

The following day the England squad met at the Lowry Hotel in Manchester. Bainesy's brother dropped us off. I felt like a new boy on my first day at school but at least I could tag along with Bainesy. John Ruddy was there and Tom Huddlestone, who I knew from Derby. Quite a lot of the squad came later as Chelsea and Liverpool played each other on the Sunday.

On the Monday we trained at Man United's facility, Carrington. Roy Hodgson came up and said: "Congratulations, great to have you in the squad. I'm not guaranteeing that I'm going to play you but I've not brought you here just for the ride. I've not made my mind up yet but I'd expect you'll play at least some part of the game." I was even more excited then.

The Sweden game was in Gothenburg and my mum, dad and Carl travelled over with my eldest son, Cole, who was seven at the time and given permission from his school to attend. Cole was made up to be sharing a hotel room with his Uncle Carl.

I went into the dressing room and saw my shirt hanging up. 'Osman 8'. I was made up because that was my number for Elmers Green years ago. But it was a long sleeved jersey. At

Everton you have two or three shirts on separate hangers. As I looked around the dressing room, pretty much everyone else had long sleeves. I was a bit gutted but I wasn't going to complain to the kit man or manager. I'd just have to get on with it, though it felt uncomfortable.

After the warm up, the players all put a tracky top over our shirts, before the anthems. There was a team photo and we took off the tracky top. As I did so, I realised almost all the players were in short sleeves. Jags spotted me and said: "Ossie, long sleeves?"

"Yeah, it was the only one on the peg."

"You wally, only the top one is long sleeves. There are two underneath that are both short sleeves. You can take your pick."

It was too late to change then so I wore the long sleeves in the first half and swapped at half-time. I'd only worn a long-sleeved shirt once before for Everton, in a League Cup when I had a cut on my arm.

The national anthem was a special moment for me. I'd watched so many England games over the years and from a very early age, I had always imagined the national anthem to be a very emotional part of it all. I know my mum and dad shed the odd tear that night. Cole was buzzing too but for a different reason. They had a guy pitchside firing T-shirts into the crowd and, believe it or not, he caught one!

We lost the game 4-2 and Zlatan Ibrahimovic was obviously the big talking point, scoring all of Sweden's goals. His overhead kick from 40-yards is up there with the most stunning goals I have ever seen. When it went in I thought 'bloody hell, how's he done that?'.

I was nervous before the game but I was much worse before

the cup final in 2009. Sometimes it's hard to go out and actually enjoy playing matches when there is so much riding on them but I was thinking 'I'm playing for England here. I'm going to try and do it with a smile on my face'. I felt I played well and Roy told me I was a plus on the night. I was comfortable playing international football, pass and move. That's my game.

I gave Mum the short-sleeved shirt, kept the long sleeved one and got it signed by everyone who was involved.

I was in the next four squads. All the regulars came back and I didn't get to play against Brazil the following February. Then it was two qualifiers, Montenegro and San Marino.

The Montenegro game was an eye-opener, it was so hostile. Their fans were screaming at us and wanted our blood. They had guys with microphones at either end, with their back to the action, orchestrating all the sing-songs. It was 90 minutes of intense noise designed to intimidate you. It would be incredible to have that noise in England. We do sing but we want to watch the match. I'm not sure they go to watch the football in Montenegro…I think their role is to intimidate the opposition!

Roy put me on against San Marino and I was delighted. I wanted to score and felt if I did it might have kept me in for a few more squads. I was on for just over half an hour and had a shot that skimmed the post as we won 8-0.

For the friendly against the Republic of Ireland at the end of May, I received a phone call about 10 days before the season finished to see what condition I was in. Unfortunately, I'd hurt my knee in a tackle with Danny Rose against Sunderland a few weeks before. I struggled on and managed to play the next three Everton games but I was struggling and could barely move. I ended up missing the last game of the season. I was gutted because that effectively ruled me out of the England squad. I knew by not making myself available, I was going to struggle to get back in. Possession is nine-tenths of the law. But there was nothing I could do about it, I had to be honest with myself and with Roy.

I am ferociously proud to have two England caps but one of my regrets is that were both away from home. I would dearly have loved to have played for my country at Wembley.

My only other regret is that my debut in Sweden came during a month when I was attempting to grow a moustache for the Movember charity. I don't enjoy looking at the photographs of me in that game! Some people have faces that can comfortably carry off a 'tache. Clark Gable, Des Lynam and Sid from the Finch Farm training ground for example. But not me! Still, it was all for a good cause.

I was recently asked in an interview if I'd given up hope when it comes to England. Realistically, the chances of me getting back in the squad are minimal but not impossible. That's the attitude I had two years ago and I ended up getting two caps. I'd never rule myself out. Will I get any more caps? Probably not but I will never say never.

16

All Change

Back at Everton, the 2012/13 season continued and we were still dropping too many points. We drew against Newcastle, QPR, Fulham, Norwich and should have beaten Liverpool but only took a point. Losing against Reading in the way we did was unforgiveable.

At the end of November, Hibbo came back into the side. He tore his calf against Newcastle in September, which is a bad injury to get, and was out for two months.

As soon as he was fit, Seamus was injured against Norwich. Tony must have had two days training and the gaffer asked him: "What do you think?" Hibbo's exactly the same as me – his answer would have been "get me back in". A lot of people would say, "I haven't had enough football" because they only want to play when they're at their peak. They don't want to embarrass themselves or get injured again.

Hibbo played 90 minutes against Arsenal on the Wednesday. If he'd then had a week to settle his body down and go again, he would have been fine. But we played Man City three days later. He limped through the last 15 minutes of the City game, broke down after that and was pretty much out for the rest of the season. It shows that a lad's character can work against him. His calf completely went. It hadn't been strong enough to cope with two quick games against top opposition but Hibbo knew he was needed and wanted to play. He had such a tough 18 months after that, including the rest of that season and the first three-quarters of Roberto Martinez's first season. I feel really sorry for him.

As the New Year arrived, we had some arrivals and departures. One man to leave us was Victor Anichebe. His Everton career had some good moments but there should have been so many more.

At one time, Moyesy and Anichebe had a couple of arguments and the manager had had enough of him. In Washington one pre-season, the players spoke about how effective Victor could be and Phil Neville and Tim Cahill went to speak to Moyesy to implore him to keep Victor because he could be unplayable at times.

Unfortunately, it didn't happen enough. We would try to gee him up but there were too many times where a tough hairy-arsed centre-half would grunt down the back of his neck and Victor could be intimidated. Victor had all the attributes to be as good as Didier Drogba but Drogba had the drive and the heart. He couldn't play through an injury and that was one of the things that frustrated the manager about him. He wouldn't play unless his fitness was perfect. He had more potential than me to be a top player. I got to where I am through drive. He got to where he is without a massive amount of drive. He is a good player but he could have been right up there. He's still got time but he's 26 now.

While Victor departed, Thomas Hitzlsperger joined as a free agent until the end of the season. He wasn't kept on but Thomas was a really nice guy and a good footballer.

He retired later that year and in January 2014, he came out as being gay. Good on him, that he felt comfortable enough to do that. I think most of our players had an idea. He didn't act any differently, it was just intuition. No-one had an issue with it. No-one inquired about it, as far as I know. It was private.

The chances are there could well have been other gay players at Everton over the course of my career. Honestly, it wouldn't be an issue within the dressing room. It wouldn't alter how we act or behave.

However, I didn't blame Thomas at all for waiting until he retired before coming out. It would certainly be an issue on the terraces. No-one wants personal chants directed at you every time you play a game. That's not going to help your career. Unfortunately, that would be the likely scenario for a gay player open about his sexuality. For that reason alone, it doesn't surprise me that no active player in this country has come out.

I don't like personal chants about any player for any reason. Look at Steven Gerrard. You have to admire how he plays while highly personal chants and songs are directed at him. Our fans do it, as do Man City's and Man United's. Liverpool supporters used to sing a derogatory song about Joleon Lescott, relating to scars from a car accident when he was a child. It's incredible to go through that on the pitch. I was embarrassed that some of our fans sang that to him after he left. He had given his all for our club for three years. Nothing will ever alter my opinion that Evertonians are the greatest fans in football and maybe because they are so brilliant, it sticks out a bit more when they turn against a former player. It doesn't happen very often though, I must stress – 99 per cent of the time our fans give every ex-player a great reception when they play against Everton.

As well as abuse from fans, a gay player could experience opposition players trying to put them off their game with a snide comment here and there. We've seen that racism still occurs on the pitch. For the sake of it, you might as well just avoid it, so I can understand why no-one has come out. But you can guarantee there are quite a lot of gay footballers. It would presumably only become less of an issue if quite a few of them were 'out'.

My strike at home to Manchester City that season was named Everton's Goal of the Month. Despite that, when it came to the end-of-season do, Kev Mirallas' goal against Stoke two weeks later somehow won Goal of the Season. They were both in March! Work that one out...

I scored with a sweet left-footer. I was quite deep on the halfway line because a few people had gone forward and I was covering. As Seamus went up, someone came back so I drifted forward. I called for the ball off Seamus. It was in the middle of my feet, it sat up, I took aim and it flew in the top corner. Joe Hart didn't even move, which made me doubt whether it was actually a goal. Then I started celebrating. In commentary, Gary Neville said I mis-hit it – "he's taken a big chunk of the ground". He apologised to me when I met up on England duty and congratulated me on such a fine goal!

Despite Pienaar being sent off, Jan Mucha had a fantastic game in goal, charging out and scaring the life out of City's players, and Jela sealed it at the end. Goodison was rocking.

As the season carried on, David Moyes' contract was running down. The talk was that he could well be off at the end of it. Other people were saying he was doing it to try to coax some transfer funds.

Eventually, with just two games remaining in the season, it was announced that he had been offered the Man United job, replacing the retiring Sir Alex Ferguson. After it was confirmed, Moyes called six of the senior players to meet him in the Thistle Hotel in Haydock – myself, Nev, Jags, Hibbo, Bainesy and Tim Howard.

We all congratulated him and told him he had earned a move like that for all his effort and what he'd done for the club. He sat us down and told us it wasn't planned but that he'd received a phone call from Sir Alex, who asked to meet him and then told him he wanted him to be the next manager of Man United. Moyesy looked us straight in the eyes and told us he hadn't expected the offer.

I absolutely believe what he told us. For me, he ran his contract down so it was easier to get offers like that but I genuinely don't believe he had United on his mind.

We had a cup of tea together and chatted about stuff as a group. We wished him luck, he wished us luck, and he spoke to the rest of the players the following day and said: "Let's finish the season in a positive way."

I was desperate to play in our final home game against West

Ham, even though I wasn't really fully fit, because we were saying goodbye to Moyesy.

He was given a fantastic send-off by our fans and it was really fitting. But what I found strange was what happened at the end. Phil Neville, a great servant and club captain, was retiring so he came on the pitch through a guard of honour. Brilliant and quite right too.

Next, our manager who has been there for 11 years. That should have been it but who comes on the pitch last? Tim Cahill! He'd come to watch the game and should have been out first, but he was last as though he was the big draw for the day. I just couldn't believe it. It was incredible. I know Tim hadn't actually asked for it to be done that way but if it was me I wouldn't have had the front to impose on such a special occasion. Tim should have declined the offer in my opinion. He'd been unbelievable for Everton, one of the best signings ever, but that was Nev and Moyesy's moment and not his.

We all went for a meal that night and when, during the evening, Tim went for a toilet break, we all stood up and clapped him back in. He didn't like it!

It's disappointing how sour it has since turned between the fans and Moyes after he bought Fellaini and tried to get Leighton Baines. He should be welcomed back to Goodison whenever he wants to come but it's not the case at the moment and that's really upsetting. I'm disappointed in it all.

Far too much was made of what happened with Fellaini and Baines. Moyes was doing what we had employed him to do for all those years – strengthen his squad in whatever way he saw fit. It shouldn't be a surprise.

Look at Roberto Martinez: He wins the FA Cup at Wigan,

gets his move to Everton and goes back to sign four players because he knows them and trusts them. It was no surprise that Davie Moyes tried to sign players from Everton. Okay, things got a bit ugly in the way it happened and the fees that were mentioned but I think he was let down by the people at United in the way it was handled.

I think, as fans, we should find it easy to forgive him. He loves the club, he really does. He's an Evertonian. He left on good terms and he should be able to come back on good terms.

After getting past Oldham in a fifth-round replay, we had set up an FA Cup quarter-final at home to Wigan during that season. It was another chance to take a step nearer getting a trophy but, ironically, all it did was give us a glimpse into the future after Moyes.

The game turned into a massive disappointment for us all. In less than four minutes, we managed to concede three goals to Maynor Figueroa, Callum McManaman and Jordi Gomez. It was a horrendous experience.

Wigan boss Roberto Martinez out-foxed us, playing 3-4-3. That should have given us a chance going forward but we weren't clever enough to figure out a method to cope with it. We're used to 4-4-2, 4-5-1 or 3-5-2, but a 3-4-3 did for us. That was one of the main reasons we lost.

It didn't allow Seamus or Bainesy to get forward as one of their front three was on a full-back. They had one centre-forward in between our centre-halves, four across our midfield marking our four and three at the back marking our two.

There were spaces in the channels but they defended man-for-man rather than zonally.

That contributed significantly to us not playing well.

The first goal was a header from a corner. These things happen. But to concede straight afterwards when Nev played it straight to McManaman was such a shock. We then pushed immediately and conceded on the counter-attack, which you should never do in the first half.

Because there is so much of the game left, you don't have to go all-out. We were getting booed after 35 minutes. It wasn't easy to be out there on the pitch at that point and there was no coming back for us. The fans were angry and Felli let himself down that day with his reaction. He was spitting his dummy out, the fans got on his case and he was the type of character to say "do one then". It was just a horrible day.

I felt sick with regret. I was 31 and felt this was the opportunity. It slipped through our fingers. Individual errors cost us against Liverpool and Wigan in consecutive seasons. Everyone makes errors in football. It's how quickly you react to them and how few you make that's important.

I spoke to players after the game and asked what they remembered from the gaffer's pre-match speech. Everyone recalled the same message: "This is our day so don't choke. Whatever you do, don't choke. Listen, don't choke." Because he was saying it, it felt like it was ours to lose rather than ours to win. City were the only other top team left in the cup and we had a good record against them. They wouldn't have worried us.

As we walked off, Roberto Martinez waited and shook everyone's hand. I said: "Well done, Roberto. Good luck. I hope you win it."

A bit later, I had a conversation with Bainesy in the showers after the Wigan cup tie in which he said: "Do you know what, I wouldn't mind if Martinez was our next manager." I responded: "He looks alright, like. He out-foxed us today and he's got a bit of class about him." Bainesy agreed and that was the last we spoke about it.

Little did we know it wouldn't be too long before I'd be seeing him again...

17

Moyes

David Moyes has been a big part of my life and career and is a man for whom I have a lot of admiration and respect.

I've often pondered how my career might have turned out if we had had three or four different managers since 2002. Would I have stayed at Everton for this long? I'm not sure I would. A new manager brings in new players, systems and tactics. It's challenging to keep on proving yourself.

Ultimately, my testimonial is down to David Moyes keeping me in the team for so long. I had to earn my place though. Moyes wouldn't have selected me if he didn't think I could do a job for the team.

There is no sentiment at this level of football, especially with David Moyes, and that's the only way it can be.

When Walter Smith and Archie Knox were in charge, I felt I was good enough and ready for the first team. But, in hindsight, I probably wasn't. Mostly because I wasn't in complete control of my knee.

Once Moyes came in, I felt I was playing well enough. I felt ready. During 2003/04, I couldn't understand why I wasn't being considered. I kept thinking 'maybe next week, maybe next week'. Kevin Kilbane came to the club in August 2003 and told me later that he couldn't understand why I wasn't in the team.

From the point I returned from Carlisle at the start of 2003 until my first start in May 2004, I felt that my dreams, my goals, my aims were so close. I could see them through a window. It was right there. But I couldn't quite reach it and wasn't given the opportunity to grab it. It was agonising and frustrating.

Senior players would come to play with us in the ressies and might have a nightmare. I'd think 'I can do a better job than them' but they were constantly in the first team. I was on the cusp but I wasn't being given the chance by Moyes.

I'd watched people like Franny Jeffers come in and make his debut, become a regular and get a move to Arsenal. Hibbo was in the first team. Nick Chadwick went ahead of me, as did Jamie Milligan, Kev McLeod, Phil Jevons, Danny Cadamarteri and Richard Dunne. All these people I'd played with.

I kept my head down and tried the best I could in the reserve games but that was as testing a period for me as the time I had out with injury. It was as if it didn't matter what I did. It was a difficult period to make sure I kept my standards up.

Our reserve coach, Andy 'Taff' Holden, was good for me. I needed someone like Taff to be on my case if my standards weren't up to scratch. I'm thankful that he was like a sergeant major with me.

Taff had been a professional player himself with a reputation as being a really tough centre-half. He got picked for Wales very soon after joining Chester City from non-league football which shows you what sort of a character he was. Where the Welsh FA found a cap to fit him though is another matter!

My starting period with Moyes was a frustrating one. Obviously we had the conversation about my contract, where the wage was reduced, and the time he remarked the club could get good money for me, but from that moment on, barring a few bumps in the road, we had a really good relationship. There were times he frustrated me but I am sure there were also times when I did his head in.

I'm glad he stayed so long. I played in more games for him than any other player but I never felt my place was guaranteed. There were certainly times when he would leave me out. Me and Hibbo would dread what we called his 'curly finger' on a Friday. This was the day he usually named the team. On Fridays he would let us warm ourselves up so me and Hibbo would do a lap or two together.

If we saw Moyes walking over to us, we knew that meant the curly finger. That was him coming to tell you that you weren't going to be in the team when he announced it shortly afterwards. A couple of times he came towards us and we ran off. But ultimately there was no escape. If one us was called over, when we rejoined the other for stretching it would be "curly finger?" "Yeah, I'm out."

I didn't always have to wait until Friday to find out if I was playing, as I would get an idea from Jimmy Lumsden on a

Thursday. I'm pretty sure Moyes would usually have chosen his team by then and, as a first-team coach, Jimmy obviously knew it.

It was probably because we were close but Jimmy couldn't look you in the eye if he knew you weren't playing. He'd avoid you, treat you differently, or give you short answers when he was usually dead friendly. If Jimmy wasn't talking to you, it wasn't a good sign. It made him uncomfortable if he knew you were going to be disappointed. At the time it used to wind me up. "He's not looking at me; he's not speaking to me. That must mean I'm not playing."

A couple times I went up to him and said. "Jimmy, what the bleeding hell's happening here? I can't believe I'm not involved. It's freezing in that stand – at least tell me to dress appropriately so I can bring my big coat." After that I'd occasionally receive a warning from Jimmy. "You might need your big coat this weekend, Ossie."

Moyes wasn't at his best whenever he'd decided to leave you out of his team. He thought it would be hypocritical to be friendly so he'd avoid you. He was all about those in the team and he cared not a jot for those left out.

That's why he sometimes operated better with a small squad. Some of Moyes' best results were when he literally had 11 or 12 players to choose from. The team picked itself and he would do his best to get all the tactical information across, wind you up and send you out.

So often that scenario led to a great result.

One of Moyes' main strengths was how meticulous he was. The management staff would study for hours in the coaching room, assessing the strengths and weaknesses of opponents.

Moyesy was also brilliant at getting you up for a game. He could get you going like an energiser bunny. He could basically turn the screw, send you out and we'd all be shouting "come on!" in the tunnel. He was really good at motivating you, making each game important and squeezing every ounce out of players. Thinking back to the 1-0 win over Man United in 2005 and the night Louis scored two against Chelsea in 2011, he really fired us up beforehand.

After the game, if we'd done well, however, he wasn't so forthcoming with praise. Moyes preferred to offer credit to the team rather that the individual.

That's something in which Moyes and Martinez are different. Martinez bigs you up. All the clamour surrounding Ross Barkley, Martinez is happy to be part of and shower him with praise. Moyes would say: "He's done well in this game but he's got a lot to learn. He did that well but what about this thing that he did wrong?"

It's two completely different styles of man-management. There are benefits to both but you have to know which players to do which with. The Martinez way, you're going to make a player love you and try harder for you. He will be extra confident but there is a chance he will become a diva and won't try as hard.

I would bet Moyes felt that if he bigged up a player, they would become soft. It was always about 'showing' people. That was the way he thought. If people put Moyes or the club down, he would say 'I'll show' you. Martinez is more, 'I'm comfy; I know how confident and comfortable I am in myself'.

For example, after one game at Goodison where I had played really well, I was in the showers – I think Bainesy was there too

– when Moyes came in. I'd scored and set one up. If that was Martinez, he would have come in and said: "Ossie, fantastic today. You should go home tonight, get your feet up and enjoy the feeling of what you've accomplished today."

Moyes actually came in and said: "You did alright there, Os. What about the one you missed? What were you thinking? Talk me through that one." It was a case of 'wow, I thought I'd played well there'.

It was his way of making sure you tried just as hard in the next game. Maybe it's because I played under him so long but that's how I am with my kids now. I don't want them to get carried away with any success or achievement in anything they do.

Players do need to self-motivate. Ultimately, it's the players who go out on the pitch but you can't deny what Davie Moyes brought to a team.

He always got an extra five per cent out of us. It was rare for a Moyes team to lose a game in the last five minutes because we had the drive to keep on going. For the most part, we'd either see a game out or nick a goal in the closing minutes under him. You would be scared of coming in if your game dipped towards the end.

Even if you had nothing left, you had to find a way to keep on going because you knew he'd go mad at you. He wasn't shy of telling you what he thought if he believed you weren't putting in a shift for him.

I remember there was some aggro in our dressing room after a dour 0-0 draw at Southampton when Moyes and Fellaini had words. Moyes accused him of not running around enough and Felli was out of his seat. "Coach, I give my maximum! I already give my maximum! Don't shout at me – I give my maximum, coach! I do." It was proper screaming, back and forth, with neither of them conceding an inch.

If we lost a match, Moyes would dwell on it and struggle to get over it. If we played on a Saturday he would still be angry on the Monday and Tuesday. And he couldn't be a hypocrite to himself so if he was feeling like that, he couldn't put on a happy face. It wouldn't be out of his system until the Thursday when he'd be clicking again. Each result meant a lot to him. If it was a Monday or a Tuesday game that we'd lost, sometimes you'd have to pick your moments to approach him for the entire rest of the week.

In terms of his tactical approach, it was a case of making sure we were secure first and foremost and going from there. He'd encourage passing but Moyes was a defender and he was de-fence-conscious. His way was always – and it served him well – everybody has a job, everybody does their job. If I let Ashley Cole go, for example, and he created something, I'd be blamed. You had to stay with your man.

It's correct, I suppose, but Martinez has come in now and he'll say: "Our right-winger is going to stay up front. I don't want him to come back at all." His view is that if the opposi-tion's left-back wants to go forward, we'll shuffle a man across and somehow cope with that. Then, as soon as we get the ball, we'll play it to our right-winger because their left-back is out of position. Suddenly we're attacking. Under Moyes, everyone came back and did their job. That left-back wouldn't have a chance to score but we wouldn't be able to break as quickly. The Martinez way is a quicker way of counter-attacking.

If we leave a man forward, are they going to let their left-back go up? With Leighton Baines, he has a decision to make: 'Do I go and attack, or do I stay on my man?' If you see yourself as a defender first and foremost and stay back, that takes away so much from Bainesy. You want him to do both.

I've heard fans moan for years: "Why don't we keep anyone forward at corners?" If you do bring everyone back, you're probably more effective at defending that corner, but it's going to take you three clearances to fully get out. If you have one or two men waiting up front, there is more chance the opposition will score but there is also more chance that you'll get out with the first clearance.

Management is like chess, even though the pieces perform themselves. They're not bits of wood – they've got their own minds, their own bodies and their own abilities. But you can position them where you want and hope the strategy works out. You try to out-fox and out-manoeuvre the opposition manager. Do you do that by leaving a piece in a certain place to affect what the opposition is going to do? Or do you keep pieces in station?

Under Moyes, there wasn't as much transition. We would defend as a team and we attacked as a team and it would take the opposition three or four clearances to turn us away. Under Martinez, it's a lot different – we will attack them and they will attack us. That's why it seems so much more exciting now. It's more to end-to-end because we're leaving three players up front who aren't helping us defend. There are more gaps.

Another difference between the managers is their approach to set-pieces. With Moyes, we could spend an hour and a half on Fridays going through routines because he was so meticulous in that aspect. If I was a manager, I'd probably do the same because fine lines can determine games. He hated losing goals at set-pieces because it was something he could influence.

Martinez doesn't really do that. It's rare for us to work on set-pieces. You're given your roles, you're supposed to understand them and if you don't, find out, think for yourself. That was a big changeover for us.

We questioned why we weren't working on set-pieces and Graeme Jones, the assistant manager, said: "How many do you have to defend in a game? Three? So why would we spend two hours standing around to defend three set-pieces when we could work on moving the ball?" There is logic to both view-points and I can see the positives and negatives in each of them.

I believe your style and personality as a player will translate to your management. Davie Moyes was a centre-half and I'm pretty sure as a player he would have been yelling "come on", clapping his hands and getting psyched up. As a centre-half, he needed to be right on his toes to win headers and tackles. I imagine he would be hyped up for games. That's how he was as a manager. He had that fire in his eyes. No matter who you were playing, you'd get sucked into it. That could help set a real tempo.

When he played, I suspect Roberto Martinez was the opposite. He would be trying to stay as relaxed as possible, slow things down, get on the ball and enjoy it. His team-talks are like that. "Relax, enjoy yourselves, come on, we can win this." It's not eyeballs out.

I'm quite happy with both approaches. If it's a game like the derby, I'll be shouting and psyched up. Against a lot of teams I try to stay as relaxed as possible. It will be interesting to see what I'm like if I become a manager.

Moyes and Martinez have different approaches to training too. Under Moyes, the usual schedule was training Monday, Tuesday; off Wednesday and then in again on Thursday and Friday. On Monday, Tuesday and Thursday, every session was hard and lasted a long time. Friday was more low-key in comparison but a Friday under Davie Moyes can be like a Tuesday under Roberto Martinez, which is the hard day.

It was a lot tougher physically under Moyes. You would come off exhausted. Moyes would set the training tempo to suit the strongest. He needed to know that even the strongest players were feeling the pace. That was all well and good but it left the not-so-strong feeling absolutely shattered. Martinez sets the training pace a bit lower.

He prefers to work at a high intensity for short periods. We only work in the red for a certain amount of time. It's aimed at hitting certain targets but it's not a slog. Moyes would work us hard and sometimes the sessions seemed to go on and on.

I think that's why he would reward us from time to time with a trip abroad during the season to regenerate. When we went away, to Spain or even the USA, we'd do a little bit of training but it was more about recharging the batteries. We'd be allowed a night out and an afternoon to go sight-seeing. Our minds would be fresh. When we returned home, the attitude would be, 'right, brilliant. Now back to work'. We would tend to play well after his trips. Getting the lads away can be beneficial.

Martinez took us Tenerife last year. We had one team meal but there was no time to ourselves. We had been looking forward to our break but it was like a mini pre-season, the opposite of what we were used to. It worked though as we finished fifth, so there are positives in all things.

Moyes' trips provided plenty of laughs over the years. In February 2007, we went to New York and I thought the weather was going to be lovely so I packed my suitcase accordingly. It was so cold I had to buy some ear muffs. We stayed in the Marriott in Times Square and had a meal with the Everton director Robert Earl at Planet Hollywood, which he co-founded.

Back then, there was a lot of talk amongst us about dress sense. Joleon Lescott was always colour-co-ordinated from his head to his toes. Joleon told me I needed help and he offered to dress me, as though he was some kind of Gok Wan for footballers.

Joleon wanted to take me shopping but I refused to go with him because I didn't want to spend my time in New York in shops. I couldn't think of anything worse. Anyway, I gave him my sizes and he came back with white and green adidas boots with bright green laces. There were jeans with a green stripe running through them and a green T-shirt. He'd also bought a green campus jacket. To top it was a white cap and a bright green rim.

I looked ridiculous. The peak of the cap was flat and it didn't fit properly so I bent it. I found a couple of stickers on the cap and removed them. Joleon took one look at me and said: "What have you done?" Apparently it was fashion – part of the look. Within two minutes I'd messed up his outfit. He never asked me again.

On another trip we went to see some basketball, the New York Knicks against the Indiana Pacers. On the Pacers team was a huge guy called Roy Hibbert. Our Hibbo loved it and we'd cheer wildly whenever his name was announced.

One time Moyesy took us to Jerez in Spain for a training trip. After our morning session one day, he told us to do what he wanted for a few hours before a team meal in the evening but made it clear he didn't want anyone drinking during the day. Quite a few of us, me and Gary Naysmith included, played golf. After our round, we walked into the clubhouse and thought 'let's just have one drink. We're grown men'.

Within minutes our physio, Mick 'Baz' Rathbone, came in, absolutely smashed, and immediately ordered a pint. Baz, Beattie, Richard Wright and about five others had been round the town. They were all falling over while me and Gary nursed our drinks. We shouldn't even have had one but we did. Moyesy finished his round of golf, came in and saw me and Gary. He gave us the evil stare, which he was good at, and walked off.

Later we met in the foyer before the meal and he made a comment about me and Gary being out of order. I trooped on the bus and got my head down but I turned to Gaz and said: "I can't believe he's just said that to us. We were the only two sober in there!"

The lads around me convinced me to get off the bus and tell Moyesy he was out of order. I did just that: "Excuse me, gaffer, I need a word. You're out of order for saying that."

His response was: "You're bladdered. You wouldn't have even come to me to have this argument if you hadn't had a drink."

I went "you're wrong", said something else and got back on the bus. The lads asked what had gone on and we all agreed to get off the bus and boycott the team meal. We told him what we were doing and that he was the one who was out of order.

While us players ended up back in our rooms, bored, the staff went out for something to eat. When serious hunger set in, we ordered room service but what was delivered you wouldn't even give to a dog. Boycotting the meal was not a clever move.

I can't believe I went up to him for an argument. He was right, I was out of order. But I'd only had a pint while some of the lads, and members of his staff, were rotten drunk.

I hope people don't get the idea I'm a heavy drinker, because I'm not, but crazy things tend to happen when we let our hair down. At our last Christmas do, at the Camp and Furnace in Liverpool city centre, I was sat down texting when Steven Pienaar and Joel Robles walked over and picked me up. As they carried me, I continued to text. They counted "one, two, three" and threw me into a Christmas tree. My phone obviously flew out of my hand and someone picked it up. Once I had untangled myself from the tree, there was no sign of my phone and I knew it was payback time for all the pranks I'd pulled over the years. We moved onto the city centre and in a bar Jags gave me my phone and said 'Ossie you'd better check it'.

I knew straight away I was in trouble. I looked at messages sent and the last recipient was David Moyes. Let's just say that the message wasn't complimentary.

I texted him the next day and wrote: "Hiya gaffer, sorry about last night. We were on our Christmas night out and someone stole my phone. I probably deserved it after all these years." He texted me back and demanded: "I want names." I've never asked who did it and I've never wanted to know because if I knew and he asked, I'd have to tell him.

While Moyesy was with us, he repeatedly showed how astute he can be in the transfer market. Think of all the players he brought in for bargain prices: Joleon Lescott, a guy no-one would touch because of a serious knee injury, was bought for £5m and sold three years later for £24m. He signed Phil Jagielka and Leighton Baines for about £5m each; Tim Cahill for less than £2m, Seamus Coleman for £60,000 and Mikel Arteta for about £2m. We could go on and on. Some of his deals were incredible. Not everything worked but, considering the players that did, Moyes was well in credit.

As I write, he is without a job after leaving Man United. I think he'll excel wherever he goes next and he'll be in that job for five or six seasons, building the club up. I did invite him to my testimonial. He wanted to come but left me a message, apologising, saying he didn't feel he could come back just yet because the time wasn't right. It was disappointing because I wanted him to be there. I think he wanted to be there too.

He certainly left us with a good base. There was a lot of talk that whoever took on Moyes' job would find it tough. I thought that was a load of rubbish. He had brought us on and put a foundation in place. The harder job was following Sir Alex Ferguson at Manchester United. They were a team in decline and needed an overhaul.

When Roberto Martinez came in, he said he was surprised how good we were as a team. Moyes left him a good set of players, good characters, who were well drilled in looking after each other. Martinez has put his own stamp on us but, because of the standard of players we had, it was a change we were very capable of making.

In his last 18 months at Everton, Moyes was much more laid-back. When he first came to the club, he felt like he needed to fine people for every offence, exert his dominance and show who was boss. He had to win all his battles. When he started out at Preston, he obviously had to do that and succeeded. He moved on to us and really did show people who was in charge and stood up to those who didn't toe the line. He showed them who the alpha male was.

It got to the point at Everton, because he had been there so long, that he didn't have to shout and bawl. He became comfortable in his style and he didn't have to show anyone who was the boss because we all knew. Towards the end, he could concede a point and he only fined people if there was a severe breach of club rules. He became easier to be around and was much more approachable. He even dealt better with defeats… although don't for one moment think he found it easy to do so!

That may have been because he had confidence in his role and had security. It made him a better manager.

What happened to Moyes at United really upset me. I wanted to go and help him. I felt sorry for him and I am probably in the minority amongst Evertonians for feeling like that. I felt he was capable of doing the job but, because he hadn't won any titles and it was a club of United's stature, maybe he felt he needed to go in with his chest out. Or was he too relaxed? It couldn't have been easy to be relaxed at United, knowing he needed to overhaul the squad.

Perhaps because it was so long since he had had to do that, maybe he wasn't as commanding at the start at United. I'm just speculating because I don't know the ins and outs, but whatever happened he didn't get the players to do what he wanted.

There were times when I didn't see eye-to-eye with him and was frustrated by him but I'm thankful that we were together for so long. It was such a settled period in my life, for club and family. I have a lot of fondness for him and would like to express my gratitude for what David Moyes did for my career.

18

A New Era

The departure of David Moyes as Everton manager was very unsettling for me. Not only was it a step into the unknown, I was saying goodbye to some good friends and the daily routine of my first-team career.

I really wanted him to stay as we'd worked together for so long. Some might say "you'd never experienced another manager" but I was happy. It was our club. It was comfortable. I could tell what Davie Moyes was going to do before he did it. We were predictable in a good way and the club had been so settled for so many years. I didn't want it to happen but change is inevitable. And you can't turn the Man United job down.

It was a sad time on a personal level. Every day I sat down for my dinner with Jimmy Lumsden, Chris Woods, Hibbo and the manager's secretary, Sue Palmer. We'd have a cup of tea, a chat and put the world to rights. Not only were we losing Moyes, we pretty much knew it meant Steve Round, Lummy and Woodsy would also be leaving. It was sad that the whole club seemed to be going to change.

As well as not knowing who the new manager was going to be, we would have to get used to his approach. Was it going to be completely new methods? Is he going to make us train at different times? Will it be easier? Harder? There was a lot of uncertainty.

I wasn't sure what to think. I decided that who I wanted was irrelevant. I would reserve judgement until the appointment was made and then I'd know how I felt about it. When Roberto Martinez was announced as our new boss, I wasn't happy or sad. Straight away it was a case of 'I wonder whether he likes me?' I looked at it optimistically, 'he likes to play football – that's a good thing'.

I was at an airport when I had a voicemail from him. The airport was busy, I was with my wife and three kids and it was just about the worst time to have a conversation with my new manager. I text back: 'I'm travelling today but I'm coming in to Finch Farm tomorrow. Can I have a chat then?' He replied: 'Perfect. Safe flight, see you tomorrow'.

My first impression was that he was nice, easy-going and positive. It was the manager's office at Finch Farm, which I was much more familiar with than him, but straight away it was his office; it was like going in to meet the new headteacher.

The people I was used to – Colin Harvey with the youth team, 'Taff' Holden with the reserves and Moyesy – were all strict and disciplined. Martinez went completely the other way; he was very welcoming and complimentary and made you feel good straight away. He told me to use my experience to help the club on and off the field.

It was obvious he was going to bring four or five new bodies with him which, in itself, was going to change the make up of the club. Under Moyes, I knew where I was. I knew he appreciated me. I was always in and around the team over the course of 10 years so I didn't have to prove myself to him. I could have two bad days in training but he knew, come game-time, he could trust me. This was a new manager and I didn't know his opinion of me; if he had pre-conceived ideas of me, good or bad. I had to prove myself again, like I did to get my youth contract and then get in the first team. At first I was a bit wary of it. 'I am 32, experienced and I've got to go through this all over again?' But it raises your game, reinvigorates you. You've got to step it up and prove yourself every day. Did I need it? Yes, probably.

From the age of 27 or so, I have returned to Finch Farm a week before we are due back to ease myself in, getting my mind and body right to try to prevent injuries. I may do it slowly over the course of a week. The first day I will walk around and meet everybody, before doing some work the following day. By the day before everyone returns, I'm running around crazily.

Under Moyes, we wouldn't see a ball for the first three days training. It was all about running. I had done Moyes' pre-season for 11 years so I knew what followed each task. My body was in tune with them, so I would get through them relatively easily while other players were on their knees. Under Martinez, everything was done with a ball. It was a nice change but I found it strange not knowing what was coming next. I actually also found it difficult at times because it was all so new. Roberto Martinez has extreme beliefs in passing and building from the back. Previously, if we were in a bad area, the instinct would be to shell it up the pitch. He wasn't happy if we did that.

At first, we had deliberation over it and we'd say "but I can't lose it here." His opinion was: "No, that's where you want to play. You want to suck them into this area and we'll pass and pass and pass." It took us time to get used to that. Martinez would rather you gamble in a bad area because it might pay off further up the pitch. There has been the odd occasion where it hasn't worked but that's a gamble he is prepared to take.

In training, he was showing us what he calls mechanisms. He taught us a few things about team shape. It was fresh, new, something to get your teeth into. You needed to be concentrating all the time to pick it up.

I'd worked under Moyes for so long that my way of playing, in terms of management and coaching, was basically his way. That was the way you play football. But as good as it was at times, it's one of hundreds, thousands maybe, of ways to play the game. Now I could see Roberto Martinez's way of playing.

If I was to be a coach or manager, I could do with experiencing another three or four manager's styles to have more of a spectrum to pull from. After a month of Martinez, it made me think, 'wow, this could be one of the best things that's happened for me in my career, short and long-term'.

However, people shouldn't believe Martinez totally transformed our way of playing. It was evolution, not revolution. Over Moyes' tenure he really developed our play, our passing and our performances.

Moyes' philosophy was that if the opposition wanted to

defend deep, we'd make them. We would pop the ball up to Felli, he'd hold it up, we'd get round him and then make something happen. Once we were up there we played some brilliant stuff and had massive confidence in each other because we had been playing good football since Nikica Jelavic, Darron Gibson and Steven Pienaar signed.

For 18 months we played some fantastic football under Moyes but we very rarely played out from the back. We never drew teams out. We didn't mess around at the back. "Get that ball in the box, get crosses in, don't disappoint." It became percentage play at times. We could be ugly as well as pretty and we were equally effective at both.

Under Martinez, we don't even try to play ugly. For the first month in the Premier League under our new manager, we weren't doing it all the way he wanted. It was still a learning process. We started the season with three draws, two of which were goalless, against teams we were expected to beat. After an international break we had Chelsea at Goodison and were desperate for that first win.

Our season could have been completely different had Gaz Barry, on his debut, not made that tackle on Samuel Eto'o when he had an open goal. We were trying to play out from the back, like the manager wanted, when Tim Howard made a bad pass and it was cut out. It looked a certain goal until Gaz somehow got across. Suddenly, the crowd was up and we started knocking the ball about in just the way the gaffer wanted. It was as if the penny had suddenly dropped. We were great and right on the stroke of half-time, I chipped to the back post, Nikica Jelavic nodded across and Steven Naismith scored.

The manager wasn't critical of Tim because he understands

mistakes will happen. He probably said "keep trying that, Tim" because that's how you play football. If Chelsea had scored then, the fans would have been screaming: "Stop messing round!" It would have made it harder for us to implement what the manager wanted to achieve.

By the time I made my mistake against Sunderland on Boxing Day, the crowd understood what we were doing. Sunderland were making it difficult for us and had stopped us getting out comfortably from the back, I decided to seek the ball to get the game started. I shouted "yes" to Tim Howard. I looked over my shoulder to see if anyone was coming and, as I looked back, the ball was almost on me. I stuck my foot out, had a bad touch and Ki Sung-Yeung was on me. I stood on the ball and he took it off me. Then you have a moment of absolute panic, praying he doesn't score. Instead he was brought down by Tim, the last man. Stonewall penalty and Tim was sent off.

I looked to the sky and groaned, "no, no, no". You try to come to terms with it and I was telling myself we had another 70 minutes and I was going to get on the ball and drag us back into the game. As I was thinking that, I looked over to the bench and Joel Robles was getting ready to come on as the replacement goalkeeper. I did the maths and realised I was playing in the role you would sacrifice. 'Oh no, it's me.' That was it. It was probably the worst minute in my Everton career on a personal level. I gave the ball away, my team-mate was sent off, I was subbed and they scored from the subsequent penalty. It was a perfect storm. It would have been better had Ki Sung-Yeung scored from my mistake. We'd have had Tim still in goal, I'd have stayed on and I believe 100% that we'd have won the game. I was actually playing well and apart from that I'd enjoyed the opening 20 minutes!

I sat on the bench for the rest of the game, head in my hands, willing the team on. It was a really uncomfortable hour and despite the lads' best efforts, we couldn't break them down.

The saddest part of the day was that Cole, my eldest, heard a lot of abuse aimed at me. Around where my family sit, people know who they are. It's usually a nice area to watch from but on that afternoon quite a few people were derogatory towards me. He was eight years old and really upset. I had a chat with him but I found the day even harder because of that.

During the early stages of the season, there was uncertainty over the futures of Marouane Fellaini and Leighton Baines as Moyesy tried to sign them for Manchester United. Felli wanted to go. He was uptight and sulked at times but he was professional on the pitch in the matches he played.

The club dug its heels in over Bainesy, while trying to see what we could get for Felli. The chairman eventually secured an unbelievably good deal. He's good at that!

I had played alongside Felli in the first three matches after Darron Gibson was injured in pre-season. Felli doesn't fit into the new manager's style of play or system in any way, shape or form. He makes a short pass and then goes and stands in the box, even though the ball might be in the right-back slot. It was very difficult to play with Felli in the Martinez system.

The manager brought James McCarthy in for £15m and Gaz Barry on loan. Again, you start thinking 'is that me out of the team?' but I realised we needed the numbers and I managed to stay in, which was pleasing.

As for our other signings, I didn't know much about Gerard Deulofeu, who came on loan from Barcelona. I'd seen Arouna Kone play a few times, and we were signing Antolin Alcaraz from Wigan as well. Unfortunately, they've both had a tough time with injuries since then.

It was pleasing that we signed so many good players. Not only were they all good players but they were really good characters. Most of Moyes' signings fitted that description. You don't know with a new manager, but we needn't have worried. Every one of his new signings was a good character. It put my mind at rest about him looking after our club. It's characters who make the club, not just players.

Victor Anichebe had already left for West Brom and we brought in Romelu Lukaku. Other departures that season saw Nikica Jelavic join Hull. After a stunning first eight months or so, he seemed to lose confidence. After he'd been with us for six months, I spoke to him in the gym and said: "Are you enjoying it? It's a good club, isn't it?" He agreed but added: "I won't be here long."

"What?"

"Yeah, 18 months and I'll go somewhere else."

At the time, things were going fantastically well for him and he was already telling me he was going to leave in a year's time. I was thinking 'how can you just say that?'. I'd never come across that before and found his comment strange. His form then dipped. Maybe he knew that he tends to go to clubs, hit the ground running and then finds it hard. Maybe he needs a fresh start regularly to keep his interest going.

Jela was a good lad, though. He started in our FA Cup third round home tie against QPR and probably already knew he would be leaving. He was a good professional because he still wanted to play in the match and scoring twice in a 4-0 win (and missing a penalty) was a nice way to say goodbye. He moved to Hull City who went on to reach the cup final but he was cup-tied because he'd played that match for us just before he left.

Ross Barkley was a massive plus for Martinez during his first season in charge. Ross really started to shine. He got into the first team two years earlier when he was 17 but Moyes didn't trust him enough. In our second league match in 2011/12, Ross started on the right of midfield against Blackburn. Early in the second half he got the ball five yards inside our own half with his back to goal and tried to turn in a bad area, the sort of thing young lads do. He was robbed, ran back and brought Mauro Formica down in the box. Tim Howard saved the penalty but Ross' head went, he made a few more mistakes and Moyes brought him off.

In 2012/13, Moyes had signed Kevin Mirallas, Steven Pienaar was back and Ross found chances few and far between. That was when Moyes decided to send him on loan to Sheffield Wednesday and Leeds. He was showing his talent but I think Moyes was of the opinion that if he was going to make mistakes while he was learning, he'd rather him make them at another club. Ross' attacking qualities weren't in doubt. If you have as much of the ball as he has, there are going to be times where you get caught. You need to learn when to keep it and when not to.

By the time Roberto Martinez came in, Ross was approaching his 20th birthday. He did a lot of maturing between 17 and 20. Ross was ready and Martinez will see the positives that you bring rather than focus on the negatives. Moyes was more concerned with, 'although you do this well, you're going to bring the team down with those negatives'. Martinez is definitely more accepting of mistakes. Moyes needed to trust that you wouldn't make errors in dangerous areas of the pitch, which Ross might have done in that 17-19 age range.

Martinez knew how to use him effectively. Also, Ross fits into his style of play more than he did Moyes'. Under Martinez, he fits into the number 10 role seamlessly.

Another young player who took his chance when it came was John Stones. Jags hurt his hamstring at the end of February and was out in the last couple of games. It was a shame for him but openings can arise from misfortune. Stones, who was only 19, stepped up and took his opportunity. He was so composed on the ball, did pretty much everything right and even earned two England caps before the World Cup.

John has the chance to have a really top career. He typifies the next generation of player – comfortable on the ball, quick, strong, tall and can head it, like a Rio Ferdinand. Opponents now know he is comfortable in possession, so they will close him down. He will have to show he is mature enough to pass it when players get close. People talk a lot about Ross and he has certainly shown his ability but John Stones can be equally as important for club and country. He'll captain England one day, no doubt about it. You read it here first!

We were the last team to lose a Premier League game in 2013/14 and when we did, at Manchester City, the manager went mad at us. We were in total control until Rom scored for us after 16 minutes but we then switched off. Martinez told us that's the time when you need to get back on the ball, do it again and show your dominance. Instead they scored straight away and got up a head of steam. The manager can be cutting, stinging, ruthless when he needs to be. He was that day. For so long we had not gone to the top teams and won and he was saying it was down to a lack of belief and expectation. He said we were going there and hoping, rather than going there and expecting.

Martinez is a very good man-manager. Against Hull, early in the second half, he brought me off for Pienaar, who then scored with his first touch before I'd even sat down. I cheered and I was happy that we had scored but I'd played quite well and I hate being subbed. The gaffer spoke to me through the week and said: "These things happen; you played well and didn't deserve to come off. I was going to take someone else off but you got booked so I changed my mind." It was one of those team bookings you take to stop the opposition breaking. It cost me and I had a tough week, mentally.

The following week against Villa I was on the bench and the manager sent me on after an hour – I set one up and scored. He waited for me on the side of the pitch and said: "Brilliant, I'm made up for you." That showed the swing you can have in football from one game to the next. The manager handled both situations very well.

In April, the long wait for a win at Old Trafford ended. I spoke to Moyesy, Woodsy and Lummy before the game and shook hands. It was good to see them again but we had a job to do.

Moyesy took quite a lot of stick off our fans that night and got a pasting every time he stood on the side of the pitch. The fans are fiercely protective of their club and if they feel they've been wronged, they will never be slow to let you know. I was really pleased when we finally got that goal and I was even more pleased it was scored by Bryan Oviedo, who finally had his chance at left-back with Leighton being injured. He'd been at the club for a while and he's a game lad, committed and tough. He had been behind Bainesy in the pecking order for 18 months. That can't be easy. He scored his first goal against Stoke and it was brilliant for him to get the winner at United. When Bainesy came back, he stayed in the team on the left of midfield because he'd raised his stock so much.

We ended up doing the double over United that season. It must have been an uncomfortable afternoon for Moyesy. He was sacked less than 48 hours later. I was disappointed for him and thought United treated him badly. At the time, United couldn't qualify for Europe so they had nothing to play for. To sack Moyes after a defeat at Goodison Park was particularly cruel I thought. And rather unnecessary.

There was a funny incident as Moyes emerged from the tunnel before the game. Jimmy Martin went to shake his hand but Moyes didn't see him and made eye contact with Roberto Martinez. As he thrust his arm towards Martinez, he inadvertently brushed Jimmy's arm away, as though he was completely and deliberately ignoring him. Jimmy looked at him, stunned, not sure what had happened, and walked sadly over to our bench. I was in hysterics. He responded: "Eff off, you. Of all people, you had to see it." Bainesy watched Football First later that night and could see what had happened with Jimmy. He 'Snapchatted' it and sent it to us all. You could hear his laughter as he recorded it

During that season, I also made my 300th Premier League appearance for the club, and scored our first goal, in a routine win over Fulham. I'm not one for statistics and I always need telling whenever I reach a milestone, but I was very proud to reach my 300th Premier League game. That's an average of 30 a season over ten years and I'm happy with that!

Following on from that, I broke David Unsworth's record for the most Premier League appearances by an Everton player, getting to 303. It was a nice moment knowing I was leading the team out and breaking the Premier League appearance record.

Me and Unsy only played together for the first team for a total of 10 minutes when I came off the bench twice in 2003. As I've mentioned, we are close and live round the corner from each other and Unsy really looked after me and Hibbo when we were coming through. On the day I broke his record, he sought me out before the game to shake my hand and congratulate me. I appreciated that but I wasn't surprised. He's a top, top bloke.

There was a big personal setback for one of my team-mates in the fourth round of the FA Cup. We were drawn at Stevenage and as Liverpool was a few days away, the manager made some changes. One of the coaches, Dennis Lawrence, pulled me to one side and told me I'd start at Anfield, so I'd be on the bench against Stevenage.

This was the day that Bryan Oviedo broke his leg horrifically. He went in for an honest tackle and when I saw him go down I knew it was serious. I had to be professional and start warming up. The manager shouted me after a couple of minutes and told me I was going on. It wasn't until later I realised the severity of Bryan's injury. It was so unfortunate – he is such a nice lad and was playing so well.

Our habit of bouncing back well from cup defeats was then shown again. Including West Ham, we then went on a seven-game winning streak, which took us into fourth position. We were wearing teams down and quite a lot of our goals came after 80 minutes because the opposition couldn't keep going.

Newcastle away was probably my favourite game of that season. Ross ran from his own half to put us ahead, Rom scored a good team goal and I managed a good one at the end, in off the bar. We wiped the floor with them. After another away win at Fulham, it was all set up for Arsenal again, a match between the two teams competing for the final Champions League qualifying spot.

It was another strange day in my career. I played seven minutes, nearly scored a volley from the corner of the box, was booked and carried off because I sliced my left eye open. I've never been so frightened on a football field. I thought I'd lost sight in that eye.

I was captain again and charged around the pitch, trying to tackle everything that moved. I'd already made a tackle that got a big roar. I decided to do the same and went in on Bacary Sagna. He saw me coming and turned to the side to protect himself. I took him out and his hip and backside came smashing into me, pushing my face down into the floor. My eye was obviously open and the impact stretched it like I never knew was humanly possible. I actually ripped my eye-lid.

The instant pain in my eye made me feel sick. Straight away I knew there was a problem. Before I'd even come to a stop on the ground, my heart was in my mouth. I couldn't see and absolute panic set in. I never get dramatic on the pitch but I was banging the floor in absolute terror. I opened my eyelid but it was pitch black. I genuinely thought my eye had fallen out. I thought my career was over. I started patting my face to feel if the eye was still in the socket. My first instinct was that it had fallen out, and was on the floor somewhere near me.

Our physiotherapist, Richard Evans, came on and the first question I asked was: "Evo, is my eye still there?" He gave me a medical pad to hold on the eye and guided me across the pitch. As he did that, the referee, Martin Atkinson, shouted "Ossie! Ossie!" Because he was on my left, I had to turn my whole body to see him. As I contorted round, he lifted his arm and announced "yellow card". That was the least of my worries.

I got to the side of the pitch and still couldn't see. The doctor said he couldn't attend to it there and then because the cut was so bad, so they ushered me down the tunnel and headed for the dressing room. The manager asked if I'd be able to carry on and they said to give them a couple of minutes. That at least assured me that the eye must still be there. But as we went down the steps, my legs wobbled and I had to grab onto the wall. Another physio, Richie Porter, grabbed hold of me. He was asking if I was alright but all I could say was, "I can't stand up; I can't stand up."

He tried to calm me down and told me to 'take deep breaths'. I didn't want to actually admit I couldn't go back out there but eventually one of them said "he's done, he's off".

I sat on the bench in the physio room, keeping the pad on my eye. The left side of my face felt like someone had had a go at me with sandpaper. I just wanted to be left alone. Over the course of about 20 minutes, I started to be able to see slightly. It was mostly grey, but there was a bit of light. That was a big relief.

The eyelid had stretched so much it had split and eventually the doctor had to stitch the cut and stuck a needle in both sides of my eyelid to numb it. That was even more painful. He did a good job because it was a jagged, horrible cut. I had to wear an eye-patch for a few hours afterwards. I was supposed to go for a meal with my wife that night. Thank God she made me cancel. I looked a mess and it wouldn't have been fair on the other diners in the restaurant to have to look at me!

The scar healed awkwardly and I was left with a lump on my eyelid, so I couldn't open my eye properly. I was seeing double of everything. I played the next game against Sunderland and had to cock my head back to see things properly. Things were going so well for the team and I didn't want to miss out.

Three weeks after the injury I visited a plastic surgeon who cut out the scarring and scar tissue. The surgeon had to cut away two-thirds of my eyelid. He did a really good job and hopefully over the course of time it will heal properly. I still see double at the very outer of my vision, while the gums in the upper left side of my face were numb for about two months, which made eating a strange experience. Even now, if I've had my eyes closed for a while and I open them, it can be blurry for a second.

While I was struggling in the dressing room, the team were destroying Arsenal 3-0. After that result, it seemed like we were on course for fourth place and a late own goal at Sunderland the following Saturday kept us in pole position with five matches to go.

We lost the initiative against Crystal Palace, who beat us 3-2 at Goodison. They were difficult to break down, we overexerted ourselves and they hit us on the counter-attack three times. That was the main difference between us finishing fourth and fifth. I know we lost another two games but it was out of our hands then.

Our hopes of fourth had gone when we played our final home game against Manchester City, who were competing with Liverpool for the Premier League title. Some of our fans didn't want us to win the match. We couldn't finish fourth even if we beat City 10-0 so I could sort of see where they were coming from, but once the whistle blows, it's impossible for a professional footballer not to want to win a football match.

We had a right go and Ross scored one of the goals of the season, but we lost 3-2. In the first half, one of their players said, tongue-in-cheek: "Why are you trying so hard? You are supposed to want us to win." It was all good banter.

I was actually late getting to the ground that day. An e-mail is sent to the whole squad telling us what time we need to meet up before every match. I usually have a glance at it and then go back and double-check I've read it right. I saw 1.45pm but then in mind that became 2.45pm.

At lunchtime I was chilling out at home, watching the final matches of the Championship season. I headed upstairs to get changed at half-time and decided to leave then, so I could see the last 15 minutes at the ground. I was in no rush at all until I checked my phone and saw that I should have been at Goodison two minutes ago! My heart sank. I scooped up my stuff and was still putting my clothes on as I rushed downstairs and got in my car.

When I arrived half an hour later, I apologised to the gaffer and he told me to get on with my pre-match routine and that we'd speak about it later. That's not like me at all. I'd rather be two hours early than one minute late.

Two days later, Liverpool blew a 3-0 lead at Crystal Palace. When it was 3-0, I decided to switch it off and watch the end of a film with Jenny. When it finished, I put Sky Sports News on and saw the score was 3-1 so I flicked back to the match. Just as I switched over, Palace made it 3-2. I made Jenny watch the last 10 minutes and when the third goal went in I was jumping up and down, going crackers. I couldn't believe it!

After three defeats in four, it was good to end the season on a positive with a 2-0 win at Hull. It was a big day for me because it meant I had played in every league game that season. It was a big accomplishment and one I'd not done before. I was really, really proud of it and I managed to set up a goal for Rom. We finished fifth with 72 points, the club's highest total since we last won the league in 1986/87. What Roberto Martinez has given us is the ability to keep the ball for long periods and overwhelmingly dominate possession in all areas of the pitch. The purists enjoy it and Evertonians have taken to it.

Everyone expected us to go through a transition period. We exceeded everyone's expectations and became easy on the eye. We seemed to do all our transition within four games, taking to the manager's new concepts in an almost seamless progression. The test now will be to continue it into the second season, which is always difficult. We're capable of it and we want to continue in the right direction.

Having spent over 12 months with Martinez as my manager, I would describe him as a people's person. He's very ruthless and determined but he likes to keep people around him as happy as possible. This can be difficult when you only have eleven slots in the team but you're constantly positive with every member of the squad who's vying for a place. It can make not being in the team a bit harder to take because sometimes you don't see it coming but that's his way and he does it very well.

As people have seen, he's a very strong character. Even if we play poorly and lose 3-1, Martinez will find the positives from the performance while identifying what we need to work on for the next game.

He's certainly capable of losing his temper but he can put the result aside and concentrate on positives within the game. What hurts you more is the disappointment he'll have in his voice. You feel like you've let him down. Moyes would be angry with you. Martinez will say, "you're capable of more."

For the manager, the big challenge now is to win a trophy. Yes, we want to impress people and finish a minimum fifth in the league, but we have to bring in some silverware. That's ultimately the challenge for any Everton manager and player. It's 20 years since we won something. That's simply not good enough.

II

Post-match

Sunday, August 3, 2014.
Goodison Park.
Everton 1, Porto 1.

"It's an honour to play for this club. Don't underestimate what we're experiencing as Everton players. This is the high point of our careers. Don't ever take it for granted. This is my 13th year and it's gone so fast. Enjoy it every time you put that shirt on..." After talking about the game and giving a little speech about me, the manager had asked me to say a few words. I meant every word I said. It really has been an honour to represent Everton Football Club for so long.

When I finally emerged from the tunnel at the start of the

game, it was amazing to see how many people turned up. It really was brilliant. The reception I was given before the game was humbling. I was probably a little bit emotional...in fact, there's no probably about it!

It's not sunk in yet about the achievement and the honour of being awarded a testimonial by the club. To be told I was having one was flattering but then you get on with your job because it's in the future. I got my committee together and basically left it to them.

I knew the game against Porto was going to be competitive. I actually prefer the old-style testimonials when you get ex-players involved and it's a bit of a laugh, a bit of entertainment for the crowd. But I understand that these days the games are part of a meticulously planned pre-season schedule.

At times we hardly got a kick against Porto, who are such a good team. We probably did well to get a 1-1 draw, with Steven Naismith getting our goal.

Unlike Hibbo in his own testimonial two years earlier, I didn't manage to score. I had a few chances, a shot with my left foot which Hibbo set me up for and two headers which, six weeks into the season, I would at least hit the target with. They both came in the last five minutes and my legs wobbled. I'd used up a lot of nervous energy during the day and probably missed because I was over-excited. That's my excuse anyway!

But I enjoyed the day.

It was great to get my three kids out on the pitch with me beforehand. I wasn't sure I'd be able to do that. I knew Cole, who is nine, would be out there – Evertonians will have seen him running about excitedly after the final home game of the season. He can't wait for the lap of honour and loves running around the pitch. He may be an actor when he's older because he loves being in the spotlight. He would have happily been a ball boy or even 'reffed' the match against Porto!

We asked Cole and Deacon's primary school to provide 90 per cent of the extra mascots. It was a case of giving a bit back to the local community and it's a school I went to as well. Also, I thought it would help Deacon if his friends and school pals were out there.

Deacon doesn't like being around too many people. As a baby, he didn't like loud noises and he has struggled a bit socially. We didn't know the reason behind his behaviour until he had a hearing test in school and it showed that he had 99 per cent loss of hearing in one ear. He is currently having further tests. He seems to have a narrow canal. They're not sure if it's glue ear or if the ear has simply not developed properly. We have been told that his lack of hearing has affected his emotional development. He prefers one-on-one interaction rather than groups surrounding him but his school has brought him on so much in the last two years. We don't know yet whether he will need an operation or a hearing aid, but at least now we know what to look out for.

That's why what he did at the testimonial can't have been easy for him. Going out on the pitch in front of thousands and having loads of people around him was a massive thing for him to do. I sat him down and told him how proud I was of him. He went out on the pitch and both he and Kendall were really good. After my little dressing room speech, I gave some gifts out to the players and staff and the manager gave me a really nice present off the club – a commemorative dish to mark the occasion.

Then I had a load of media interviews to do before I went into the lounge to meet my family and friends. I got to meet up with my former first-team coaches Jimmy Lumsden and Alan Irvine; Colin Harvey and Les Helm, who looked after me in my youth-team days, plus John McMahon and Ted Sutton, my under-16 and under-15 coaches. Former Everton players Graeme Sharp, Ian Snodin and Graham Stuart were there too. So were my youth-team friends Nick Chadwick, Keith Southern and Matt McKay.

It took me ages to get round the lounge and greet everybody. I just wanted to sit down, take a moment, relax and take in the day but it was another hour-and-a-half or so before I could do that. Eventually I sat there, took a couple of breaths and settled myself down. It was an amazing day, I will look back and cherish the memories, but it was frantic from the moment I got to Finch Farm. Like I said earlier, it was just like a wedding day.

The whole experience really meant a lot to me. I can't put it into words, the gratitude I feel for the people that turned up and the people who planned it. To get a reception just for me was weird. Good or bad, the reaction we get off the fans is usually for the team. This was just for me. The fans were cheering my name and I felt a bit embarrassed actually.

I'm so grateful for the testimonial committee for everything. They'd already organised a golf day which raised a lot of money for my chosen charities, the Make-A-Wish Foundation and Claire House Children's Hospice.

During that dinner, the comedian went to town on Bainesy, who was talking to someone in the corner of the room. His dress sense came in for plenty of criticism.

I hired a DJ we use for family parties who was playing tunes and singing a few himself until Matt McKay demanded the microphone and sang Deacon Blue's Real Gone Kid. It then turned into karaoke.

The testimonial committee chairman, Mark Manley, marched me on stage and basically forced me to the front to sing. I asked for Boom! Shake The Room by Will Smith and DJ Jazzy Jeff. I rapped my way through that, dancing up and down the stage. Hibbo, as usual, was egging me on but staying well out of the spotlight.

As you will have gathered by now, Hibbo and I are very close friends. He's Godfather to Kendall and is like my big brother – he will always come to my rescue.

Hibbo's testimonial against AEK Athens was something else. You couldn't script what happened with his goal from the free-kick. The club had promoted "Hibbo scores, we riot" and that's exactly what happened. The AEK players absolutely freaked out – they didn't know what was going on. I was loving it, though. It was a real feel-good night. And at least Hibbo scored in his testimonial (I actually felt sorry for Naisy who scored the most forgotten hat-trick in the club's history!).

Hibbo's always looked after me. We're not the type to share feelings but if you need him, he'll be there. We shake hands and wish each other good luck before every game.

Running out on to the Goodison Park pitch is still an amazing feeling and it always will be. I love the place. It has got so much history. You think back and Dixie Dean, Pele and Eusebio have all played there, as well as all the great Everton players and teams.

But football, like life, moves on. It has to.

When I was injured in December, 2011, I travelled south to the Arsenal game where Robin van Persie scored a whopper to beat us. What a stadium the Emirates is. Everything about it is top class. There are lounges throughout the ground and the executive boxes are twice the size of the ones at Goodison. The seats in the stadium are so comfy and roomy and there is not an obstructed view anywhere.

If the club is going to go to the next level, we need a stadium like that to be able to compete. It's sad to say but we need a new ground, or a massive redevelopment of Goodison Park, which I don't think is possible.

At first I felt we couldn't and shouldn't move from Goodison. But look at Manchester City. They were a 'yo-yo' club for many years. Fortunately for them, Manchester was able to host the Commonwealth Games and suddenly there was a spare stadium which they took over. Because it's such a nice stadium with plenty of lounges and the potential to generate serious money, businessmen are interested because they can make a big return. We have something like eight or 10 executive boxes and a handful of lounges. We are not in the same league.

The chairman, Bill Kenwright, has run the club fantastically well and we can certainly compete at the top end of the Premier League. But even Bill, who I am proud to say is a friend, has publicly stated that he would welcome some investment to help us compete at the very top.

If there's a better chairman in football than Bill Kenwright, then I'd be surprised. He absolutely genuinely cares for the club. He cares for the staff, the players and the fans. You go to some grounds and the chairmen are all over the dressing room, in people's faces and generally wanting to be seen around the players. Bill's never been like that. He leaves us well alone and allows the staff to get on with their jobs. He looks after us when we're in London or New York and things like that, but it's always private. He's not one for trying to share the limelight and I respect him for that. What he will do on a matchday is make the players' families welcome. My mum and dad love him!

Will we ever leave Goodison Park? Who knows? I personally think we will but I hope it's all done correctly with no controversy and that we can give Goodison the send-off it deserves. Can you imagine the atmosphere at the last ever game at Goodison? I can't even begin to. I'll cry for a week!

It's a fine line because we don't want to lose the history that this club possesses. But, based on our history, we expect to be winning things. We are operating really well and have gradually progressed over the past decade. Not many clubs in Europe will have been as consistent, year on year, but to make that next step, we need something extra. A new stadium would bring investment.

Even without any more investment, I believe we can win something before I'm finished. After my testimonial speech, the manager said: "There is only one thing missing from Leon's career and that's silverware. Let's make sure we get some this year."

I may be 33 now but I still have a lot to offer and ambitions I want to achieve. I'm not ready to retire yet.

I've not put a figure on how long I want to keep playing. As I write, my contract takes me up to the end of the season. I'm hoping to negotiate at least another one. Having only started playing regular first-team football at Everton as I turned 23, I still feel like I have a lot of football left in me.

Some who start at 17 can be burnt out at 31 or 32. Being a footballer can be quite stressful – the pressure of game-to-game, season-to-season. It can wear you down. A footballer can have a set number of years physically and mentally. Some players retire because physically they can't do it any more; some have had enough mentally. We love the game but it's not like playing in the park with your mates.

I would like another contract at Everton but what if they don't offer me one? Will I decide to go and play elsewhere? Or would I decide I want to finish here? It depends on what I feel at the time. Having been at this club for so long, I think I'd find it strange to seek football elsewhere. But if I still want to play, I might have no choice.

If I do stay, one thing I'd love is for our supporters to do something with my chant. The only one anyone's come up with is: "Le-on, Le-on, Le-on." I could understand it if my surname was Stracqualursi but Osman must fit into a song somehow! I was hoping someone would have come up with a really catchy tune by now. Even Hibbo's is quite upbeat. I need a bit of excitement with my song. I've had fantastic support over the years and it would be great to hear something new before I finish!

Another ambition away from football is to learn a new language. At the start of my career, pretty much everyone spoke English in the dressing room. That's changed as the years have passed. There could be four players speaking to each other in French on my left, or three players talking in Spanish on my right. In jest, I have said: "Oi, you're in England now. Speak English so we can all understand." But it's actually me who's the ignorant one because I can only speak one language. Some of them can speak three, four or five. I can't criticise them.

I decided I'd learn Spanish properly but I kept putting it off. In the summer of 2014, I have finally started. At training we have electronic boards that show a message of the week. It might be about belief, insight or desire. One at the end of last season said: 'The best time to plant a tree was 20 years ago. The second best time is now.' At first I was thinking, 'what does that mean?'. After a while it started to sink in. It really struck a chord with me and I've finally decided to plant that tree.

Long-term, I have no definite plan. I want to keep as many options open as I can. I've done media work – a few columns with the Daily Mail, commentary work for evertontv and a bit for radio. I've really enjoyed it, although my delivery would need to improve. That's a route I might want to follow but that would mean me not working day-to-day within football and that's all I've known since I was 17.

I feel I have a lot to give with regards to teaching young kids to develop and helping young adults in making the next step from the youth team. I'd also like to work with first teams day-to-day, as a coach or manager, building towards a game that really means something. I've passed my UEFA 'B' licence coaching qualification and want to get my 'A' licence at the end of the season. But I don't want people to think I'm doing my badges because it's the end of my career. I just want to make sure I have as many options as I can when the end does eventually arrive.

I would hate to finish playing and have nothing to go into, or only have one avenue available to me. I would like to have at least three options. The favourite has to be to stay within football and hopefully within Everton as a club. I'm trying to help David Unsworth with the Under-21s this season and will get to as many games as I can.

My career has gone so quickly. It's 10 years since we finished fourth. Wow!

I am part of the one per cent who progresses right through the ranks to become a first-team regular. I've been very lucky to have had so many fantastic experiences and I'm very grateful for all the support I've had along the way, from family, friends and Evertonians.

To absolutely everyone who has contributed to the Leon Osman story…cheers. It's not over yet by the way, there are still a few more chapters left in me!

III

The Two Jimmies

Before you go, I asked our kit man Jimmy Martin and our club masseur Jimmy Comer for their opinion of me. They know me better than most. Here's what they said...

JM: When I first met him, he was as quiet as a mouse.

He's always been a good kid, full of laughter and full of fun. The other one, Hibbert, is the most miserable git you'll ever meet in your life. He would come in on a push bike and not speak to anyone all day. Until he went over that white line and then he'd kick you for a shilling.

JC: They were always like an item.

JM: And when Leighton Baines came, they were called the 'three amigos'. Up to tricks. Mischievous.

They'll drown you in water out of the window. We went to Austria a couple of years ago and they were co-ordinating the operation with walkie-talkies. One was sitting at the window and the instruction would be given: 'Now!' They've done everyone.

When I returned to work after my heart attack, he and Hibbo got me again with the cold water. The club doc, Dr Thomas, went mad, telling them we were out of order and that it was dangerous. Because he had a go at them, they did the doc five minutes later!

JC: One time Hibbo went to Taskers to buy a paint gun. Me and Jimmy were playing head tennis and Hibbo came into the gym. Next thing we're getting peppered with sticky yellow paint. One time they shot the health and safety man in the back at Bellefield.

JM: I'd say Ossie's worse now. You go for a night out, you go to put your shirt on and all the buttons are missing.

JC: There will be peas flying over to your table during formal dinners, like the Everton awards.

JM: Last year, he brought his formal clothes in and asked one of the girls to iron his shirt. I told the young lad who works with me, Sean, to fetch Ossie's white shirt. I printed his name and squad number on the back, before putting it all back in his suit carrier. He took it home and I had a phone call from him at 5pm: "You little so and so! But I like it, Jimmy. Good one!" He was the only one wearing a black shirt with a black dickie bow that night. We always get him back.

The worst one he did to us was when we were playing head tennis in the indoor gym. My missus was using my car and we arranged that she would pick me up at Finch Farm. She was supposed to call me but I carried on playing, waiting for the phone to ring. The next thing little Mo from reception called me over and said: "Jimmy, your Marie's here and she's going berserk."

My wife said: "I've been ringing you all afternoon." It was 4pm and I should have been going home at 2pm. Ossie had taken the SIM card out my phone and pinned it to the noticeboard. I had down the banks off the wife because of him.

JC: He's a sod for the phones. If you leave your phone lying around, he will text anyone that's on there.

JM: He texted Walter Smith from my phone and wrote something I can't repeat!

JC: He's so well known for it that you'll get a reply 10 minutes later saying: 'Jimmy, tell Ossie I said hi'.

JC: He did Stephen Hunt from Steve Brown's phone – one of our performance analysts. Browny used to be at Reading at the same time as Hunt. He texted Hunt, who had gone to Hull, that he was made up that Ireland were beaten by France after Thierry Henry's handball in 2009. Stephen Hunt replied to Browny, going mad. Kevin Kilbane, who was then at Hull, told Hunt that Jimmy the kit man would be responsible.

We played Hull away just a few weeks later and Hunt scored the first goal. He smashed one in from the edge of the box and ran over to our dugout, yelling at us. Everyone was saying: "What's all that about?" He came to the dressing room at the end of the game looking for Jimmy.

JM: I said: "I don't know what he's after, I don't know what he's on about." I got hold of Kevin Kilbane and made him tell Hunt it wasn't me. I never said it was Ossie because it would have caused chaos. We all knew it was Ossie.

JM: In Australia on pre-season a few years ago, another of our kit men, Tony Sage, prepared all the staff kit and left them on a table by the dining room. Ossie, Bainesy, Hibbo and Phil Neville went in and swapped all the labels so that the sizes were completely mixed up. The manager came down wearing a really tight shirt. Jimmy Lumsden's was swimming on him. We got the fella at the hotel to check the CCTV and you could see them all.

JC: It is a professionally run place but if he sees an opportunity, he'll take it. He can't help himself. If a fitness coach sets up cones for a running session, he'll kick over what's taken an hour to prepare. That's his mentality.

JM: You can't fall asleep on a plane because if you do, he'll tie your shoelaces together.

JC: He gets bored. In Austria, I was put in a room with Craig Mazur, the masseur, and Shiggsy, the kit lad. It was their first trips and I told them: "Don't leave the door open. Don't let Osman or Hibbert into the room. Whatever they say, whatever they do, tell them to go away." I gave them a key each and told them not to lose them. We went down for training and within 10 minutes I asked Craig if he had his key. It was missing. I went back to the room and I had no bed. It was gone – the whole thing.

You come in of a morning for work and check the injury board. You don't want to see the names Hibbert and Osman up there. If they're both out for a long time, they're bored and that's when anything can happen. They'll cut ice bags. Stupid things.

There is a hot and cold plunge at Finch Farm. Some days you'll walk in and it's got massive suds in because those two have put Fairy Liquid in it.

JM: Osman is always the ringleader.

JC: He has the ideas. He stimulates others. We were going out for a stroll around Sydney Harbour one evening, before a meal. Under Moyes, we had to be in uniform. One of the squad, a young lad called Craig was on his first trip and I told him to wear our club gear. He said: "It's just that, with us going out after tea, I thought I might wear my jeans and T-shirt."

I said: "No, Craig. Always be in uniform." He said: "It's just that Ossie, Baines and Hibbo have asked me if I want to join them on the harbour and have a walk round. They've said they're putting their jeans on." I said: "Craig, no. Put your club gear on and get changed afterwards." If he'd come down dressed in jeans, the manager would have gone mad. They were trying to set the new lad up.

JM: Football-wise, it was always going to happen for him because he had great ability, great feet.

JC: I'm a big fan of Ossie's.

JM: We both are.

JC: I was talking about him recently and said I wished he was 21 again but sometimes I wish he was at Tranmere Rovers, so we could have some peace.

JM: His banter's brilliant.

JC: He grew up here; he's part of the family. He's learned off Davie Weir and Alan Stubbs. What they were good at, he's carried that on. Good captains who understand the club.

JM: He's a great lad to have around the place. When people like him and Hibbo go, it's going to be sad.

JC: The players now have a different mentality. He understands the importance of the kitchen staff, the backroom staff, the

groundsmen. If Osman has a family do, there will be groundsmen there. He's carried on that Everton tradition. You get
invited to everything when those people are involved. Phil Neville was the same.

JM: They are old school.

JC: If you are away on tour and there's a night out, you're
never left out of it. It's the likes of him that has kept that tradition up. He makes you feel important – you feel valued.

IV

Leon Osman
Career Statistics

Compiled by Gavin Buckland

CARLISLE UNITED

	Division 3		Other		Total	
	Starts (subs)	*Goals*	*Starts (subs)*	*Goals*	*Starts (subs)*	*Goals*
2002-03	10(2)	1	3	2	13(2)	3

DERBY COUNTY

	Division 3		Other		Total	
	Starts (subs)	*Goals*	*Starts (subs)*	*Goals*	*Starts (subs)*	*Goals*
2003-04	17	3	-	-	17	3

EVERTON FA YOUTH CUP

	Starts (subs)	Goals
1997-98	7	2
1998-99	8	2

EVERTON

	Premier League		FA Cup		League Cup		Europe		Total	
	Starts (subs)	Goals	Starts (subs)	Goals	Starts (subs)	Goals	Starts (subs)	Goals	Starts (subs)	Goals
2002-03	0(2)								0(2)	
2003-04	3(1)	1			0(1)				3(2)	1
2004-05	24(5)	6	3	1	2(1)				29(6)	7
2005-06	28(7)	3	3(1)	1	0(1)		1(1)		32(10)	4
2006-07	31(3)	3	1		2				34(3)	3
2007-08	26(2)	4			4	1	7	2	37(2)	7
2008-09	32(2)	6	6	1	1		2		41(2)	7
2009-10	25(1)	2	0(1)	1	1	1	6(1)		32(3)	4
2010-11	20(6)	4	3		2	1			25(6)	5
2011-12	28(2)	5	3		1				32(2)	5
2012-13	36	5	5	2	1	1			42	8
2013-14	27(11)	3	1(3)		1				29(14)	3
Total	280(42)	42	25(5)	6	15(3)	4	16(2)	2	336(52)	54

SUMMARY

	Starts (subs)	Goals
League	307(44)	46
FA Cup	25(5)	6
League Cup	15(3)	4
Europe	16(2)	2
Other	3	2
Total	366(54)	60

EVERTON GOALS BY CLUB (54)

Aston Villa	6	Derby County	1
West Bromwich Albion	4	Huddersfield Town	1
Fulham	3	Larissa	1
Manchester City	3	Leyton Orient	1
Sunderland	3	Liverpool	1
West Ham United	3	Macclesfield Town	1
Wigan Athletic	3	Millwall	1
Arsenal	2	Oldham Athletic	1
Hull City	2	Plymouth Argyle	1
Newcastle United	2	Portsmouth	1
Norwich City	2	Stoke City	1
Southampton	2	Swansea City	1
Birmingham City	1	Tottenham Hotspur	1
Blackburn Rovers	1	Watford	1
Brann Bergen	1	Wolverhampton W.	1
Cheltenham Town	1		

FACTS AND STATS

❑ Leon Osman has won 145 Premier League games with Everton, a club record and 14 more than next-placed Tim Howard.

❑ Leon's first career goal came for Carlisle at Macclesfield in a 2-2 draw on 19 October, 2002, on the same day as Wayne Rooney's famous strike at Goodison against Arsenal. Curiously, Leon also scored at Macclesfield for Everton in the FA Cup in January, 2009.

❑ Leon has scored twice in a game for Everton on three occasions: against West Brom at Goodison in August, 2004 – his first goals on the ground – and then at Aston Villa in February, 2005, and at Fulham in May, 2009.

❑ Leon did score a hat-trick in a reserve game against Manchester United, during a 4-1 away victory in January, 2003. It remains the only treble at any level by an Everton player against United since Johnny Morrissey in a Lancashire Senior Cup tie in 1964.

❑ Leon scored the winner against Southampton at Goodison in October 2004, with a late strike at the Gwladys Street end. Eight years later he scored Everton's next Premier League home goal against the Saints, also at the Gwladys Street end, in a 3-1 victory in September, 2012.

❑ Leon is one of only seven Everton midfielders to score 50 or more goals in all competitions for the club and one of only five (with Kevin Sheedy, Tim Cahill, Alan Ball and Andy King) to do so from open play.

❑ Leon has scored more Premier League goals from open play from outside the box than any other Everton player – seven in total, two ahead of Andrei Kanchelskis and Louis Saha.

❑ With Kevin Campbell, Leon has the highest tally of Premier League goals at the Park End, a total of 15 goals.

Index

OSSIE

LEON OSMAN
MY AUTOBIOGRAPHY

Sport Media